P9-DUJ-936

DATE DUE

SE 30 '97			
DE 1 '98			
DE 1 8 '0?			
JE 24 04			
AP 12 '08			
DE 19 08			

DEMCO 38-296

Books by Nolan Pliny Jacobson
from Southern Illinois University Press

*Buddhism and the Contemporary World:
Change and Self-Correction*

Buddhism: The Religion of Analysis

The Heart of Buddhist Philosophy

Understanding Buddhism

Buddhism and the Emerging World Civilization

Essays in Honor of Nolan Pliny Jacobson

Edited by
Ramakrishna Puligandla
and David Lee Miller

Southern Illinois University Press
Carbondale and Edwardsville

Riverside Community College
Library
4800 Magnolia Avenue
Riverside, California 92506

BQ 120 .B8123 1996

Buddhism and the emerging
  world civilization

Copyright © 1996 by the Board of Trustees,
  Southern Illinois University
All rights reserved
Printed in the United States of America
Production supervised by New Leaf Studio

99 98 97 96   4 3 2 1

Library of Congress Cataloging-in-Publication Data

Buddhism and the emerging world civilization : essays in honor of
  Nolan Pliny Jacobson / edited by Ramakrishna Puligandla and
  David Lee Miller.
    p. cm.
  Includes bibliographical references (p.   ) and index.
  1. Buddhism. 2. Buddhism and culture. I. Jacobson, Nolan Pliny.
  II. Puligandla, R., 1930–   . III. Miller, David Lee, 1940–   .
  BQ120.B8123   1996
  294.3—dc20   93-3267
  ISBN 0-8093-1842-3   CIP

The paper used in this publication meets the minimum requirements
of American National Standard for Information Sciences—Permanence
of Paper for Printed Library Materials, ANSI Z39.48-1984. ⊚

To the Memory of Nolan Pliny Jacobson
in
appreciation of his friendship,
wisdom, and humanity

Contents

Acknowledgments

We wish to thank Kathy Skurzewski for her fine work in preparing this manuscript to be delivered for final editorial work at Southern Illinois University Press. Marian Crooks did a very helpful early proofreading of the manuscript, providing a variety of suggestions for improvement.

Our thanks also to several people at Southern Illinois University Press for responding so positively to *Buddhism and the Emerging World Civilization* in every stage of its development. Our special gratitude to Curtis L. Clark for his work on this volume. It is very fitting that Mr. Clark be directly involved, since he worked with Professor Jacobson on earlier books published at Southern Illinois University Press.

Finally, we offer our appreciation to Professor Jacobson's wife, Grace, and his children, Page and Susan, who were always positive catalysts for his thinking and writing, and to whom his books were frequently dedicated.

Editors' Introduction

Nolan Pliny Jacobson was a profoundly motivated interdisciplinary thinker, who sought always to find, to explicate, and to synthesize points of similarity among leading thinkers of different Oriental and Western cultures. His interest was expressed for nearly half a century in a hopeful vision of an emerging world civilization in which all people can feel and express more naturally and fully their creative, constructive powers for the benefit of others and themselves. The following essays comment on Jacobson's interest and vision, and are grouped into four parts: Historical Context, Central Issues, Practical Implications, and The Japan Emphasis.

In this continuing quest for new and more humane personal and social experience, Jacobson focused his energies on numerous comparative studies of philosophers and philosophies, East and West. In particular, he understood and clarified many themes in the writings of the classic American philosophers (Whitehead, Dewey, Peirce, James, Hartshorne, Wieman, and others) that he found also in the major emphases of the Buddhist traditions. He thus saw American philosophy and Buddhism to be a living stream of confluence, forming a powerfully constructive and rich fount of hopeful possibility for the emerging world civilization.

Opening out and embracing the enormous problems and projects of the sprawling natural and human creation, Professor Jacobson's philosophic perspective was rooted in the conviction that novelty is the center of a creativity that lives beyond all words, arguments, and rational paradigms, and is the driving and informing source of experience that is vividly and memorably alive. He thought that philosophy and the work of philosophers should be understood as a vital force of all civilizational experience, bringing integrity and meaning to the rapidly passing pulses of life.

Jacobson was negatively impressed by the lure and power of settled knowledge pools and belief systems. He was persuaded that they inevitably inhibit, distort, and minimize the blooming impetus of creativity. He always sought the live insight, the fresh meaning that broke through the self-assured and self-isolated collection of established civilizational values and achievements. His search and commitment were directed toward enhancement of the living, emerging moment of meaning, the unfolding fullness of the passing *now*.

Nolan Jacobson discovered a good deal of his fuel for thinking, writing, and living in a lengthy exploration of Buddhist texts and personalities. He did this work in various parts of the United States and throughout the Orient, most particularly in Burma and Japan. The story is incomplete, however, without emphasizing his debt to the classic American philosophers and to an early, exhaustive study of the thought of Karl Marx. In all these sources, he stressed the confluence of new insights, the coming together of human thought from different continents of the world, bringing with it the irrepressible attraction for serious thinkers of informed inspiration to contribute divination to the emerging world civilization by articulating their novel intuitions beyond all traditions.

Professor Jacobson's personal and philosophic life was one of passion and reason focused on offering whatever he could to nurture the birthing efforts everywhere for a positively shared human experience in which there is gentle regard for the nonhuman natural elements that support and make possible this human experience in the first place. His writings celebrate all that brings together and brings out the joyful and vibrant qualities of the whole earth and the living creatures that inhabit it. These writings are philosophic exultations, moving through the shadows and darkness of suffering and despair.

The contribution of Jacobson is powered by the conviction that the revelatory character of each passing individual droplet of experience is intrinsically motivated and directed toward the enjoyment and support of all else that is natural and alive. This contribution takes as its starting point the natural passing of events, each of which is always ready and able to demonstrate that it is an important forming ingredient in the interrelatedness of all experience. The individual develops his/her identity as he/she expresses a whole-Earth consciousness, which recognizes, protects, and honors each individual as indispensable for its life and health.

The Jacobson philosophical corpus rejoices in all things natural. The texts are generous with references to the blooming flowers, the warming sun, and the delicate walkways that we call earth. All things natural, sadly, are overlaid with artificial and blighting human constructions, spawned by the fundamental problem of ego-craving. Jacobson worked hard to return individuals and cultures to this natural matrix of spontaneous and lovely forms. He thought that such a matrix is the proper starting point for any global civilization that can be termed sane and caring.

Jacobson welcomed all efforts of individuals and countries to get beyond themselves to more variegated and inclusive values. In this regard, we believe that he would applaud the present efforts of the peoples of Russia, eastern Europe, South Africa, and elsewhere to rethink and revise traditional orientations and outlooks. These efforts manifest the pulsebeats of new perspectives on what the forms of civilizational and individual experience mean. They express the struggling concerns to recast, speak anew, and embody in behavior an enlarged feeling and idea of what it means to be human in a whole-earth context.

As we near the year 2000, the original Buddhist insight of universal suffering remains entirely relevant, but it must be reinterpreted in different ways and with different meanings. Perhaps we can see suffering in the context of a world more generously endowed with possibilities for global consciousness than ever before in history. As we look into the thought of Nolan Pliny Jacobson, we see a sustained focus on the possibilities for awakened consciousness, a beck and call that should challenge us to break out of our narrow and suffocating personal and cultural shells. This invitation for reflective and compassionate response means that we should endeavor to critique everything within and before us, not for the purpose of proving anything right or wrong, but for that of seeing and putting to good use some new values from consciousness that exemplify deeply and fully the emerging world civilization.

The task as understood by Jacobson, then, is entirely comprehensive, and the aim of philosophy should be commensurate with it. In this way, the task is far beyond any acceptance of the cherished professional paradigms of philosophers, beyond the best that has been thought and prized throughout the world, and radically beyond the sum of all that is and has been.

Our task is to embark. Nay, the embarkation has always been with us. We ride most satisfactorily within the waves, as individual interlacing waves within waves within waves, facilitating the coming and breaking into consciousness of the emerging world civilization. This is the lucid poetry of experience, the reason of no-reason, the mysterious burgeoning unity that pervades everything, reassuring as it gives shape to the forming world.

The lucid poetry of experience lights up and trails off, leaving marks of evocation, following the feeling side of thinking, hearing the explosion of the nerve cells of experience, giving up the acquisitive impulses, offering energy and effort to all that is freely disciplined and charitably disposed, and to all that is comprehensively embodied in the forever evanescent forms of the emerging world civilization:

> Spontaneous resolve
> Open reserve
> Luminous flow,
> A creative
> Self-corrective
> Civilization.

Part One
Historical Context

1.
The Possibility
of Nonattachment   *Bart Gruzalski*

Theravāda Buddhism has always been of interest to intellectuals in the West, but it has come increasingly to the attention of philosophers in the analytic tradition in the past twenty-five years. Nolan Pliny Jacobson stimulated the analytical philosopher's interest in Buddhism with his book *Buddhism: The Religion of Analysis*, and Derek Parfit's recent *Reasons and Persons* reveals a respect for Buddhism at the heart of one of the contemporary classics of analytic philosophy.[1] One attraction of each of these works to an analytic philosopher is a focus on the metaphysics of Buddhism, specifically on the Buddhist account of the nature of the self. The philosopher who moves from this contemporary interest to the broader themes of Buddhism discovers a practical philosophy that promises a solution to the problem of suffering.

Buddha expressed this solution in the Four Noble Truths: (1) there is suffering in the world, (2) its cause is desire (*tanhā*), (3) the cessation of desire is the cessation of suffering, and (4) the Eightfold Path leads to these cessations. The prescription suggested by these statements is to do what causes the cessation of desire. Since the cessation of desire would result in desirelessness, western thinkers have puzzled over difficulties of the following sort: if the thrust of Buddhism is to encourage desirelessness, then that is to encourage persons to desire desirelessness, which itself seems contradictory. Such concerns raise the possibility that the Buddha's path is as impossible as squaring a circle.

In what follows I shall address three serious intellectual problems that are often raised when someone first notices that Buddhism presupposes the possibility of a meaningful life without desire or attachment. Although there is a marked difference between the cessation of desire and the cessation of attachment, I shall overlook this difference in order to focus more directly on these three problems. For this reason I shall explicitly discuss Buddhism as if it presents a solution to the problem of suffering that involves the cessation of desire. What I say can, *mutatis mutandis*, be applied to Buddhism understood as promoting the cessation of attachment.

The first problem focuses on the desire to become desireless. The second focuses on the concern that, even if we can show that it is logically possible to be desireless, a person who attained "desirelessness" would need a desire to remain that way. The third is whether we can make sense of a fully coherent pattern of human activity without desire. If any of these problems is insoluble, then the Buddhist program, whatever insights it may offer into human life, would not be a coherent view. But these intellectual puzzles can be solved in their own terms, and these solutions can help the Western philosopher more easily appreciate the merits of Buddha's ancient path.[2]

1.   The Desire for Desirelessness

If a person who wanted to stop suffering tried to move toward becoming desireless, that person would naturally desire to become desireless. If the person now desired to remove this new desire, the desire to do so would be an additional desire, and, apparently, to remove the new desire would require another desire and so on *ad infinitum*. If this criticism of Theravāda Buddhism were accurate, then there would always be at least one desire present in the person trying to remove all desires, and hence the aim of the Buddhist program could never be attained.[3] It would follow that the Buddhist program, at least as I have characterized it, would be logically impossible.[4]

There are several ways a practitioner of Buddhism might resolve this puzzle. For example, assuming that the Eightfold Path leads to liberation, becoming an exemplar of that path would lead to the cessation of suffering. Likewise, one might *intend* to work toward the cessation of craving and desire, rather than *desire* to achieve anything, and there is good reason for thinking that the frustration of an intention does not cause suffering.[5] Nonetheless, these two ways of resolving the problem may seem, to the analytical Western mind, more like in-house disguises than solutions.[6] Since the thought that Buddhism might rest on a logical inconsistency has the potential for blocking a person from investigating it further, we have a strong practical reason for resolving the problem in its own analytical terms and without any subtlety.

There is a solution to this problem that does not involve the Theravāda Buddhist in inconsistency. What we are asking is whether there is any state that a person can desire which, if attained, would result in the person's being desireless. One answer to this question is

that a person could desire to rid herself of all desires except the desire
to do so. Once all other desires were extinguished, the desire to be rid
of them would be satisfied, and hence it too would be extinguished.[7]
This solution also has a more intuitive formulation. When we think of
the desires that typically cause us suffering—the desire for comfort,
for the well-being of others, for affection, for health, for reputation,
for money—it makes sense to think that if we did not have these desires, we would no longer suffer the corresponding frustrations and
dissatisfactions. If all such desires were removed, the person in question would no longer desire to be rid of them and, hence, would be
without any desires.

It may be objected that this solution is contrary to Buddha's insights, for the thought that one can rid oneself of desire through the
satisfaction of desire is one of the illusions about reality that Buddha
attempted to correct.[8] In addition, the desire to *become* desireless is
itself a cause of suffering, as Buddha clearly implies in the Second
Noble truth when he states that desires or cravings which are the origin of suffering include the "craving for becoming." Nonetheless, insofar as we are trying to solve a problem about logical consistency, the
solution either stands or fails on its logical merits. From a logical point
of view we seem to have established that reaching a momentary state
in which there are no desires is possible.

2.   The Desire to Remain Desireless

We have assumed, in discussing the problem generated by the
puzzle of the desire for desirelessness, that when a desire is satisfied, it
is gone. This is true for what are referred to as "felt" or *occurrent*
desires. For example, if I have a desire for a particular orange, and am
given that orange, then I no longer have that desire. A "felt" or occurrent desire involves a favorable regarding or viewing of an object, and
typically involves an inner tug, a warm feeling, an empty feeling, a
tingle, or some other inner sensation (hence the name "felt").[9] Not all
desires, however, are occurrent or felt. Smith, for example, may want
more money, even though Smith has no tugs or tingles at this moment
about the prospect of having more money because Smith is totally
involved in watching the first robin of spring. Nonetheless, Smith wants
more money, and under the proper conditions this want will become
occurrent. Such background or "waiting" wants are referred to as
dispositional desires. The more basic of the two kinds of desires is the

occurrent desire, since a dispositional want is only a disposition or propensity to have an occurrent want under certain conditions.

The desire to reach a goal that, when reached, leaves one desireless is a desire to be a certain kind of person. Such desires are typically dispositional. For example, if I desire to be a good tennis player, and become one, is my desire to be a good tennis player extinguished—or only temporarily satisfied? What happens if, the following season, I fail to practice, and I slip into mediocrity? We might say that the original desire was extinguished and that I may or may not now have a new desire to become again a good tennis player. Or, if I do find myself desiring to be a good tennis player, we might say that the original desire was a dispositional desire and was always "in the background." In the case of Buddhism, however, the desire to be free of all other desires would not be just to become a certain kind of person, but rather to become and remain a certain kind of person *without backsliding*. The only way such a desire can be satisfied is if one never backslides. If one does backslide, the desire to be that kind of person would no longer be satisfied and, one might hope, would again motivate the person to regain his lost character. This suggests that the desire to extinguish all other desires is not only occurrent but is also dispositional, and that the person who has extinguished all occurrent desires might yet have a dispositional desire to remain free of any occurrent desire.

It follows from this that although we have shown the logical possibility of the cessation of all occurrent desires, we have not yet established the plausibility of the cessation of all dispositional desires. To make plausible the cessation of *all* desires, occurrent *and* dispositional, and so to make plausible the possibility of nonattachment, requires that we investigate another fundamental factor that leads to suffering: ignorance. From the Buddhist perspective, because we would not have the desires that cause suffering if we were not ignorant of the way things are, overcoming ignorance is a crucial part of the path of liberation.

3. Ignorance Conditions Desire

Having the knowledge that overcomes ignorance is more than possessing justified correct information. Buddhists distinguish between knowledge that only requires information and knowledge that involves direct and unmediated awareness.[10] For example, a person may be as well informed about grief as anyone. This person may later experience grief and subsequently report that, prior to the experience, she did not really know what grief was, whereas she now knows the nature of grief, even though there is no new information she can pass on. It is only in the sense in which knowledge is realization that the Buddhists claim knowledge is essential to the solution of the problem of suffering.

One chief insight a person gains in overcoming the ignorance that leads to desire is that everything with which we are familiar, everything we value and prize, is in the process of ceasing. Partly as a result of this radical impermanence, desire leads to suffering. If we desire and gain anything ordinarily considered to be "permanent"—health, home, reputation, family, well-being of friends—our desire typically involves an attachment or a desire to keep what we have. Because everything is changing and passing away, this desire will eventually be frustrated. A realization of the impermanence of all phenomena is central to liberation.[11] The following example illustrates and makes plausible how the awareness of impermanence can undermine our desire for anything to remain unchanged.

Suppose Sara, an adult, has lived her entire life in a part of the world that has snowy winters and, as a result, is quite familiar with the fact that a snowman built in early autumn might easily melt the following day if the temperature becomes unseasonably high. Suppose that Richard, a six year old, is visiting the same part of the world and that, during this late autumn visit, Richard experiences his first snowfall. Sara and Richard each build a snowman. The next day the temperatures become so warm that it is clear to Sara that her snowman will melt away before late afternoon. Precisely because Sara knows, almost as well as she knows anything from experience, that her snowman will melt that afternoon, we can easily imagine that it will be very hard for her to desire that the snowman not melt and that, even if she has such a desire, it would be unlikely for her to have that desire to the same degree as a person who lacks her knowledge. Richard, however, who has a radically different awareness of what is going on, might well attempt to keep his snowman from melting by adding snow and trying to prop up what is sagging. Importantly, what distinguishes between Sara and Richard is their knowledge: no other factor seems able to account for their markedly differing degrees of desire. The most plausible account we can give of the difference in the degree of the desires of these two people is their knowledge of the nature of snowmen (in the sense in which knowledge is realization and different from mere information). Because Sara knows that snowmen melt on warm autumn days, she does not desire her snowman not to melt to the same degree as Richard desires his not to melt. Hence, it is at least plausible to claim that the awareness of the impermanence of entities makes it more likely that we will not desire them to be otherwise.

We may use this conclusion to illustrate the plausibility of a much larger point. According to Theravāda Buddhism, everything that we are involved in trying to get, maintain, or protect—health, relationships, job, professional status—has the same essential characteristic of Sara's and Richard's snowmen: all this is passing away. Hence, it is at least plausible that the person who clearly sees this will not, or at least not as likely, desire to get or keep anything at all.

It may be objected that the awareness of impermanence often heightens desire and its corresponding suffering. Suppose I learn, for example, that someone dear to me has died. Since my desire for the person to be alive may even increase, it may seem to follow that an awareness of impermanence does not diminish desire. This objection, however, draws its apparent strength from the complexity of human grief. When someone dies the bereaved often suffers from an array of unfulfilled desires (in addition to such emotions as anger and resentment). Not only is there an unfulfilled desire for the deceased to be alive, but there are also desires of many other sorts: desires to be free of guilt for past actions or omissions; desires to be able to communicate some feeling or thought; desires for continuing whatever supports and sense of well-being were provided by the deceased; desires not to be like the deceased and hence vulnerable to dying; and so on. Plausibly these desires were present before I learned of the death, and this event only caused me to become aware of them. These realistic complexities, combined with our own lack of practice in being mindful about our emotional responses, prevent us from clearly identifying any individual desire caused by the awareness of impermanence in the example of the death of a loved one and prevent us from drawing any reliable conclusions about the relationship between desire and the awareness of impermanence. By contrast, the snowman case is very narrowly circumscribed. If we again reflect on it, knowledge is the only clear differentiating factor—and it does make a difference. Hence, the straightforward snowman example provides reason to find the Buddhist view plausible.

Furthermore, reflections on how we do grieve provide further evidence for the plausibility of Buddha's insight. The relevant fact about human beings is that we are better able to accept death losses after we have directly experienced the fact of loss—for example, by viewing the body. In contrast, those who deny losses by avoiding any experience that might make them more real (for example, by avoiding a funeral) typically have a significantly more difficult time grieving and moving toward a state of acceptance. This suggests that experiencing the impermanence or loss of anything does undermine, or at least helps undermine, our attachment or desire for reality to be otherwise. This evidence provides further plausibility to the Buddhist claim that becoming aware of the impermanence of everything undermines our having desires for any of it to remain unchanged. In short, it is plausible to think that undermining ignorance undermines desire and attachment.

If the arguments above are correct, we have shown the possibility of desirelessness and nonattachment. It is plausible to think that the person who has an awareness of the nature of reality, including its radical impermanence, will not be able to have occurrent desires again. Since there can be no occurrent desires, it makes no sense to claim that there are any underlying dispositional desires, because a dispositional desire is nothing more than a disposition for occurrent desires to arise. Hence, there need be no background dispositional desire—no desire to remain desireless—for a person to remain free from occurrent desire. For such a being, there will be no desires or attachments of any kind at all.

4. Action Without Desire

The possibility of a living human being lacking desires leads to a third concern often raised about Buddhism: the worry that without desire a person would be so indifferent as to be unable to act in any coherent way at all, much less in the compassionate way indicated by Buddhism.[12] We can begin answering this concern by reflecting on our ordinary actions. Imagine that you turn your key to the right in an automobile's ignition. As you turn the key, you have no apparent desire to turn it and no thought of having to do so; likely you are thinking about something entirely irrelevant to the action. Or imagine leisurely walking down a street and coming upon an elderly person who is struggling to keep from dropping some shopping bags. You help without wondering if helping is in your interest or if it is something you ought to do. Or again: someone asks you for directions and you know the information requested; you act, giving the directions without any conscious decision or desire to do so. Or finally: someone calls out your name, and you respond "spontaneously."

In each of these examples we can imagine a person acting only after a conscious decision or a felt desire to do so, and for each of us there probably was a time when such a mental event was required to turn the key in the ignition, help with the bags, or give directions. But now that such ways of acting have become habitual, that's the way we are. We just do such actions. This indicates that coherent action is possible without desire. Such actions do occur, simply because of the way we are.[13] Habitual actions show that coherent human action is possible without a desire to act in the requisite way. Perhaps most of our actions are desireless in this way—the way we sit, hold a pen, walk, eat soup, raise a hand to ask a question, call out someone's name, and so on.

This response to the concern that action is impossible without desire may seem incomplete for three reasons. First, habitual actions are rooted in desire. At one point, for example, we desired to learn how to start a car, and our first attempts were filled with the appropriate inner tugs until we mastered the actions involved. Second, a life of habit does not seem to be a good way to avoid suffering, because when habitual action is blocked, frustration and suffering often result. And third, actions like my starting a car occur within a context of desire. When I start my car, presumably I am doing so because I want to go somewhere.

The first concern—that habitual actions are rooted in desire—poses no difficulty for the Buddhist, since the Buddhist does not claim that we *begin* without desire, only that there is no desire when the process is *completed*. The second concern—that the frustration of habits causes suffering—requires a longer answer that enlarges the scope of our understanding of human action.

In the foregoing I have deliberately referred to patterns of coherent human activity as *habitual*. It is more appropriate to refer to these patterns of activity as *skills*. Acquiring a habit is troublesome for the Buddhist in two ways that acquiring a skill is not. If I am a person who sails in a habitual way, and if I always tack as I sail past the yacht club, I may be frustrated when the winds are such that I can not do this. But if I am a person who sails in a skillful way, there is nothing about my way of sailing that will lead to frustration in these conditions. For a person to sail skillfully simply requires that the person exemplify good sailing principles to the extent possible for that person in that boat and in those conditions. Insofar as acting skillfully is the whole account of what I am doing, then frustration will no more occur when I am forced aground than it would if I, while only trying to play skillfully, lost my most skillful game of chess to a player whom I knew to be much better than myself. Secondly, habits are notoriously blind, as blind as desire, whereas skills require constant awareness and adaptability to changing conditions.[14] The sailor who habitually sails in a particular fashion will go aground in an unusually low tide, whereas the skillful sailor will be aware of the new conditions and take these into consideration.[15] If she goes aground, and of course conditions may occur in which going aground is unavoidable, her going aground will not be caused by her lack of awareness or her attachment to a particular way of sailing.

Although these and other skillful activities may, like habits, account for coherent patterns of human activity unmotivated by desire, these patterns of activities typically occur *in contexts* in which desires play a fundamental motivational role. This brings us to the third concern, that is, that actions always occur in a context of desire. Nothing discussed above about skillful action shows that it is possible for an *entire life* to be devoid of desire. We have not yet resolved the question whether coherent human activity is possible without desire. To answer this question we will turn to an apparently unrelated question, that is, why Buddhism not only points to desirelessness but also points toward compassion.

Compassion is a natural antidote to desire.[16] For example, a person suffering a significant monetary loss may find her pain and underlying desires are diminished when she only focuses her mind and heart on the plight of recent war victims who have lost loved ones, possessions, and communities. Her pain over her monetary loss would also likely diminish if she began to help these war victims. But even compassion may embroil us in desires for the well-being of others. I may begin to identify with the desires of those whom I am trying to help and may become frustrated at my own inadequacy. At best, then, compassion may seem only an adequate antidote to egoistical desires. Nonetheless, this move away from egoistical desires is really a move toward an entirely new way of being: toward being an exemplification of compassion.

Once a person is fully compassionate, there is never an occasion for the frustration over the suffering of others that would lead to suffering. If there is suffering that cannot be relieved, an understanding of this reality would prevent additional suffering for a fully compassionate person, much as Sara, once she realizes the nature of snow on a warm autumn day, need not suffer because her snowman is melting. The way of compassion is a practical path toward desirelessness. Once compassion is fully exemplified, once a person becomes totally and skillfully compassionate, that person no longer desires to conform to this way of being. This is that person's nature, that person's entire life, so these traits are naturally exemplified by that person's nature, without the need for some larger context or even a desire to be that way. That is just the way the person is. Such a person, a skillfully compassionate being, fully awake and nonattached, is a Buddha.[17]

Notes

1. Nolan Pliny Jacobson, *Buddhism: The Religion of Analysis* (Carbondale and Edwardsville: Southern Illinois University Press, 1966); and Derek Parfit, *Reasons and Persons* (Oxford: Clarendon, 1984). The last two pages of Parfit's text, pp. 502–503, appendix J, entitled "Buddha's View," is composed of eight primary Buddhist selections on the nature of the self.

2. Although much of what I shall say in this chapter applies to most of orthodox Buddhism, I am explicitly referring only to that Buddhism referred to as Theravāda Buddhism, Early Buddhism, Original Buddhism, Pali Buddhism, or sometimes "Hinayana Buddhism." In so doing, I am explicitly only focusing on the canonical Pali texts.

3. In Parfit's recent terminology, we would thereby say that Buddhism was "indirectly self-defeating" because "it is self-defeating when applied to certain people, during certain periods." See Derek Parfit, op. cit., pp. 3–5.

4. One might wonder whether the desire for desirelessness problem is a product of careless translation, because the word we have translated as "desire," *tanhā*, is literally translated "thirst" and is often translated as "craving" rather than as "desire." But translating *tanhā* as "craving" will not mollify one who has this doubt, because there is a problem in drawing a meaningful distinction between desire and craving within the context of a solution to the problem of suffering. If I desire something, I am no less liable to suffer when that desire is frustrated than when a similar craving is frustrated. Hence, if the cessation of suffering is of prime concern, then so is the cessation of desire. In English the words *craving* and *desire* point to attachments that are no different in respect to the Buddhist theme of the cessation of suffering, except that cravings are typically stronger than desires. Because of this interrelationship between desire and craving, I do not think that this distinction is useful in trying to answer the analytic philosopher's worry over problems like the desire for desirelessness. Furthermore, note that although *tanhā* is often translated as "craving," it is also not uncommonly translated as "desire" (see, Walpola Rahula, *What the Buddha Taught* [New York: Grove, 1974], passim, and Huston Smith,

The Religions of Man [New York: Harper & Row, 1965], p. 113). Other meanings of *tanhā* include "transience, i.e., as motion opposed to calm dispassion" [see *The Book of Kindred Sayings* IV (London: Pali Text Society, 1980), p. 37, note 2]. In short, the desire for desirelessness problem is not the result of careless translation.

5. I am indebted to Ajahn Sumedho for this observation.

6. Compare, for example, a Kantian reply that a person could just "will" to become desireless and act accordingly. However, because it is controversial whether such "willings" fail to express desires, to rest the defense of the rationality of Buddhism on such a controversial claim would not satisfy those who took the problem seriously.

7. This solution is discussed by Wayne Alt, "There Is No Paradox of Desire in Buddhism," *Philosophy East and West* 30, (October 1980), p. 527. Neither Alt nor his critics consider the objection discussed in the text about the problem of dispositional desires.

8. I am indebted to Piyadassi Thera for this objection.

9. Here I am following Alvin Goldman's account of occurrent and dispositional wants in *A Theory of Human Action* (Englewood Cliffs, N.J.: Prentice-Hall, 1970), pp. 86–99.

10. "The adoption of views is a term discarded for the truth-finder, who has had actual vision of the nature, origin and cessation of things material—of feelings—of perception—of plastic forces—and of consciousness. Therefore it is that, by destroying, stilling, suppressing, discarding and renouncing all supposings, all imaginings, and all tendencies to the pride of saying 'I' or 'mine', the truth-finder is Delivered because no fuel is left to keep such things going" (*Majjhima-Nikaya*, I, 486).

11. After Buddha's first sermon, "the venerable Kondanna obtained the pure and spotless *Dhamma-eye* (that is to say, the following knowledge): 'Whatsoever is an arising thing, all that is a ceasing thing'" (*Sanyutta-Nikaya*, V, 423).

12. Thomas Nagel expresses this kind of concern in "The Absurd," in *Mortal Questions* (Cambridge: Cambridge University Press, 1979), p. 22.

13. It may be objected that every action, habitual or otherwise, is motivated by an occurrent desire. The chief problem with this objection is that nothing will count against it. If upon introspection no desires are discovered, then, because the criticism is assumed true, the critic assumes either that a desire was present which was overlooked in introspection or that the desire in question was unconscious. Such criticism assumes an answer to the question we are asking, and in this way simply begs the question. Do I have a desire to turn the ignition key a quarter to the right? I may, but the key point is that I also may not, and that is all the Buddhist needs to defeat the claim that all acts are motived by desire.

14. Gilbert Ryle makes similar observations about skills. See *The Concept of Mind* (London: Barnes & Noble, 1949), pp. 42 and 45.

15. As Ryle points out, having a skill involves being able to innovate in situations that are new. For example, the skillful driver has never "foreseen the runaway donkey, yet he is not unprepared for it. His readiness to cope with such emergencies would show itself in the operations he would perform, if they were to occur" (ibid., p. 48).

16. I am indebted to Moreland Perkins for this observation. There is another answer to this question, however, and it is that compassion is a natural outcome of laying aside egoism and desire. Ajahn Sumedho, Moreland Perkins, and Marion Gruzalski have independently suggested that Right Attitude—which includes the four *Brahma-vihāra*: compassion (*karuna*), loving kindness (*metta*), sympathetic joy (*mudita*), and equanimity (*upekkha*)—is a natural outcome of the *samādhi* and *sīla* groupings of the Eightfold Path.

17. I am indebted to Professor Moreland Perkins for demonstrating how to use the analytical concerns around which this chapter is organized as a way to appreciate the plausibility of Buddhism. Versions of this chapter were presented at a Northern New England Philosophy Association Meeting, a Central Division American Philosophical Association Meeting, George Mason University, Northeastern University, Rensselaer Polytechnic Institute, and the University of Dundee. I am grateful for the comments I received on those occasions, to Ajahn Sumedho and Geshe Lobsang Tharchin for helping me gain a deeper appreciation of Buddha's path, and to Marian Wilson-Gruzalski for her helpful comments.

2.
To End Is to Begin   *Cedric Lambeth Heppler*

As I work independently on this essay, I have confidence that some—if not most or all—of the other contributors to this volume will corroborate my thesis that Nolan Pliny Jacobson's career of thought and deeds was consistent from its beginning until its end. This thesis appears to fly in the face of the evidence of his career. On the surface, it would appear that Jacobson began his career by writing his dissertation, "The Religious Naturalism Implicit in the Writings of Karl Marx," in 1948 at the University of Chicago. He then wrote some articles on general themes of religion and Christianity, such as "Religion and the Fragmentation of Man,"[1] "The Problem of Civilization,"[2] "The Uses of Reason in Religion: A Note on David Hume,"[3] and an article based on his dissertation, "Marxism and Religious Naturalism."[4]

Then somewhere in the midst of his career, it appears that Jacobson was converted to Buddhism. A further surface reading of the evidence of his career seems to indicate that Jacobson had no considerations left for his previous thoughts. My thesis is that this is not the case. Some years ago I discovered that four years prior to the completion of his dissertation, Jacobson published a major article that he described in volume 2 of *The Nature and Destiny of Man* as "a critique of Niebuhr's philosophy of history," together with a naturalistic interpretation of the same data to which Niebuhr appeals.[5]

Niebuhr's Philosophy of History

Jacobson began his writing career with the article on Reinhold Niebuhr's philosophy of religion, and in his last book, *The Heart of Buddhist Philosophy*,[6] he returned to an analysis of Niebuhr's thought within the context of the theme of his career. Jacobson very early in his career developed a naturalistic worldview, especially philosophically and religiously. He found that Henry Nelson Wieman's philosophical and religious categories of creative good, created goods, and the creative event with its dimensional subevents were the most adequate means by which to explicate a naturalistic worldview; and he thought that supernaturalistic philosophical and religious worldviews were detrimental to humankind's quality of life, and by extension, to that of the universe. Reinhold Niebuhr's supernaturalistic worldview was not the only such worldview of the day. However, it was the most popular and the best articulated. The critical analysis that Jacobson brought to his interpretation of Niebuhr's supernaturalistic worldview by means of naturalistic categories would have been applied to all supernaturalistic worldviews.

In "Niebuhr's Philosophy of History," Jacobson identified eight "empirical data employed as evidence for super-history" by Niebuhr. To Niebuhr, these eight empirical data were based on the biblical revelation that proved that the answer to history comes from outside of history, super-history. The data were:

1. Man can look before and after, and dream of what is not.
2. Man realizes his own finiteness.
3. Man can extricate himself from the causal forces in history sufficiently to achieve freedom.
4. All the meanings of history are fragmentary and frustrated in time.
5. Man has a sense of failure to fulfill the absolute demands of God; this sense issues from the image of God that is in him.
6. Man looks forward with anxiety to the end of history and to death.
7. History is involved in conflicts that appear on each successive cultural level, never to be escaped.
8. The sacrificial love that was manifested in Christ points to super-history.[7]

Jacobson concluded his study and critique of Niebuhr's philosophy of history with "A Naturalistic Interpretation."[8] He paid tribute to Niebuhr's incisive analysis of the development of meaning in history, of the ambiguities of existence—the survival of meaning in the midst of defeat and the emergence of new meanings from the old, and the problem of sacrificial love in the ambiguities of existence. Niebuhr saw the answer to these empirical, historical ambiguities of existence in super-history. Jacobson established his position on "two particularly fundamental points of variance between the Niebuhr interpretation and one open to naturalism": "We confine all that is, all causal efficacy, to time and space and further affirm that all such efficacy is in the form of structured energy in motion. A non-temporal, non-spatial, non-material activity which Niebuhr interprets super-history to be is rejected. And our method of investigating this causal efficacy is confined to the public observance of relationship between events.[9]

Jacobson's naturalistic categories of interpreting history led him to state that there is "a correlate to Niebuhr's super-history," to be found operative in nature and human history: "It is a matter open to public investigation that whatever have been the individual fates of nations and cultural epochs, there has been a *continuing*, though spasmodic and faltering, *development of meaning*, a *progressive growth of mind*, a widening of mental horizons in a *more appreciable world*. ...The creation of this sensitive community of minds in a wider, more appreciable world is the work of that activity which we call God.[10] These naturalistic categories are Wiemanian in origin.

Marxism and Religious Naturalism

For anyone, especially at the University of Chicago, to write a dissertation on Marxism in 1948, an act of courage was necessary. More accessible than the dissertation is the 1949 *Journal of Religion* article, "Marxism and Religious Naturalism." It is obvious from a reading of both the dissertation and the article that Jacobson had read all of Marx (and Engels) that he could come by. Jacobson's thesis was that "Marx seeks the key to an understanding of human history in man's own practical, labor activity....The life activity that Marx identifies with human labor embodies both self-creation and self-transcendence....The elements that are intrinsic to this history are real historical men, their emerging needs, their practical, critical life-activity, the social matrix of their life-process, and the material conditions under which they live.[11]

Marx is famous, or infamous, for the assertion that religion "is the opium of the people,"[12] so why did Jacobson go to Marx for any views on religion? Jacobson believed that what Marx developed out of his study of human work and human history could be instructive with regard to the significance of human beings having aspirations for finding in human work and human history evidence of the source of all human good: "Is there in Marx's philosophy of history a structured process of identifiable and intrinsically observable events, which functions in and through human living as the source of all human good?...does this structured process *bring forth* values that men cannot foresee; *transform* human likes, needs, values, and goals; and develop value loyalties that tend *mutually to support* rather than to conflict and destroy one another?"[13] These three events of the structured process that is the source of all human good, elaborated throughout the rest of Jacobson's article, are Wiemanian and áre drawn from Jacobson's intimate, involved study of Wieman's naturalism and its categories,[14] as well as from the religious naturalism that he found to be implicit in the works of Marx.

The historical context of Jacobson's dissertation (University of Chicago, 1948) is epoch making. Because I lack enough study and insight into the work of Marx, I leave it to others to judge whether Jacobson was successful in bringing out religious naturalism implicit in the works of Marx. I think, however, that Jacobson's elaboration of the three events of the source of all human good constitutes one of the clearest statements made on this basic principle of religious naturalism. Jacobson's elaboration of the emergence of the first event into the life and affairs of human existence and history is clearer than Wieman ever was able to state it.[15]

In the late forties and early fifties, just about every American philosopher and theologian brought his/her soteriology (worldview) to bear on the human situation, under the influence of various analyses of the human situation by various existentialist philosophies and theologies. "Religion and the Fragmentation of Man" was Jacobson's attempt to point out that religious naturalism had answers to the problems created by the fragmentation of man. Although he alluded to and quoted briefly from Kierkegaard and Berdyaev (plus Horney and Fromm), Jacobson chose to use insights drawn from George Herbert Mead (and to a lesser extent, from William James) to analyze the fragmentation of man that needed healing.

What was the fragmentation of man according to Jacobson?

The increasing lack of warm mutuality and fellow-feeling, the loss of opportunity to bring one's total personality to bear upon the world, the overruling and mechanical linking-together of specialized functions, and the loss of spontaneity, all reap a harvest of moral depravity, mental disorder, alcoholism, suicide, and barbaric wars that are shocking and in themselves demoralizing to behold....

As yet modern man seems almost totally in the dark as to what he must *know* and how he must proceed in order to heal his dividedness.[16]

I emphasized the word *know* in the citation above to call attention to the difference between the existentialist (and neoorthodox) philosophers and theologians and a religious naturalist when it came time to give an answer to this fragmentation. The distinction is between the existentialist leap of faith (into either the wholly other or nausea) and the empirical and experiential knowing that can lead a person or a community of persons to make rational and purposive decisions. The distinction is between irrationalism and a reasoning approach to the search for the answer to the brokenness of human existence: "*What men must know*—If we mean by knowledge the ability to predict what conditions will yield what consequences, we must strive to identify the conditions in the problem at hand which will deliver man from his dividedness.[17] The irrationalism of a Barth or a Reinhold Niebuhr sought—or rather announced—the conditions for the solution to the brokenness of the human condition either in a grace of God that was infinitely and qualitatively different from the human spirit—this grace gave humans the faith to "believe" in it—or in a super-history that contradicted all human effort.

Jacobson's analysis of the conditions that will deliver people from their dividedness is both a further refutation of supernaturalism and a further explication of his naturalistic categories. Given the definition of knowledge above, Jacobson identified the conditions as:

> constitut[ing] an external structure *in the midst of human life*, controlling the process by which the individual transcends his dividedness and expands his powers. They are external, not in the sense of operating outside of man, but in the sense of forming a structure not dependent upon human thought, to which our thinking must conform. They are external in the sense that they are not something that man can accomplish. ...They have brought man out of bestiality into civilization and are something to which no man, and no group of men, can ever gain title. Because they create man, they must be considered as part of the nature of God. In so far as man lives in the keeping of these conditions, he finds fellowship with God.[18]

These conditions are Wiemanian, and they are five in number.

1. The first condition is the opening of the individual to a felt need, a sense of requiredness, a feeling or inadequacy.

2. The second condition is the emerging of a new quality, perspective, insight, or meaning.

3. The third condition is the sharing of each new meaning, quality, and perspective with other people in a manifold of social interchange, so that it becomes an avenue for repeated communication, an occasion for connective growth.

4. The fourth condition is the integrating of each new meaning, quality, or perspective that has stood the test of social interchange, within the individuals involved so that old attitudes are transformed and borrowed perspectives transcended.

5. The fifth and final condition in the process of personal becoming is the integrating of the new qualitative meaning or perspective into already existing avenues of social interchange. Without this integration, nothing is rescued from *the processes of death and corruption that overflood the generations of social living.*[19]

Jacobson summarized the analysis of the five conditions that can heal the fragmentation and brokenness of human existence by admonishing that "these five conditions must not be understood in their separateness but in their togetherness."[20] The conditions (or events) cannot be controlled by human ideals and planning. The conditions come into human existence as the required conditions are present. Humans lay no claims on the conditions, and humans hold present understanding of the conditions that is open to change as the dimensional aspects of the conditions lead humans through new felt needs, emerging values, sharing of values, integrating of values, and integrating new and shared values into existing social interchange.

Faith, as articulated from the perspective of religious naturalism, operates in two dimensions: at the level of the symbolic expression of the present understanding of where the conditions have brought the human scene, and at the level of remaining open to the possibility that the conditions can lead humans beyond any controllable or imaginable state of affairs. Jacobson summarized it as follows.

he can learn to place his anchorage in the vortex of conditions which alone are capable of delivering him from his dividedness and pseudo-self.

...what is involved here is commitment to something that transcends life as presently patterned and understood. ...This is the faith that overcometh (*sic*) the world, that cures every dividedness, every evil and disintegrative tendency, every incapacity for maximum self-realization.[21]

"Religion and the Fragmentation of Man" is a good example of Jacobson's commitment to a naturalistic worldview, of his explications of Wieman's philosophical and religious categories of the creative good, created goods, and the creative event, and of his care to show that worldviews are tentative at best but that a naturalistic worldview can be humble enough to await newness and destruction.

The Problem of Civilization

Jacobson wrote "The Problem of Civilization" during the rise of anticommunism in many national and local governmental agencies, the building of nuclear weapons by major nations, and the implementation of the cold war containment strategy of the United States with regard to the Soviet Union internationally. Some of the anticommunism displayed on the local and national scenes was well-intentioned in its purpose of making the world safe for democracy, but most of the anticommunism displayed on the local and national scenes was hysterical and wrongheaded in its method of passing judgment through guilt by association. So Jacobson saw the threat of the potential decline of civilization—and perhaps even the annihilation of human existence and history.

For Jacobson the potential decline of civilization threatened because leaders of the major nations did not understand the dynamics of the growth of civilization and did not seem to understand the dynamics of the decline of civilization. The actions of nations that gave rise to the headlines in news of the day in 1952 gave evidence of the decline of civilization rather than of its growth and renewal. In Jacobson's estimate, "...the concept of 'civilization' means the progressive diversification and interweaving of relationships joining individual human beings with one another and with the rest of nature."[22]

Jacobson was quick to point out that "civilization is not something that *does* this to men; a series of such transformations *constitutes* the process of civilization." For civilization to be rising instead of declining, there should be evidence of the following events: (1) a growth in the sensitivities of the individual person; (2) exercising and maturing of new capabilities of the individual; (3) increasing self-awareness; (4) growing effectiveness of the individual as a source of social change; (5) broadening diffusion, interweaving, and communication of each individual's sensitivities and responses with the thought and action of others; (6) increasing interdependence between men; and (7) increasing assimilation of non-human nature into the expanding relation-manifold binding men together.

Jacobson was so bold to state, "The events gradually disappearing during a period of decline will be found to be the ones to which our concept refers.[23]

Given the nature of human history, the problem of civilization has been "the problem of promoting the growth of individual men in mutually compatible rather than divisive and mutually destructive directions.[24] And given this, especially in view of the tremendous destructive power that humans have at their disposal, is there any unitary power, force, or process capable of "promoting growth in mutually compatible directions and protecting the civilizing process against its enemies of mutual annihilation and destruction?"[25] Based on his continued commitment to a naturalistic worldview and to the soteriological efficacy of the source of all human good, the creative event, Jacobson answered that there is such a unitary process, and that it "is constituted by seven types of occurrences, functioning together to promote man's progressive growth."[26]

The first occurrence in any kind of individual growth whatsoever is the opening of the individual to a felt need, a sense of requiredness, a feeling of inadequacy....

The second type of occurrence...is the emergence of a new sensitivity within the psychosomatic organism....

The third type of occurrence...is the emergence of some new insight, perspective, or qualitative meaning on the trail of emerging sensitivity and need....It [the sensitivity] has found a relationship with other events in man's conscious awareness....

The fourth type of occurrence...is the exercise and maturation of a new capacity, talent, or power....

...the fifth type of event...is the sharing of each new qualitative meaning, perspective, or power with other people in the social manifold, so that it becomes the avenue of repeated interchange....

The sixth type of occurrence...is the integration of each new meaning-illumined, effective sensitivity and need, when it has survived the test of sharing, with all the rest the individual can see, feel, know, anticipate, and do....

The seventh type of event in the process we are seeking to identify in the midst of civilization is the integrating of the new illumined, need-driven power into existing avenues of interchange, man to man and man to the rest of nature.[27]

Although a great deal of emphasis is placed on the individual, Jacobson stressed that "the process described...promotes simultaneously the growth of both individual as *such* and community."[28] Without the mutually enhancing growth of the individual and the growth of persons within the social manifold, civilization stagnates, declines, and dies. Jacobson challenged ingrained institutions—government, education, industry, religion, and the family—to become open and responsive to the unitary process of the source of all human good. The challenge still stands.

"The Uses of Reason in Religion: A Note on David Hume"

Jacobson's "The Use of Reason in Religion: A Note on David Hume" is the most intriguing, yet the most perplexing, of his early articles under consideration in this essay. It is intriguing because it sheds much-needed light on the philosophy of Hume. It is perplexing because its six and one-half pages leave the reader hungering for more.

Without rephrasing the positivistic and sensationalistic aspects of Hume's empiricism, Jacobson proposed

to show that Hume's analysis of reason terminates in the identification of a subrational matrix which has unassessed religious significance. It might be said that Hume has assigned reason a task in the ultimate issues of life and that this task is to study the case history of thought, following the trail backward into a mothering matrix of fellow feeling and interper-

sonal relations. The natural history of believing is traced to
this matrix, and it is here that we are saved from the full
force of our dilemmas. It is this matrix that breaks the force
of all skeptical arguments and which, "by an absolute and
uncontrollable necessity," determines us "to judge as well as
to feel."[29]

This "mothering matrix of fellow feeling and interpersonal relations" is prior to logical analyses of human existence and its attendant
pain. The biosocial basis of human existence—where we are when we
hurt, when we feel with, or sympathize with, our fellow human beings
in their hurts and pains—is the subrational matrix: "Reason, for Hume,
finds its ultimate function in keeping men alive to this psychosocial
foundation which is the very ground under our feet....Biosocial interchange is the natural element in which all believing takes place. It is
what we are already in when we arrive.[30]

Jacobson argued that Hume's insights into this biosocial interchange as the process from which we are nurtured through sympathy
and fellow feeling is "the fundamental bonding agent of human society." This biosocial interchange is not based on reason or intellect. It
is not based on anything at all. It is "the 'ultimate propensities' of
human nature in a kind of sympathetic communication wherein individuals share the deeps of what they are privately undergoing and
touch the inmost reality of each other's lives....Spiritual communion
of this sort is possible, and, according to Hume it constitutes the reality 'beyond which we cannot hope to find any principle more general'
or more basic. It is the ultimate and irreducible fact."[31]

Reason, rather than leading to a fixation of belief through a controlling intellect, has its main function in the guidance of human life
through a world with a weltering, teeming flow of qualities. We become human, and religious, when we allow reason to function in at
least three dimensions of our biosocial natures. Although the function
of reason may be analyzed in these three dimensions, it is unitary in its
causal efficacy.

First, reason functions "to keep us from those forms of thought
which alienate us from the creative sources of mind and personality."
Second, the world of quality is characterized by change, and as minds
and personalities come in contact with each other and the world, the
world and minds and personalities will undergo change, by virtue of
the quality of the world and of minds and personalities. There must be
some efficacious agency that can guide this change, or else there will

be chaos and insanity. Thus, "the chief function of reason is to furnish such control by a knowledge of the relevant conditions."[32]

Third, reason teaches us humility. We soon learn that we are not able to summon forth the flow of the quality of the world and the changes that take place in our minds and our personalities as we are nurtured in and by the biosocial interchange of human life. We are only able to open ourselves to one another and to the qualities of the world. As we open ourselves, we marvel at our "capacity for undergoing progressive transformation of mind, yielding up inherited theories and attitudes in order to make room for organized unities more sensitive, on the one hand, to the world of nature and man and, on the other hand, to the full capacities of each individual organism for experiencing the world in the developing light of all native endowments."[33]

"The Uses of Reason in Religion" is not only intriguing and perplexing but a masterful introduction to the basis for religion in human history. Because it is so short, its pregnant meaning for religion, especially our Western varieties, could easily be overlooked or ignored. I have found it rewarding to supplement it with the further rich insights that Jacobson developed in the other essays I have discussed here and in his chapter "The Buddha and Hume," in *Buddhism: The Religion of Analysis* (see note 3).

Conclusion

My concern in this essay has been to highlight Jacobson's earlier career, when he was still writing about normal Judaeo-Christian themes, and to attempt to illustrate that he established a thematic commitment that remained consistent throughout his career. I leave it to others more knowledgeable of his later career to explicate its dimensions. Jacobson's later writings turned to the East, especially to Buddhism. From that perspective, he analyzed religion. His analysis during this later period remained consistent with the theme of his career: a naturalistic worldview, a commitment to the saving efficacy of the creative event in our biosocial life, and, an empirical and rational challenge to supernaturalistic worldviews.

This consistency ranges from his essay "Niebuhr's Philosophy of History" to his last book, *The Heart of Buddhist Philosophy*. In a key passage of this book, Jacobson quotes Whitehead, emphasizing that "We see here [Niebuhr's view] the antipode to process thought in religion. 'Any appeal,' Whitehead writes, 'to a reality outside nature—the

Absolute, Brahma, The Order of Heaven, God—to which we may appeal for the removal of perplexity, constitutes the great refusal of rationality to assert its rights.' Wieman and Buddhism agree."[34]

Notes

1. Nolan Pliny Jacobson, "Religion and the Fragmentation of Man," *Journal of Religion* 32, no. 1 (January 1952), pp. 18–30.
2. Nolan Pliny Jacobson, "The Problem of Civilization," *Ethics, an International Journal of Social, Political and Legal Philosophy* 63, no. 1 (October 1952), pp. 14–32.
3. Nolan Pliny Jacobson, "The Uses of Reason in Religion: A Note on David Hume," *Journal of Religion* 39, no. 1 (January 1959), pp. 103–109. This book is not the only writing Jacobson did on Hume. See especially: "Hume on the Uses of Reason in Religion," *The Iliff Review* 15, no. 2 (Spring 1958), pp. 49–59; "The Possibility of Oriental Influence in Hume's Philosophy," *Philosophy East and West* 19, no. 1 (January 1969), pp. 17–37; Chapter 8, "The Buddha and Hume," in *Buddhism: The Religion of Analysis* (New York, Humanities 1965; Reprint, Carbondale and Edwardsville: Southern Illinois University Press, 1966, 1970).
4. Nolan Pliny Jacobson, "Marxism and Religious Naturalism," *Journal of Religion* 29, no. 2 (April 1949), pp. 95–113.
5. Nolan Pliny Jacobson, "Niebuhr's Philosophy of History," *Harvard Theological Review* 37, no. 4 (October 1944), pp. 237–268.
6. Nolan Pliny Jacobson, *The Heart of Buddhist Philosophy* (Carbondale and Edwardsville: Southern Illinois University Press, 1988).
7. "Niebuhr's Philosophy of History," p. 241.
8. Ibid., pp. 261–268.
9. Ibid., p. 262.
10. Ibid., pp. 262–263 (emphasis added).
11. "Marxism and Religious Naturalism," pp. 95, 96, 97.
12. The context is Marx's statement in his *Critique of Hegel's "Philosophy of Right,"* trans. Annette Jolin and Joseph O'Malley (Cambridge: Cambridge University Press, 1970), p. 131: "The wretchedness of religion is at once an expression of and a protest against real wretchedness. Religion is the sign of the oppressed creature, the heart of a heartless world and the soul of soulless conditions. It is the opium of the people."
13. "Marxism and Religious Naturalism," p. 101 (emphasis added.)
14. In the elaboration of the second event—the integration of a new, active relationship within an existing context of relationships, person to person and person to the rest of nature—Jacobson cites Wieman specifi-

cally on p. 107, n. 26: "Cf. H. N. Wieman, *The Source of Human Good* (Chicago, 1946), pp. 59–61.

15. Jacobson, "The Religious Naturalism Implicit in the Writings of Karl Marx" (Ph.D. diss., University of Chicago, 1948), pp. 322–325; "Marxism and Religious Naturalism," pp. 103–105.

16. "Religion and the Fragmentation of Man," p. 18 (emphasis added).

17. Ibid., p. 25.

18. Ibid., pp. 25–26 (emphasis added).

19. Ibid., pp. 26–27 (emphasis added)

20. Ibid., p. 28.

21. Ibid., p. 29.

22. "The Problem of Civilization," p. 15.

23. Ibid.

24. Ibid.

25. Ibid., p. 21.

26. Ibid., p. 22.

27. Ibid., pp. 22–26.

28. Ibid., p. 27.

29. "The Uses of Reason in Religion: A Note on David Hume," p. 103. In this passage, Jacobson had two notes: "1) David Hume, *A Treatise of Human Nature*, ed. Selby-Bigge (London, 1896), I, iv, 1 (187)," and "2) Ibid., I, iv, 1 (183); also, 12, iv, 2."

30. Ibid., pp. 104–105. At "arrive" in the passage above, Jacobson's footnote 11 reads: "In his recent book, Hocking quotes Whitehead as having remarked at a Harvard seminar, 'Hang it all! *Here we are*: we don't go behind that, we begin with it.' (W. E. Hocking, *The Coming World Civilization* [New York, 1956], p. 27)."

31. Ibid., p. 104.

32. Ibid., p. 106.

33. Ibid., p. 108.

34. *The Heart of Buddhist Philosophy*, pp. 99–100.

3.
C. I. Lewis and Buddhism   *Robert L. Greenwood*

It will seem surpassingly strange to anyone at all conversant with the received view of C. I. Lewis to see his name associated with Buddhism. Is not Lewis a member of the school of positivism, an exponent of the verification theory of meaning, a phenomenalist? According to the view I shall develop here, Lewis is a great American philosopher, working within the tradition of American philosophy. Anyone conversant with the writings of Nolan Pliny Jacobson will anticipate immediately the kinds of connection I see between Lewis and Buddhism.

Lewis himself was entirely silent on questions of religion and Eastern thought, and it is unlikely that he was influenced consciously in any way by Eastern thought. But we can easily find a ripening of preceding American thought in the work of Lewis, and hence compelling parallels with the Buddhist intellectual tradition. For example, like the Buddha, Lewis did not argue for a particular metaphysical view.[1] It is not difficult to establish, however, a high probability that he favored process philosophy; that is, he rejected ontological and epistemological dualism. In addition, Lewis did not condemn metaphysics as meaningless. With respect to empirical knowledge, Lewis denied that we could ever enjoy absolute certainty. For a pragmatist, the only correct method for philosophy is the method of hypotheses and a complete rejection of the traditional a priori method. That is to say, philosophy has no special method that can afford us insight into ultimate reality.

Why Lewis Is Not a Phenomenalist

The first task before us is to clear away the lush undergrowth of misinterpretation Lewis has suffered at the hands of such critics as Roderick Chisholm and E. M. Adams. These scholars regard Lewis as an exponent of traditional Western philosophy—as a person committed to the Platonic-Cartesian soul, with all the attendant difficulties that such a view brings in its train, such as the infamous mind-body problem, the problem of other minds, the egocentric predicament, and the problem of the existence of the external world. That Lewis never discussed these problems, except to point out that they are not meaningless, seems not to have discouraged scholars from regarding Lewis as a typical substance philosopher.

Chisholm and Adams regard Lewis as a phenomenalist, and as a result of their powerful influence, Lewis is dutifully described, depicted, and classified as a phenomenalist at every turn. Several textbooks of readings in epistemology contain an excerpt from Lewis, allegedly defending linguistic phenomenalism. The selection is invariably from his discussion of so-called terminating judgments found in his work *An Analysis of Knowledge and Valuation*.

A strong superficial resemblance exists between Lewis's view, especially as expressed in *An Analysis of Knowledge and Valuation*, and linguistic phenomenalism. According to the latter view, a statement about physical objects is equivalent to an infinite number of sense-datum statements. A sense-datum statement does not mention physical objects but only sense-data. According to the view of Lewis, an objective statement (a "nonterminating judgment" in Lewis's terminology) entails a limitless number of terminating judgments.

The following is in the form of a terminating judgment: "If this appearance is that of a cat and I should seem to myself to stroke it, then in all probability I shall seem to myself to experience purring." The word *appearance* does not connote a sense-datum in the classical sense. Lewis quite specifically rejects the sense-datum theory in *Mind and the World Order*.[2] The word *appearance* and its cognates signify for Lewis what they signify for anyone who speaks ordinary English. When a philosophically innocent person says that something "appears to be a cat," all other speakers of English understand that the person is telling us that she/he is in some doubt about the correct interpretation to put on that experience at the moment; this might be a cat and it might not, but it probably is. We understand perfectly the distinction between her/his subjective experience and the object of that experience. The locution, "seem to myself" no more connotes a sense-datum than does the term *appearance*.

Lewis writes that terminating judgments are phrased in expressive language. One very important difference between sense-datum language and expressive language is that the former denotes logically private experiences, while the latter expresses contingently private experiences. By logically private, I mean that their privacy is the result of theoretical considerations. Thus, Descartes's and Locke's ideas are logically private. By contingently private, I mean that I cannot feel the pain in your toe—no matter how much I may empathize with your suffering—and you cannot taste the food in my mouth—although you may be starving. Expressive language attempts to capture immediate experience without making objective claims. It is an instance of the epoche.

A linguistic phenomenalist finds her/himself constantly embarrassed by impurity of analysis. She/he can never rid her/his sense-datum sentences of references to physical objects. As long as this is so, she/he can never produce a pure sense-datum sentence, and her/his program of cashing objective statements in terms of sense-data cannot be realized.

For Lewis, impurity of analysis is clearly not a problem, because he is not in the business of casting objective statements in terms of sense-datum sentences. A terminating judgment is based on what Lewis calls principles of interpretation. These principles are our concepts as applied to our experience of objects. They bear a close relation to Charles Sanders Peirce's theory of meaning: "Consider what effects, that might conceivably have practical bearings, we conceive the object of our conception to have. Then, our conception of these effects is the whole of our conception of the object."[3]

Meaning and the Pragmatic A Priori

Lewis's theory of meaning is part of his theory of the a priori. This latter theory is unique to Lewis and represents a contribution to process philosophy. Although for Lewis, as for Kant, the a priori is universal and necessary, the account each gives of these characterizations is entirely different. For Kant, the universality and necessity of the a priori springs from innate structures of the human mind. For Lewis, they arise from the definitive nature of all concepts.

All concepts have a linguistic meaning and a sense meaning. The linguistic meaning can be found in any good unabridged dictionary. The sense meaning is a criterion in mind—understood as a schema or prescribed routine—by which we are prepared to recognize an instance of the concept, should one occur. The linguistic meaning and the sense meaning together make up the intension of the concept. Lewis calls the intentions of concepts the principles of interpretation. The principles of interpretation contain everything that we believe about a concept. My concept of cat includes not only such things as "if a cat, then a mammal," but such things as "if handled roughly, may scratch." Concepts also include the facts of perceptual relativity. My concept of a white object includes the belief that if it is seen in red light, it probably will appear pink.

For Kant, certain basic concepts—the categories of the understanding—are fixed for all time. This is not so for Lewis, who holds that any concept is subject to change over time. It is entirely possible that some future biological taxonomy will no longer classify cats as felines along with lions and tigers. In that event, the concepts of cat and feline will have undergone change. Such change does not, however, effect their status as a priori. The older a priori has simply been abandoned and replaced by the new.

Knowledge

Lewis's theory of knowledge builds on his theory of meaning. An objective statement, such as, "This is my cat, Mei Ling," connotes a set of statements that Lewis calls terminating judgments. A terminating judgment has the following form: "If this appearance where *appearance* does not denote a sense-datum is indeed that of Mei Ling, and if I should reach out and stroke, then in all probability I should feel soft fur." The if-then relationship in this case is not material implication but a natural connection learned from experience and part of the concept of cat. If I should perform the action of reaching out and stroking and am rewarded with the feeling of soft fur, my objective statement, that this is Mei Ling, has been confirmed. It has not been conclusively verified, because that would involve drawing a conclusion by means of the logical fallacy of affirming the consequent. If I should feel something hard and cold, I am mistaken in my objective statement. I am not in the presence of Mei Ling, but perhaps of a porcelain representation of a cat. Because of the probability factor involved in the terminating judgment, the failure of my action to elicit the expected experience does not decisively falsify my objective statement.

In Lewis's view, we can claim to know something that is actually false. This comes about because empirical knowledge can never, in the nature of the case, be certain. Lewis rejects the Western quest for certainty in claims to knowledge. Empirical knowledge claims can be confirmed or disconfirmed, but never established beyond preadventure.

Metaphysics

Because of the misapprehension about Lewis's philosophy to which I have called attention, he is usually not mentioned in the pantheon of American philosophers. I believe this is a tragic mistake. His theory of meaning puts him clearly in the pragmatist tradition founded by Peirce. Although he studied under William James, Lewis did not write about something called the pragmatic theory of truth—probably because no such thing exists outside the imagination of such writers as Bertrand Russell. It is now widely recognized that James regarded the success of an idea a necessary condition for truth, but not a sufficient one. I think that James was attempting to formulate a theory of knowledge that he mistakenly put in terms of truth. I further think that Lewis produced the pragmatic theory of knowledge for which James was reaching. The writings Lewis left to us indicate that he was influenced by Whitehead's metaphysics. Lewis's pragmatic theory of the a priori is consistent with a process metaphysic.

Classical American pragmatist philosophers, including Lewis, did not condemn metaphysics as meaningless. They condemned arguing for metaphysical theses from innate, self-evident, or any other a priori basis. If the term, *pragmatic method* means anything, it means using the method of hypotheses, to use Quine's term. Peirce called it the scientific method. Dewey called it the empirical method. Lewis called it the reflective method. All stress that philosophy begins and ends with experience, no matter how high the intermittent flight. This has the effect of removing the spurious distinction between physics and metaphysics. Whitehead states:

> Philosophy has been haunted by the unfortunate notion that its method is dogmatically to indicate premises which are severally clear, distinct, and certain; and to erect upon those premises a deductive system of thought.
>
> But the accurate expression of the final generalities is the goal of discussion and not its origin. Philosophy has been misled by the example of mathematics; and even in mathematics the statement of the ultimate logical principles is beset with difficulties, as yet insuperable. The verification of a rationalistic scheme is to be sought in its general success, and not in the peculiar certainty, or initial clarity, of its first principles.[4]

Lewis offered examples of meaningful metaphysical statements in "Experience and Meaning," his presidential address to the Eastern Division of the American Philosophical Association at Amherst College.[5] Included in the metaphysical concepts Lewis defended as meaningful were immortality, the external world, and other selves.[6] I think that Lewis would also have defended certain Buddhist concepts as meaningful. For example, Jacobson identifies the denial of any immutable substantial self, the affirmation of change with no substance undergoing the change, and the proposal that reality is a social process empty of anything transcendent or with independent existence as the core of the Four Noble Truths, the Noble Eightfold Path, and the Doctrine of Dependent Origination.[7] Lewis subscribes to all three of these views.

Process Metaphysics

Jacobson has pointed out that process philosophies have made an appearance on three separate occasions. The first was associated with the teachings of Gautama Buddha. The second is found in Heraclitus. And the third, "this time in a fully rounded-out and systematic form, came during what Max H. Fisch calls 'the classical age of American thought,' beginning about 1880 with William James and Charles Peirce and continuing to the eve of World War II in the work of Josiah Royce, John Dewey, and the Anglo-American Alfred North Whitehead."[8] Lewis rightfully belongs in this list.

Other than stating in a number of places that he favored realism, Lewis failed to give a positive account of his metaphysics. By looking at various pronouncements that he made on the subject, we can infer that he favored process philosophy. Perhaps the most direct evidence is found in this quotation from *Mind and the World Order*: "The long-persistent problem in physics of action at a distance increasingly comes back to haunt us and to unite with new problems of physical interpretation which threaten to drive us once more to dissipate the 'material thing' throughout all time and space; to find its manifestation and even its very being in a spatio-temporal spread of events indefinitely extended."[9]

More evidence exists in Lewis's sympathetic account of Whitehead under the title "The Categories of Natural Knowledge," in which Lewis aims to emphasize what he takes to be "the permanent significance of this philosophy of natural knowledge."[10] In "Realism or Phenomenalism?" Lewis writes: "I would set over against this traditional conception of substance a thought drawn from Whitehead—even though I do some violence to his way of thinking in so extracting it. An object is an event: some continuous volume in space-time comprising a history of enduring. Characteristically, the process of change in this kind of event is never too abrupt or too pervasive; and what we recognize as an object is so recognizable only by some persistence of character."[11]

The Self

The Buddhist view of the self differs pragmatically from the traditionally prevalent Western view. According to the latter, the self is a nonspatial, uninterrupted, and simple substance. Because no one ever experiences such an entity, as can easily be ascertained by a moment's reflection, and because no one can even imagine what it would be like to be nonspatial, simple, unchanging, and uninterrupted in experience, the concept is pragmatically meaningless. It answers to no criteria in mind. The Buddhist view makes no such metaphysical claims. The five *skandhas* are found in experience, hence that concept is pragmatically meaningful.

It is a common prejudice among philosophers that Lewis should be counted among the mentalist philosophers, especially because of the title *Mind and the World Order*. Lewis, however, makes it perfectly clear in his contribution to the Schilpp volume devoted to Whitehead that he is well aware of the insurmountable difficulties of substance dualism. He writes: "Some modes of…persistence, or continuities of a distinctive type, are very precious—our own continuity of memory, for example, or other aspects of our self-recognition. But if some exquisite and superprecious 'being-in-itself' is to be attributed, then I think that at least it is inexpressible."[12] Lewis is no more sympathetic with the idea of a Kantian transcendental ego: "We cannot, unless dogmatically, construct experience from a hypothetical and transcendent mind working upon a material which likewise is something beyond experience." He says, "That the phenomenalist treats mind as transcendent is a fallacy which is correlative to his treatment of the independent object as beyond knowledge."[13]

Lewis devoted an appendix in *Mind and the World Order* to the concept of mind. He made it clear that the term *mind*, to be meaningful, must conform to the same experiential strictures as any other meaningful concept. In another place, however, he admitted that he could not "express precisely and clearly what you and I mean by 'mind.'" "But," he added, "if anything I have to say should be found incompatible with that common meaning, then I should not wish to persist in maintaining it."[14]

Dependent Origination

Buddhists speak of dependent origination and Lewis speaks of natural connection. Both terms name a fact of our experience, namely, that we observe regularities in nature and that we expect, for whatever reason, that these regularities will continue to hold for the future. The doctrine is pragmatically meaningful because we all know what it is like to have our expectations met. I believe that there is a natural connection between being a cat, being a mammal, and being carnivorous. Consequently, I confidently expect that Mei Ling, if she gives live birth, will suckle her young. I also believe that she will find fresh meat a rewarding repast. I know what it would be like to confirm all of this, because of the criteria I possess in mind regarding cats and what pertains to them.

The doctrine of karma holds that through the operation of dependent origination, the five *skandhas* making up my empirical self will remanifest in a future birth. According to Lewis's criteria of meaningfulness, such a view is quite meaningful. I can easily imagine what this would mean not only for myself, but for another. I might seem to remember a past life or lives. Even if I do not remember any past lives, the doctrine has not become meaningless, because I know what it is like to suffer forgetfulness and, at least in the case of others, to suffer amnesia. Suppose that I encounter a young child who claims to have been my father in a former life, and suppose that most of the statements he makes can be confirmed for me. He reminds me of conversations between us that could not possibly have been overheard by third parties. He directs me to look for certain lost documents that turn out to be precisely where he has indicated. All this would be good empirical confirmation of his claim to be the person he claims to be. We would be hysterically dogmatic if we denied his claim to know who he is.

Reality and *Śūnyatā*

About reality and philosophic truth, Lewis writes:

The reflective method necessarily leads to the repudiation of any reality supposed to be transcendent of experience altogether. A true philosophic interpretation must always follow the clues of the practical reasons for our predications. A philosophy which relegates any object of human thought to the transcendent, is false to the human interests which have created that thought, and to the experience which gives it meaning. Philosophic truth, like knowledge in general, is about experience, and not about something strangely beyond the ken of man, open only to the seer and the prophet. We all know the nature of life and of the real, though only with exquisite care can we tell the truth about them.[15]

For Lewis, reality is experience categorized. This means that the real is the interpreted given in the here and now and that the given and the conceptual interpretation put on it are abstractions. One salient difference between Lewis's view and that of Buddhism is that Lewis doubts that the given can be experienced free of interpretation: "The given, as here conceived, is certainly an abstraction. Unless there be such a thing as pure esthesis (and I should join with the critic in doubting this), the given never exists in isolation in any experience or state of consciousness."[16] Even this is not laid down as dogma, however: "If there be states of pure esthesis, in violent emotion or in the presence of great art, which are unqualified by thought, even these can be conveyed—and perhaps even retained in memory—only when they have been rendered articulate by thought. So that in a sense the given is ineffable, always."[17]

The point at issue between Lewis and Buddhism represents not a disagreement over the facts but a disagreement of how the facts should be expressed in language. Lewis wishes to reserve the term *reality* for the conceptualized given. The Buddhist wishes to reserve the term for experience free of interpretation. Both agree that everyday experience is overlaid with interpretations, and that this overlay is subject to change. This is Lewis's theory of the pragmatic a priori. But the theory of the pragmatic a priori would be gratuitous nonsense in conjunction with a substance view. It gains real point in a world that is in process of becoming.

Lewis, then, has made an important contribution to process philosophy in his epistemological studies. This gives the look of dogmatism to Jacobson's remark that "Buddhism has been more successful than the West, moreover, in avoiding what has been called 'the epistemological industry,' emphasizing from the very beginning that what is needed is not a better theory of experience but to free experience from the facile artificial formulations of self-encapsulated, ego-aggrandizing cultures and peoples."[18] Epistemology is not confined to substance philosophies, as Lewis's work makes abundantly clear. When we understand how our experience of the world is influenced by the interpretations we place on it and that these interpretations can be not only modified but overthrown, real power is given to the Buddhist view of śūnyatā.

I am comparing Lewis's given with Nāgārjuna's śūnyatā. The same problem that arises for śūnyatā arises for Lewis: is not talk of emptiness a kind of theory? If it is, Nāgārjuna, despite his protestations to the contrary, has a theory. In the case of Lewis, at least, there must be a frank admission that the theory is just one theory among many. It can be evaluated only by its fruits.

I do not claim that C. I. Lewis may be regarded as a crypto-Buddhist. He should be regarded, however, as a typical member of the school of American philosophy according to which process philosophy replaces substance philosophy, an immutable substantial self is repudiated, and what is given in experience is overlaid with interpretation. In light of these observations, Lewis's work should be of interest to Buddhist scholars.

Notes

1. Lewis did commit himself to metaphysical realism: "There are, in my opinion, metaphysical presuppositions which are essential to epistemology: for example, the nature of knowledge itself presupposes a reality to be known which transcends the content of any experience in which it may be known. And my own metaphysical convictions are, as it happens, realistic." *Collected Papers of Clarence Irving Lewis*, ed. John D. Goheen and John L. Mothershead, Jr. (Stanford: Stanford University Press, 1970), p. 333; hereafter cited as *Papers*.

2. Clarence Irving Lewis, *Mind and the World Order: Outline of a Theory of Knowledge* (New York, Chicago, and Boston: Charles Scribner's Sons, 1929), chapter 2, especially pp. 61 ff; hereafter cited as *Mind*.

3. Reprinted in Justus Buchler, ed., *Philosophical Writings of Peirce* (New York: Dover, 1955), p. 31.
4. Alfred North Whitehead, *Process and Reality: An Essay in Cosmology*, corrected ed., ed. David Ray Griffin and Donald W. Sherburne (New York: Free Press, 1978), p. 8.
5. The address was published in *The Philosophical Review* 63, no. 2 (1934), pp. 125–146, and reprinted in *Papers*, pp. 258–276.
6. Lewis did not defend these concepts as theses.
7. Nolan Pliny Jacobson, *The Heart of Buddhist Philosophy* (Carbondale and Edwardsville: Southern Illinois University Press, 1988), p. 66.
8. Ibid., p. 10.
9. *Mind*, p. 235.
10. *Papers*, pp. 113–114.
11. Ibid., p. 341.
12. Reprinted in Ibid., pp. 341–342.
13. *Mind*, pp. 30, 176.
14. *Papers*, p. 294.
15. *Mind*, p. 35.
16. Ibid., p. 54.
17. Ibid., pp. 52 ff.
18. Op. cit., p. 4.

4.
Creativity and the Emerging
World Civilization   *David Lee Miller*

Much in the thought of Nolan Pliny Jacobson recommends it as an expression of philosophy of creativity. From the very early influences of Charles Hartshorne and Henry Nelson Wieman as teachers at the University of Chicago during the 1940s through his last published book in 1988, Jacobson's thinking and writing have been permeated by the notion of creativity. In his several books and numerous shorter essays, he sought to elucidate and find application for creativity in many different spheres of human experience, including science, technology, art, economics, politics, and religion.

Much influenced by Karl Marx and several Existentialist thinkers, especially Sören Kierkegaard, Jacobson moved into a year-long systematic study of Buddhism in Burma. It was a year of intense study and personal struggle, and it was a philosophically decisive year for Jacobson, because this experience provided the focus for the major work that he did over the next twenty-six years until his death in December 1987. As he explains:

> Since 1961 when I accepted a Ford Foundation grant for study at the International Institute for Advanced Buddhistic Studies, Rangoon, the major focus of my work has been in the confluence between Buddhism and the other great international "process" philosophy associated with Heraclitus, a few minor European figures, and the "golden age" in American thought—William James, Josiah Royce, John Dewey, Alfred North Whitehead, and Charles Hartshorne, the only major American to have pondered Buddhist thought throughout his professional career.[1]

Notably omitted from this list of American thinkers is Henry Nelson Wieman, the American philosopher/theologian who concentrates his work entirely on the problem of creativity. Jacobson has a good deal to say about creativity in his books published in English after the publication of *Buddhism: The Religion of Analysis* in 1966, and he often refers to Wieman. I suspect that the Wiemanian influence was so fundamental for the forming of Jacobson's philosophy that at times it did not occur to him that such influence needed explicit explanation. Both men were steeped in the deeps of the experience of creativity and were committed profoundly to clarifying its meaning and relevance for human civilization over the whole earth.

The Problem

Throughout his writings, Jacobson addresses the difficulty that individuals and entire civilizations have in breaking free from all manner of conventional, passive, forced, and misdirected thought, feeling, and action. It is the problem of massive bondage to the countless ways that humankind is caught in the snares of suffering. It is the problem of wasted energy, scattered energy, and energy offered up for the selfish, the pointless, and the demonic. It is the everywhere present choking-off of the spontaneous joy of living that can come only from a deep receptivity and painstaking discipline. From this individual point of view, "it is not the world that we are called upon to deny, but the illusory, distorted, smothered and tangled world that results from our egocentric, conditioned, unconscious compulsions."[2] And from the perspective of the social order, "civilizations up to now have thwarted and destroyed the intensity and wholeness of human experience, confining feeling to insatiable wants, local, habit-ridden, parochial views, reducing life to its lowest common denominator."[3]

The confluence of Buddhism and the major American thinkers on the difficulties experienced by individuals and entire civilizations is striking, and a major dimension of Jacobson's thought is at the center of this East-West confluence. Riding waves of inspiration from the insights of Buddhism and of Dewey, Wieman, Hartshorne, and the like, Jacobson continually challenges each individual person and all existent social orders to come out of their long-standing and sometimes comfortable deep sleep, to feel the problem(s) deeply and sincerely and to be seriously motivated to positive alternative orientation and action.

It is difficult to read for long in the Jacobson corpus without harkening back to his 1948 dissertation on Karl Marx and without imagining the impetus that Marx's work provided by suggesting that the final home for philosophical analysis and reflection is in the rapidly passing concreteness of experience. Unfortunately, in the West, historically, the chief thrust of reason has been removed from such experience, thus contributing to the tangled web of universal suffering that is the lot of the human race. Nowhere is Jacobson more Buddhistic than at this point that is so deeply shared by the already-named American philosophers.

Important here is the return to experience, the taking up of the vital powers of analysis, cognition, and meditation for the practical tasks of eradicating the impurities and agonies from the human situation and directing the flow of that joyful spontaneity that enables all human beings to live most freely and fully out of the centers of their unmatchable individualized experience. Life lived in this way is vivid and memorable, escaping, commensurate with its thoughtfulness and commitment, the pits of impoverishment and incarceration. The return to experience redefines human thinking and provides an angle of feeling and seeing that loosens our chains and grants sanguine possibilities within the passing moment.

The West has, however, given us formidable obstacles that stand in the way of the vivid joyfulness at the heart of our fleeting experiences. Healthy life seeks extrication from these obstacles, and as Jacobson says, it has as its basic motivation "to be free from the forced striving of the self, that illusory fabricated custodian of awareness to which men and women cling as the center around which everything appears to revolve."[4] The individual self cherished as a separate and self-reliant entity is here understood to be the taproot of the world's individual and social woes.

Freedom from the self is central to the basic problem of civilization. Freedom from the self as an independent and self-sufficient entity is the necessary condition that must be met if one is to move from under the cloud of compulsive clinging into the fresh possibilities in emerging experience. Freedom from gives rise to freedom to, but without the freedom from, Buddhism and Jacobson instruct us, civilization will continue to pass through its stale and sterile forms, carrying with it life-robbing realities of greed, hatred, war, and the like.

Much and increasing theoretical knowledge is relevant to the many-sided problem of civilization and the individuals who comprise it. Theoretical knowledge, however, has its fundamental relevance in its liberating effect on the delicate fabric of our fleeting human experience. This knowledge needs context—the context of cultivating the awareness that knowledge becomes sacred as human beings become increasingly aware of its awesome powers to decrease the misery of life, and to open the way for health, sanity, and wonder to fill the lives of individuals and the civilizational matrices through which they hope for the increase of meaning and value in their lives.

For Nolan Pliny Jacobson, theory and practice are one, and this oneness should permeate the passing of experience, leaving it more refreshed and more informed, freer and fuller, richer and deeper, in attentive awareness to the problems and options, and to the tragedies and joys, of living. Jacobson emphasizes that "fundamentally, Buddhism is not a teaching or doctrine at all; it is a matter of practical involvement, a method for dealing with the pervasive and enduring problems of life."[5] John Dewey stressed the same point throughout his career and life, as did C. S. Peirce, William James, Alfred North Whitehead, Charles Hartshorne, and Henry Nelson Wieman in their distinctive ways.

Our problem, as Jacobson explains it, is to liberate people and civilization from the circumscribing and crushing weight of a self-contained, self-seeking, and self-justifying self that imagines deeply that its worth and that of society depend on each person's going his/her way, irrespective of the fragile web of unfolding, shared experience. To this problem, Jacobson speaks and writes eloquently, drawing deeply from the Buddhist traditions, American pragmatism, and American process philosophy and theology.

Creativity

A spirit of jubilation pervades Jacobson's writings. He speaks repeatedly of "the wonder of being vividly and memorably alive" and of "the joyful response of life to life."[6] His jubilation of hopefulness is fully aware of the deep-seated and many-sided problem of individual and civilizational suffering. The only idealism, or optimism here is that rooted in the dark realities of life, the realities of opportunities missed, of potentialities wasted, of disease, hunger, and tragic death all over the planet.

Jacobson takes care to respond in detail to these dark realities. He does so with poetic and prophetic zeal, and always with the Buddhist perspective in mind. He urges us to become celebrants, to feel and to express the sustaining rapture of the precious and passing moment. For example, he writes, "Buddhism is thus the celebration of the joy of living, the joy being the natural expression or 'voice' of the vivid quality and heightened awareness flowing in those original centers of experience where life is becoming ever more fully a work of art."[7]

All the jubilation felt, expressed, and shared by the celebrants—the joy, the memorableness, the vividness—is the presencing of creativity throughout individual and civilizational life. This supporting and sustaining creativity is deeper than words, deeper than laughter and tears, the fundamental energy and voice of life. This theme of creativity becomes increasingly important as Jacobson's work unfolds through its more mature stages. In *Buddhism and the Contemporary World*, he declares that "the ultimate source of one's identity, therefore, is found in casting oneself as fully as possible into the keeping of the creativity that sustains the world, the creativity that is forever unifying and enriching the diverse, divisive, and disparate nature of things."[8]

Buddhism is the superlative embodiment of creativity, as Jacobson indicates when he writes, "Buddhism may be called humankind's most persistent thrust toward fuller and freer participation in the creativity incarnate in the passage of temporal fact."[9] As the locus of positive meaning in life, the passage of temporal fact is faith in the generosity of the natural order of things that ties together the main emphases in Buddhism and our golden age American philosophers. Both traditions call attention to the need to form, test, and continuously sharpen our commitments within the matrix of the rich and diverse processive flow to avoid an escapist flight to some type of supernatural realm and a futile search for meanings through the desire for pleasures, honors, and monetary success and power.

One fundamental way to understand the passing fullness of creativity is as the unimpeded aesthetic flow of life. It is open becomingness, the spontaneous and enabling possibilities resident in the natural cells that are coming to be, which suggest to one another the options for freedom and joy, the ways out of the mire of bondage and suffering. For Jacobson, it comes to mean the understanding that "in the Buddhist view creativity never ceases. The opposite of creativity is not the *absence* of it, for this is impossible: The opposite is *suffering*, which is where we are when we begin to reflect upon our life in the world."[10]

Creativity and suffering are focal ideas for understanding the thought of Nolan Pliny Jacobson. Universal suffering is the starting point of life, and creativity is the redemptive power that enables us to continually overcome suffering. Creativity is bright, beckoning, bringing the rush of opennness of feeling and free play concerning the most serious and pressing issues of life. It is trustworthy, people cannot merely summon it at will, and it will carry away the unwholesome, poisonous propensities to action. Creativity transforms us toward the greater good in ways we cannot by will, tradition, or good intention transform ourselves.

We live best on the waves, waves within waves within waves, sighting our course as the waves rise and fall, taking care not to wall off the life-infusing creativity as our sense of insecurity and vulnerability tempts us to do. This is the way of adventure—that quality that Whitehead identifies in *Adventures of Ideas* as indispensable for the health and sanity of civilization. The adventure is the way of music and healing, of poetry and compassion, of the luminous embodiment of the surprising transformative qualities within the pervasive and passing creativity.

The way of Buddhism is the way of creativity, which is the transparent character of the whole world. Jacobson stresses this point when he emphasizes that "creativity, then, is the universal feature of a world that is alive in every pore." He continues: "Buddhism is humankind's most persevering effort to participate in the creativity incarnate in the passing now."[11] The way of creativity found profoundly stated and practiced in Buddhism is the way of casting off the traps and manacles, the calculation and deceit, the pseudoexplanations and conceptual structures, that tie and gag the promising energy patterns that are the inalienable possibilities for all that lives and has some iota of feeling for the emerging richness of quality in the innumerable events that constitute the passing nows.

Most of the difficult work toward liberation lies ahead of us. The existing social order has been mainly concerned with developing, protecting, and expanding various paradigms for the guidance and control of human thought, feeling, and expression. These models provide order, insight, and meaning. They also afford restricted thinking, inflexible perspectives, and definition of individual identity in terms of some niche or another in civilization. Individuals need to embrace the metaparadigmatic power of creativity and be central participants in the making of an emerging civilization beyond all existing civilizations. Jacobson urges that "individuals discover their identity not in any cultural pattern or empirical social class, but in the flow of unstructured quality sweeping like a kaleidoscope across their feeling systems, enlarging their one-sided fraction of experience with the inexhaustible energy of the world."[12]

Self-Correction

Creativity provides the inexhaustible currents of energy for the coming and flourishing of life in its many and changing forms. The capacity for ongoing self-correction at the human level of existence provides an intelligent focus for this energy, and self-correction is essential for the emerging world civilization. The connection between creativity and self-correction reveals the heart of Professor Jacobson's philosophical perspective. It is the key to understanding his hope and work on behalf of a more bountiful human civilization that is more fully endowed with interlocking harmonies and still provides diverse possibilities for individual development. As he puts it in the concluding paragraph of his last book:

> The Buddhist solution to the problem of civilization is for each individual to live self-correctively in ultimate dependence upon the creativity operating in the original individualized experience of people everywhere in ways that bring forth the novel forms of togetherness without which human civilization would have come to an end long ago.... Whoever would participate in the new levels of advanced civilization must break the compulsive unconscious grip of their noblest ideals and stay in touch with the original concrete events that speak out of the soft underside of the mind, echoing with the strange togetherness of everything alive.[13]

The pushes and tugs of encapsulated individual behavior are powerful, and the equally (if not more) powerful demands and expectations of the social order constitute formidable threats to the positive effectiveness of self-correction. Nevertheless, two clearly defined, longstanding communities have self-correction as one of their chief values. In this connection, Jacobson writes: "The issue of survival serves to single out for the attention of all humanity the two clearly defined communities where the greatest joys of life have been associated with the process of self-correction. One of these is the community of modern science. The other is the venerable Buddhist legacy, where self-correction has operated on the personal level for twenty-five hundred years."[14]

These two communities have carried on their work in relative independence of each other. Personal and social habits and ingrained and highly prized self-isolating behavior have prevented them from

acquiring a greater constructive power that would surely add momentum to the Jacobsonian aspiration of the coming world civilization.
The need is for a new openness, a deliberate effort on the part of the
practitioners in each community to appreciate and incorporate from
each other their distinctive capabilities and strengths. Such coming
together heralds the coming together of science and religion, or the
coming together of the spirit of science and the spirit of religion.

Here Buddhism and the American philosophers of the golden age
have one of their most important areas of agreement. Both are deeply
persuaded of the need for mutual reinforcement of science and religion and of the role each system has to play in the life and destiny of
the other. Particularly in the West, science and religion opposed one
another as severe critics, exacting enormous human energy for the
keeping and promulgating of treasured truths. It is a most conspicuous expression of the wastage of human energy, driving men and women
back into themselves and their narrow range of like-minded colleagues,
sowing the seeds of intellectual and spiritual arrogance and dogmatic
pronouncement.

Jacobson would have it the other way. Congruous with Buddhism
and the golden age American philosophers, he understands that science is profoundly in religion, and that religion is profoundly in science; both are different and basic manifestations of the resplendent
flow of creativity. Self-correction is the distinguishing characteristic of
each, as they together promote searching, flexible, and receptive habits
in thinking, feeling, and living. Such is the coming out of our cultural
shells, the breaking of our inveterate tendencies to try to mask our
deepest insecurities in conceptual absolutes of various types. Now the
chick is out of the shell. The shell is broken, giving way to the long,
risky search for an increasingly satisfactory civilizational experience.

This self-corrective character of human thinking adds a vital dimension to the human mind. With the habit of self-correction, human
beings are at least as interested in falsifying their truths as in gathering
them. We are persuaded of the value of the open stream of human
thinking and deeply committed to the passing and provisional nature
of all things. The self-corrective orientation means a living saturation
in the sobering realities of criticism and change, an opening up of
undreamed about and unthought about possibilities. The positive lure
is that "both self-corrective communities serve to challenge humanity
to burst provincial cultural, intellectual, and spiritual bonds. The human world has become inextricably interlocked with itself; the sepa-

rate parts are being forced to converge toward one self-corrective community."[15] Jacobson believes the stakes are exceedingly high: "The destiny of the human and the more-than-human world may well depend upon the mutual understanding and support now possible between the two self-corrective legacies together as the Yang and the Yin of the self-corrective community of tomorrow."[16]

Despite problems and imperfections in these two self-corrective communities,[17] they serve as beacon lights toward the living unification of the Earth's people, a growing sensitive regard for all nonhuman living things, and a resonating appreciation for other things natural and beautiful. The self-correction is replete with feeling content. It deepens and vivifies the sources of empowering creativity and brings individuals within the helping service of each other. In this way, individuality is preserved and enriched as civilization brings individuality into enhanced unison. The emerging world civilization suggests that the whole world is where the individual is, and that the individual is where the whole world is.

Postscript

The emerging world civilization depicted in the writings of Nolan Pliny Jacobson is characterized by a fullness of presentness in the fleeting nows. The fullness and the passing away of it are foundationally free from both causal and teleological influences. Cause and purpose, as far as we know, will always condition human action and civilization to a certain extent. But insights from the Buddhists and the golden age American philosophers show presentness—those moments in the rapidly vanishing present in which the individual is alive with the primordial creativity, awake to the need for self-correction, and resourcefully reaching out to the life and energy over the whole Earth.

It seems much easier for the individual to live in the midst of this presentness than for civilization to do so. Yet individuals make civilizations, and it is important that we think carefully, fluidly, and long about the possibilities for civilizations to express presentness—or more exactly that we consider how the emerging world civilization might express, as a matter of its structure and function, the qualities of presentness.

According to Jacobson, we must start with the awesome suffering, living in it with open and compassionate interest, and seeking to penetrate its secrets so that we might eradicate as much of the suffer-

ing as possible. In this context, we very much need to develop our
spontaneous resolve to experience creativity, and we need to permit
our rational capacities to acquire and utilize the skills of self-correction. In this way, we will be "Pioneers on a New Frontier,"[18] participants in and fashioners of a new global lifestyle in which conflicts and
tragedies are minimized and cooperation and harmony are lived out
as the natural and preferred values of the human race. The whole
earth and its civilizational component can move out of the present
into a succession of new presents with as much dynamic rapture and
peace as the enabling power of possibility permits. Such a lure is best
expressed in the language of poetry:

> Vividly, memorably alive
> here, now, connected
> through the creativity
> self-corrective and moving
> the emerging world civilization.

Notes

1. Curriculum vita, sent to author, 5 February 1983, from Nolan Pliny Jacobson.
2. Nolan Pliny Jacobson, *Buddhism: The Religion of Analysis* (New York: Humanities, 1965; reprint, Carbondale and Edwardsville: Southern Illinois University Press, 1966, 1970), p. 91.
3. Nolan Pliny Jacobson, "A Buddhist Analysis of Human Experience," in *Buddhism and American Thinkers*, ed. Kenneth K. Inada and Nolan Pliny Jacobson (Albany: SUNY Press, 1984), p. 48.
4. Nolan Pliny Jacobson, *Understanding Buddhism* (Carbondale and Edwardsville: Southern Illinois University Press, 1986), p. 60.
5. *Buddhism: The Religion of Analysis*, p. 36.
6. Professor Jacobson used these phrases frequently in personal conversation and in class lectures.
7. Nolan Pliny Jacobson, *Buddhism and the Contemporary World: Change and Self-Correction* (Carbondale and Edwardsville: Southern Illinois University Press, 1983), p. 68.
8. Ibid., p. 57.
9. Ibid., p. 56.
10. Ibid., p. 45.
11. Ibid., p. 49.
12. Jacobson, *Understanding Buddhism*, p. 109.

13. Nolan Pliny Jacobson, *The Heart of Buddhist Philosophy* (Carbondale and Edwardsville: Southern Illinois University Press, 1988), p. 135.

14. *Buddhism and the Contemporary World*, p. 122.

15. Ibid., p. 148.

16. Ibid., p. 149.

17. See "The Cultural Disintegration of Modern Science," in *Buddhism and the Contemporary World*, pp. 123–133.

18. The title of a class offered by Professor Jacobson at Queens College, Charlotte, North Carolina, after his retirement from full-time teaching.

Part Two
Central Issues

5.
The Standpoint of
Early Buddhist Philosophy   *Hajime Nakamura*

In the West, scholars tend to approach Buddhism as an object of philological or linguistic study. They are apt to be indifferent to the basic philosophical problems posed by Buddhism. Professor Nolan Pliny Jacobson was quite different in his approach. He sought to elucidate philosophical problems posed by Buddhist philosophers. He wished to evaluate Buddhist thought in the contemporary setting. He discussed problems of Buddhist philosophy in relevance to Western philosophy, such as that of Whitehead. Jacobson engaged earnestly in discussing the Buddhist and Eastern philosophy for the sake of mutual understanding and cultural interchange in a global perspective. Considering his wish for the future, I have ventured to point out the fundamental standpoint of Buddhist philosophy in relation to the thought of contemporary thinkers.

The Attitude Toward Other Philosophers and Religions

Buddhism has been regarded by Indians as a philosophy (*darśana*) and a religion (*dharma*). Although it was not a rationalistic philosophy achieved by ratiocination alone (*ānvikṣiki*), Buddhism has developed a variety of philosophical systems in different Asian countries. Buddhist philosophy has been more or less religious in the eyes of Westerners. No matter how one understands Buddhism, the human condition has been the central problem of Buddhist philosophy.

In the days when the Buddha lived, great freedom of thought was allowed to all people. The various philosophical and religious systems prevalent then can be classified in two categories, orthodox and heterodox. The orthodox religion from the standpoint of the Indians in general is Brahmanism. Brahmanism is the religion that admits the authority of the Vedic scriptures. The heterodox thinkers of those days did not acknowledge the authority of the Vedas. They engaged in a free and often arbitrary way of thinking. They subscribed to materialism, hedonism, asceticism, determinism, skepticism, denunciation of the moral, and so on. Mahāvira, the founder of Jainism, was one of these thinkers. What attitude did the Buddha show to these various dissenting opinions?

The Buddha noted that many of the systems of philosophy prevalent in those days were contradictory to each other and that philosophers disputed with each other on various philosophical problems. Each philosopher claimed that his own doctrine was absolutely true and that the other doctrines contained falsehoods based on various fallacies. "What some say is truth, the reality, that others say is void, false; so, having disagreed, they dispute. Why do not the thinkers [*samanas*] say one [and the same thing]?" "Here they maintain 'purity'; in other doctrines [*dhamma*] they do not allow purity; what they have devoted themselves to, that they call good, and they enter extensively upon the single truth." "Because, he holds another [to be] fool, therefore he calls himself an expert; in his own opinion, he is one that tells what is propitious; others he blames."[1]

If, however, someone who stands apart from any particular philosophical point of view considers these conflicting ideas from an objective, synoptic standpoint, each philosophical system is relative and partial in those respects in which it conflicts with and opposes another philosophical system. Then where shall we find the truth? We have the postulate that "the truth is one, there is not a second,"[2] yet we suffer from such fatal contradictions. How can we explain this?

The Buddha commented on this situation as follows: These philosophers get into disputes over insoluble metaphysical problems and are entangled in confusion. Hence, they are apt to fall into moral evils: "Saying that there is something firm in his own way, he holds his opponent to be a fool; thus he himself brings on strife, calling his opponent to be a fool and impure"; "They are inflamed by passion for their own [philosophical] views."[3] The Buddha regarded all such disputes as valueless and did not care to participate in any metaphysical disputes: "He overcame such disputes."[4] He maintained the perspective that "having left all resolutions, nobody would excite strife in the world."[5]

The early Buddhists did not want to be entangled in disputes held at public places. "Those wishing for dispute, having plunged into the assembly, brand each other as fools mutually; they go to others and pick a quarrel, wishing for praise and calling themselves [the only] experts." "Engaged in dispute in the middle of the assembly, wishing for praise, he lays about on all sides; but, when his dispute has been repulsed, he becomes discontented; at blame, he becomes angry, he who sought for the faults [of others]." "Because those who have tested his questions say that his dispute is lost and repulsed, he laments and grieves, having lost his disputes; 'he has conquered me'; so saying, he wails." "These disputes have arisen amongst the ascetics, in these [disputes] there are blows [and] striking; having seen this, let him leave off disputing, for there is no advantage to obtain from gaining praise." "Or he is praised there, having cleared up the dispute in the middle of the assembly; therefore, he will laugh and be elated having won that case as he had a mind to." "That which is his exaltation will also be the field of his defeat; still he talks proudly and arrogantly; seeing this, let no one dispute, for the wise do not say that purification [results] from that."[6]

The early Buddhists refrained from getting into disputes with others. In comparison with other world religions, this tendency is conspicuous throughout the Buddhist world. Religious discussions do not lead to heated antipathy among the participants.

Silence on Metaphysical Problems

Early Buddhism discouraged metaphysical speculation concerning problems not related to human activities, such as whether the world is eternal, whether the world is infinite or finite, whether the soul and the body are identical with or different from each other, and whether a perfect person exists after death. Many ascetics in those days asked such questions. But to all such questions, the Buddha refused an answer.

Why did he not answer? According to a Buddhist scripture, many ascetics complained that when they asked the Buddha, they did not receive any answer to their questions. The Buddha said: "The jungle, the desert, the puppet-show, the writhing, the entanglement of such speculations is accompanied by sorrow, wrangling, resentment, the fever of excitement. It conduces neither to detachment of heart, nor to freedom from lusts, nor to tranquility, nor to peace, nor to wisdom, nor to the insight of the higher stages of the path, nor to Nirvāna."[7] The Buddha stated that answering all these questions would leave no time for finding the way to salvation or to liberation from suffering, and he illustrated this by means of the following parable. A man is hit by a poisoned arrow. His friends rush him to a doctor. The latter is about to draw the arrow out of the wound. The wounded man, however, cries, "Stop! I will not have the arrow drawn out until I know who shot it, whether a warrior, a *brahmin*, a common man, *vaisya*, or a slave, *sudra*, to which family he belonged, whether he was tall or short, and of what kind the arrow was and its description."[8] But what would happen before all these questions were answered? That man would die!

In the same way, the disciple who wished for answers to all his questions about the beyond and the like would die before he knew the truth about suffering.[9] The theories held by philosophers in general purported to explain the origin and end of all things, to be able to give a clear and absolute decision about the finiteness or infiniteness of the world, about the eternity of the soul and of those bigger souls, the gods, and about other problems. But all of them were repudiated by the Buddha.

Even in our daily life, we meet with these kinds of questions to which we cannot give any definite answers. And not to give any answer evidences a definite reply, in a way. Henry Clark Warren, the pioneer in Buddhist studies in America, explains the situation in the following way: "I think that he [the reader] will see that the Buddha considered all such questions to be out of court....Hence he refuses to give a Yes or No answer, just as any one of us might be excused for doing, in case any one were to be so impolite as to ask, 'Have you stopped beating your mother?' The truth of no one of these theories could be allowed."[10]

There is this story in the scripture. A man went to various gods in turn to resolve a doubt on the question "Where now do these four great elements—earth, water, fire, and wind—go, leaving no trace behind?" Finally, Brahma, the highest god, said to him, "I do not know, brother, where those four great elements—earth, water, fire, and wind— go, leaving no trace behind."[11]

The attack made on this sort of metaphysical speculation was the most formidable one made so far in the history of the world on theology and metaphysics. We find here two propositions: do not discuss things for which we do not have good evidence, and do not discuss things that are of no use, no good, for us. Whether true or false, both propositions seem to us quite intelligible. Such metaphysical arguments as these, however, have been brought forward to show that behind the deliberate silence of the Buddha lay, after all, a covert and firm belief. The Buddha was perfectly firm. He refused not only to answer but even to discuss such matters. They were constantly being raised. His answer was simply a list of indeterminates. Such questions were barred. The problem of God's existence is also one of the metaphysical subtleties against which he protested. In this respect, the Buddha was apparently an atheist in the Western sense of the word, but basically he was very religious.

This attitude of dealing with metaphysical problems that lead us to antinomies has contemporary significance. According to Wittgenstein, this kind of metaphysical speculation is meaningless. The endeavor to solve these problems is not only useless but impossible. He says, "The correct method in philosophy would really be the following: to say nothing except what can be said, that is, propositions of natural science—something that has nothing to do with philosophy—and then, whenever someone else wanted to say something metaphysical, to demonstrate to him that he had failed to give a meaning to certain signs in his propositions. Although it would not be satisfying to the other person—he would not have the feeling that we were teaching him philosophy—this method would be the only strictly correct one."[12] Bertrand Russell also reflects this view, saying, "The right method of teaching philosophy would be to confine oneself to propositions of sciences, stated with all possible clearness and exactness, leaving philosophical assertions to the learner, and proving to him, whenever he makes them, that they are meaningless."[13]

The Buddha was often compared to a doctor. According to him, human nature is afflicted with disease. He conceived his role to be that of the physician. His doctrine was presented as therapy, a treatment or cure, a method and a process of healing, for those who wanted to follow it. He offered his advice in the practical manner of a spiritual physician. The art of Indian medicine seems to have been adapted by him to the sphere of spiritual problems. So the Buddha's doctrine can be regarded as practical. Because the main concern of early Buddhists was moral and psychological practice, Buddhism did not attempt to develop natural sciences even in later days.

Everything that does not make for "quiescence, knowledge, supreme wisdom, and Nirvāna" should be set aside. Among the questions that the Buddha thus dismissed are several that have been persistently debated in Western religion and philosophy. We see this sort of thought expressed in the oldest stratum of the scriptures of early Buddhism. Gautama did not want to found a new religion or to advocate any particular metaphysics.

Eliminating, as far as he could, any metaphysical doctrine that might lead to antinomies, Gautama wanted to elucidate the true practical knowledge of the law of human activities. The Buddha was neither a positivist nor a pragmatist. But extracts from the scriptures show that it is not necessary to read metaphysical notions between the lines, as later scholars have wanted to do. Buddhism, as a philosophy, is described by some scholars as a dialectical pragmatism with a psychological turn. Here dialectic means the method of seeking knowledge by questions and answers, as was done by Socrates. In origin and intention, Buddhism has always been marked by its intensely practical attitude. Speculation on matters irrelevant to salvation was discouraged by Buddhism from the time of its very beginning. Although Mahāyāna Buddhism has set forth something like a philosophical system that might be called metaphysics, Buddhists in general have not wanted to discuss problems that would lead to antinomies.

Partial Truth of Ideas

How should we regard the wrong metaphysical views prevalent in those days? The Buddha said:

On such points brahmins and recluses stick,
Wrangling on them, they violently discuss;
Poor folk! They see but one side of the shield.[14]

All metaphysical views are only partial apprehensions of the whole truth that lies beyond our cognition, beyond rational analysis. This point is well illustrated in scripture by the famous parable of the blind men and the elephant. Each blind man touches an elephant and makes a claim as to what an elephant looks like. Various metaphysical views are like the opinions of these blind men, and the whole truth is like the elephant.

Some ascetics and Brahmins once met together and began to quarrel. Some said, "The world is eternal," and others, "The world is not eternal." Some declared, "The world is finite," and others, "The world is infinite." Again, some taught, "Body and soul are separate," and others, "Body and soul are but one." Some said, "The perfect man is after death"; others maintained, "The perfect man is not after death," and so forth. All this led finally to a quarrel and to harsh and insulting words. The monks told the Buddha of this quarrel, and he told them the following parable.

There once was a king who had all those who had been born blind brought together. When they were all assembled, the king commanded an elephant to be "shown" to them. An elephant was brought, and he told some of them to feel his head, others his ear, others his tusk, others his trunk, and so on, and the last one the elephant's tail. Then the king asked them, "How does an elephant look?" Those who had touched the elephant's head said, "An elephant is like a pot"; those who had touched the ear said, "An elephant is like a winnowing basket"; those who had touched the tusk declared, "An elephant is like a plow-share"; those who had touched the trunk said, "An elephant is like the pole of a plow"; and those who had felt the tail maintained, "An elephant is like a broom." A great tumult arose. Each one maintained, "An elephant is like this, and not otherwise; he is not like that, he is like this," until at last they came to blows, at which the king was mightily amused.[15]

Similar, concluded the Buddha, is the case of the ascetics and Brahmins, each of whom has seen only a portion of the truth, and who then maintains, "Thus is truth and not otherwise; truth is not so, but thus."[16] Ordinary teachers, who have grasped this or that small part of the truth, dispute with one another. Only a Buddha can apprehend the whole truth. Buddhists assume that rational analysis is useful in clarifying the limitations of rationality. By detaching from metaphysical conflicts, a person is able to grasp the truth. Thus the way of thinking that acknowledges the raison d'être of all dissenting philosophical opinions was established.

According to scripture, Gautama would not say, "[My doctrine] is true," nor would he say, "[Your doctrine] is false."[17] He does not conflict with other philosophers,[18] because he does not dispute with others who adhere to any definite standpoint. He said, "I do not fight with the world, but the world fights with me, for one who knows about the truth [dhamma] never fights with the world. And what the learned in the world regard as non-existent, that also I teach as non-existent. And what the learned in the world regard as existent, that also I regard as existent."[19] The teaching of the Buddha transcends comparison; it is neither inferior, nor equal, nor superior to other doctrines.[20] "After investigation, there is nothing amongst the doctrines which such a one [as I would] embrace, and seeing [misery] in the [other philosophical] views, without adopting [any of them], searching [for truth], I saw 'inward peace.'"[21]

Skepticism made an appeal to many unphilosophic minds. People observed the diversity of schools and the acerbity of their disputes and ascertained that all alike were pretending to knowledge that was unattainable. This fact betrays the other side of the ideological fact pointed out by the Buddha. By detaching from philosophical conflicts, a person is able to grasp the truth and to attain inward peace. Thus, in Buddhism, no dogma opposes other dogmas or claims to be believed. Buddhism as a historical and cultural product developed many different systems of thought in the course of time. But in the early days, such systems were not in accord with the ideals of the starting point of Buddhism. And even later Buddhists did not want to coerce the followers to believe what seemed irrational. They always sought to avoid obscurantism and coercion.

Concerning the fundamental standpoint of Buddhism, Irving Babbitt says: "The comparative absence of dogma in the humanism of Confucius and the religion of Buddha can scarcely be regarded as an inferiority. On the contrary, one can at least see the point of view of a young Chinese scholar, Mr. H. H. Chang, who complains that the man of the Occident has introduced unnecessary theological and metaphysical complications into religion; he has been too prone to indulge in 'weird dogmas' and 'uncanny curiosity.' He has been guilty to a degree unknown to the Far East of intolerance, obscurantism, and casuistry."[22]

Babbitt says that the Buddha's avoidance of the form of obscurantism is a matter of great importance. The conflict between the head and the heart, the tendency to repudiate the intellect in the name of what is above or below it, which has played such an enormous role in the Occident from some of the early Christians to Bergson, is alien to genuine Buddhism.[23] Obscurantism has been lacking in Buddhism as a general trend. That is why there has been hardly any problem of conflict between religion and science in the East, unlike in the West. Buddhism aims at nothing but peace of mind. The supreme illumination of the Buddha was associated with the precise tracing of cause and effect, with the following out of the so-called causal nexus, which should be accepted by all people.

Professor Jacobson's philosophical perspective is thoroughly and richly Buddhist in many of the ways discussed in the preceding pages. His view seeks the more inclusive, holistic truth and avoids confrontation, argumentation, and explication on behalf of partial truths. The Jacobson philosophy always seeks to understand and appreciate essential points of similarity, and it does so through the activities of silent, meditative reflection and wise action. Through his long study of Buddhist traditions, Nolan Pliny Jacobson made important contributions to the emerging world civilization.

Notes

1. *Suttanipāta* 882, 824, 888, in *Pali Canon* (London: Pali Text Society, 1980), vol. 1, p. 847.
2. *Suttanipāta* 884.
3. *Suttanipāta* 893, 891.
4. *Suttanipāta* 907.
5. *Suttanipāta* 894.
6. *Suttanipāta* 825–830.
7. *Majjhima-nikāya*, in *Pali Canon*, vol. 1, no. 63.
8. T. W. Rhys-Davids, trans., *Dialogues of the Buddha*, vols. 2 and 3 of *Sacred Books of the Buddhists*, ed. F. Max Muller (London: Oxford University Press, 1899, 1957), vol. 2, pp. 186 ff.; cf. Henry Clarke Warren, *Buddhism in Translation*, Harvard Oriental Series, vol. 3, no. 9 (Cambridge, Mass.: Harvard University Press, 1947), pp. 117–128.
9. *Majjhima-nikāya*, no. 63; cf. Maurice Winternitz, *A History of Indian Literature*, trans. S. Ketkar and H. Kohn and revised by the author, 2 vols. (Berkeley: University of California Press, 1927, 1933), vol. 2, pp. 70–71.
10. Henry Clarke Warren, op. cit., pp. 111–112.
11. T. W. Rhys-Davids, op. cit., vol. 3, pp. 280–281. The attitude not to think of a person's past and future existences is expressed in *The Sabbasava-suttra*, in T. W. Rhys-Davids, trans., *Buddhist Suttras*, vol. 11 of *Sacred Books of the East* (Oxford: Clarendon, 1881), pp. 298–300. It is somewhat similar to agnosticism, but Gautama was very positive.
12. Ludwig Wittgenstein, *Tractatus Logico-philosophicus* (London: Routledge & Kegan Paul, 1961), T. 6.53, p. 151.
13. Bertrand Russell's introduction to Wittgenstein, op. cit., p. xxi.
14. *Udāna* VI.4. F. L., in Woodward, trans., *Udāna: Verses of Uplift* and *Itivuttaka: As It Was Said*. The Minor Anthologies of the Pali Canon, pt. 2. Vol. 8 of *Sacred Books of the Buddhists* (London: Pali Text Society, 1935), pp. 81–83.
15. *Udāna* VI.4., in ibid. The Chinese version of the *Arthavargiya-sūtra* (*Taisho Tripitaka*, in *Pali Canon*, vol. 4, p. 178 a–c.) This parable of the blind men and an elephant (*andha-gajahyaya*) is a favorite one for both Hindu and Jain philosophers (see Winternitz, op. cit., vol. 2, p. 88n).
16. Winternitz, op. cit., vol. 2, pp. 87–88.
17. *Suttanipāta* 843.
18. *Suttanipāta* 847.
19. *Samyutta-nikāya*, in *Pali Canon* (London: Pali Text Society, 1972), vol. 3, pp. 138 ff.; cf. *Suttanipāta* 73.
20. *Suttanipāta* 842 ff.; cf. 855, 860.
21. *Suttanipāta* 837.
22. Irving Babbitt, "Buddha and the Occident," in *The Dhammapada* (New York and London: Oxford University Press, 1936), pp. 67, 72.
23. Ibid., p. 69.

6.
Buddhism and the
Theistic Question   *Charles Hartshorne*

Nolan Pliny Jacobson is an outstanding example of the power of Buddhism to appeal to people of countries and cultures other than those that produced this ancient religion. According to Levi-Strauss, Buddhism, which is older than Mohammedanism and Christianity, should have come last, implying that it is the most civilized or sophisticated of the three. According to Whitehead, Christianity was a religion seeking a philosophy, and Buddhism was a philosophy seeking a religion. Charles Peirce called his own view Buddhisto-Christian. All these philosophers together imply that these two religions (and I would add Judaism) might do well to try to learn from each other. Whitehead explicitly said as much.

What should Westerners of Christian or Judaic background learn from Buddhism? Jacobson said they should learn the importance of the creativity of moment-by-moment experiencing that is in each person but that tends to be stifled by culture-induced habits and over-valued theories. I see in this a fusion of the Buddhist idea of dependent origination with the Whiteheadian (also Bergsonian, Peircean, and Berdyaevian) idea of creativity. Bergson said that each of us is an artist and that our primary art-products are our momentary experiences, each of which is unique compared to any other in all history. This uniqueness, illustrating Peirce's firstness, or creative aspect, is suggested by the word *origination* in the Buddhist idea; but *dependent* implies the lack of self-being that is so much stressed (and overstated) by Buddhism. Whitehead's term *prehension* has both implications (in better balance) and also implies that the data prehended are all temporally antecedent to the prehending, so that the relation corresponds to traditional causality, except that causes are necessary but not strictly sufficient conditions for the new experiences; thus the latter are indeed originative or creative.

My primary emphasis on what Buddhism can give us is somewhat different. Bergson, Peirce, Whitehead, and Berdyaev seem to have arrived at the idea of the creativity of experiencing with little help from Buddhism. Also, as Jacobson points out, Hume had already challenged the idea of the self or soul as strictly identical entity into which becoming inserts new qualities and from which it extracts qualities. How strict identity or nondifference can be reconciled with these insertions and extractions has always been a puzzle. The Buddhist "No soul" or "No substance" doctrine was finally arrived at by the West on its own. Hume, after first attempting to derive sympathy from love, rejected this attempt and declared the irreducibility of sympathy. Western theology and ethics scarcely noticed until recently the positive importance of this theoretical point in Hume. Paul Weiss, with all his brilliance, seems still to feel that the "No soul" doctrine is a threat to ethics. Peter Bertocci takes a similar line. I think they miss the positive importance of this negation. Even Hume did not use his denial of personal identity in treating religious or ethical questions. Peirce did, however; and he was followed independently by Whitehead, when (with a smile) he said: "I sometimes think that all modern immorality has been caused by the Aristotelian doctrine of substance," as defined by the proposition that qualities are in a substance but the substance is not in anything other than itself.

The West has lacked most an adequate sense of the absurdity of taking without qualification the concept of self, soul, or identity through change, of the person and equally without qualification the nonidentity among persons. Buddhism alone among religions or ancient philosophical traditions has the glory of having made both qualifications. Yet one New Testament text sharply implies them: "Thou shalt love thy neighbor as thyself." This counsel means nothing much unless it means a denial of the Aristotelian idea of substance as it stands. Consider also the statement of Paul, the apostle to the Gentiles, that "we are members one of another." Is it intellectually honest (or if honest, is it insightful) to consider this philosophy compatible with Aristotle's?

Plato on this issue (as in some others) is not Aristotelian. Nor was Aristotle, whom I call the first great neo-Platonist, a good Platonist on this point. For Plato, reality does not consist of a plurality of Aristotelian substances. In the *Timaeus,* qualities belong to the receptacle, a vague, insufficiently clarified cosmic something that keeps acquiring and losing predicates. In the *Phaedo,* Plato does seem to take individual souls as actually immortal, but this is a loose end, as far as I can see, in his mature thought. As I learned from one of my mentors on Aristotle, Chung Hwan Chen, a former colleague, the famous doctrine of substance was a pluralization of the receptacle. Plato's view was unacceptably vague and unfinished. But to go to an opposite extreme from Plato's too monistic stance was not to arrive at the balanced truth.

According to Tzscherbatski, an opposite development occurred in Buddhism. In Theravāda or Southern Buddhism, a rather extreme pluralism was presented. But in Medieval China, in Fa Tsang of the Hua Yen tradition, an equally extreme monism seemed to take its place. Fa Tsang held that earlier and later events mutually require each other. There is no freedom in the genuine libertarian sense. Not only were my ancestors necessary conditions for my being and becoming, but I was a necessary condition for their being and becoming. Effects are as necessary to their causes as vice versa. There is no piecemeal contingency, no individual freedom or creativity, at all. According to this, Peirce, Bergson (also Descartes, Cournot, and many other French philosophers), Whitehead, Popper, Dewey, and James were mistaken about freedom, and Spinoza and his disciple Blanshard were right.

If we are to love others as we love ourselves, how do we love ourselves? For a Buddhist, our present self is the latest in a series of successive selves. What is called self-love or self-interest is the concern of each momentary self or mental state for its definite predecessors and possible successors. There is no absolute difference between self-interest and altruism. Suppose someone has in the past insulted or injured me. If I then say to the injuror, "You insulted me, you injured me, therefore I hate you," a Buddhist may (in the words of one of them) term my behavior "writhing in delusions." Why? Because the injuring self is no longer the other person's active self and the injured self is no longer my active self. If personal identity is not absolute identity (I and virtually all Buddhists agree (that it is far from absolute), nonidentity among persons is not absolute.

I was about twenty years of age when I thought through the question of self-interest and altruism. I knew nothing of Buddhism or of Hume, Peirce, Whitehead, or Plato, but I knew the Pauline saying quoted above. I reached the conclusion that interest in other persons is the presupposition of being a person (I did know Royce's great essay on community) and that both interests are equally and in their own right rational. Since then I have read many ingenious arguments for the notion that altruism is rational only because it is to our own long-run advantage to be good to others. Neither then nor now have I found these arguments acceptable. Rational valuation is valuing truly valuable things. Rational interest is interest in interesting things. Interest exclusively in self (as much as this is possible) is unenlightened, no matter how shrewdly and farsightedly it takes the interested person's own future advantage into account. If I am important, it is because persons, properly so-called or with anything like normal degrees of intelligence, are important. We should leave it largely to animal instinct to make us care about ourselves (at least in the near future) and should not dignify self-concern by calling it peculiarly rational. Even animal instinct takes some care of species' interests, not just individual ones. Reason generalizes self-concern and other-concern and makes both types of concern far-sighted and comprehensive.

The Buddha is reputed to have said that our human identity through change is least radically qualified when our bodies are concerned and most radically qualified when taking us as conscious individuals. This qualification is fairly obvious. Our hearts go on beating in dreamless sleep when our consciousness is, as far as we know, reduced to zero. So does our breathing. So do many other bodily processes. Moreover, our gene combinations, unique except in identical twins or more numerous cases of the same genes, were already there in our fetal stages, when our consciousness had nothing like the qualities that make us superior, if we are superior, to the other animals. Buddha really did tell it like (as) it is in this respect. Many other thinkers have not done so.

Theistic belief is the big issue debated between Buddhism and all other high religions except Jainism. T. R. V. Murti has said that India "is the most theistic country of all." Buddha asked his followers to think primarily not about Brahman, Íśvara, or God but about how a human individual can live to escape suffering and achieve the highest possible form of positive good, called Nirvāna. Buddhism is not atheistic, but it is not explicitly theistic. Shall we call it agnostic? Suzuki, the scholar who did his best to instruct Westerners about Buddhism early in this century, has written that he was not sure whether Zen Buddhism is or is not theistic. One Buddhist text reads as follows: "There is an eternal being, unborn and undying; if this were not so, we could not ourselves escape from birth and death."

Also debated is whether the careers of human individuals are bounded by birth and death, or whether there are posthumous experiences related to those before death, somewhat as the later were to earlier experiences in the same personal careers. Buddhism does not limit a human career to a single life span. It values the reincarnation belief as enabling us to find karmic justification for misfortunes in this life by attributing them at least partly to actions the individual has done in a previous incarnation. The belief also enables us to hope that in a long series of reincarnations, each of us can achieve a closer approximation to Nirvāna or eventually Nirvāna itself.

Nirvāna is sometimes described as escape from suffering or from birth and death. But this is a negative description, like that some theisms give of deity. Surely this end of all ends or purpose of all purposes must have positive character. I have seen Nirvāna described as pure bliss. To this I take exception. Here Buddhism seems finally ambiguous and unsatisfying. In Mahāyāna, a wonderfully high ideal, the Bodhisattva, achieved clarity. To transcend egoism, with its painful conflicts and frustrations, the individual needs to realize the dependence or lack of self-being and, in the end, the complete impermanence of all worldly things. The individual should generalize his/her concerns into universal compassion and good will. This belief leads to the standpoint that a person seeks not simply personal enjoyment of Nirvāna but Nirvāna for all. Until this is possible, the person renounces final personal achievement. I take this to mean that the person stands by love as the highest principle, not mere self-enjoyment. Reality, including divine reality, is essentially social. No feeling or experiencing is mere self-feeling or mere self-experiencing. As far as that is the meaning of Trinitarianism, I am not a Unitarian monotheist. But God must love the creatures, not just other divine persona.

Jacobson did not stress his difference from me in regard to the God question. But he did, I think, dissent from the theological aspect of my thinking and Whitehead's. However, if Buddhism is nontheistic, does it solve the religious problem? As Plato said, there have always been atheists, but has any society done really well on an atheistic basis? And on that basis, what, in final analysis, is the meaning of our existences between birth and death? Also, how do we understand the possibility of an orderly world if each individual at every moment is to some extent self-moving, self-determining, creative, or free? Should the laws of nature be taken as final facts with no further explanation possible? I see only two explanations. One is that these laws are the only laws possible for some mathematical or logical reason that, so far, we have not discovered. The other is that these laws are contingent: there could be, and may have been, other laws, and the selection and establishing of the existent laws has been the act of some supreme form of freedom worthy of being called divine. This explanation must attribute eternal and noncontingent existence to the divine power. Otherwise we would need some action to produce this power, which would lead to an endless and vicious regress.

One great advantage of theism over any nontheistic cosmology is that it has an explanation for contingency that applies even to the laws of nature. This explanation is the creativity inherent in mind, in experiencing, thinking, and feeling, in any form of the psychical. Plato said long ago, "What has soul is what is self-moved," self-determined.[1] In the recent form of philosophy of mind found in many thinkers, from Descartes to the writer of this sentence (with many intermediaries), it is not enough to say that a person's present experience is determined by that person's previously formed character and environment. Each new momentary experience must be somewhat self-determined, not fully determined by a person's previous character and environment. That all this should make a world possible (rather than hopeless disorder and mutually frustrating conflict) without some cosmic form of self-moving mind to inspire the local acting singulars or agents with some sense of common direction, some outline patterns of order, seems unintelligible.

Second to the "No soul" or "No substance" dictum, the Buddhist saying "Mind only" is another aspect of Buddhism that surpassed the thought of all the ancient Greeks, even Plato, who thought there were some parts of nature devoid of self-acting agents, including the rocks that compose the earth. Hence, he could not say "Mind only." Nor could Aristotle. Epicurus, the materialist, attributed self-movement and a germ of freedom to atoms; he should therefore have attributed some lowly form of mind to them also. The Buddhists were the first to get rid of a mind-matter dualism without falling into a counterintuitive materialism. They did so long before Leibniz or Berkeley. They could not, however, do much with this project, because its development required scientific advances of many centuries. Peirce and Whitehead were the first to be in a good position for this, and quantum theory has since made the idea seem even more credible.

Some physicists and biologists since Whitehead have used these new possibilities. The notion of mere matter, mere stuff or process, devoid of feeling and hence of quality in any positively intelligible sense, in contrast to mere relational structures, is less and less relevant to science. It never was very helpful in philosophy of religion or ethics. Wordsworth's poetry, supported by Shelley's, did not have use for it. Nor did that of Robinson Jeffers. Unluckily Jeffers was a determinist, which tied his hands and kept him from reaching a satisfying form of theism. Thomas Hardy, Mark Twain, and Ambrose Bierce were similarly handicapped.

Because of their concept "Mind only," when Buddhists refer to the bodily continuities through change, we should know they are talking about some type of mind or the psychical that is much more primitive than our consciousness but suitable for cells or smaller active units. When certain of our cells are damaged or ill-treated and we feel pain, we can interpret the pain as our sympathetic participation in the feelings of those cells. In this semi-identity theory of sensation, the mind-body relation is a mind-mind relation involving more than one level of feeling. Because the body is physical, if anything is, no Cartesian dualism need exist in this doctrine.

My former colleague at Texas, Richard Zaner, makes it clear, I think, that before Descartes finished his work, he came to the conclusion that what has been called Cartesian dualism is not true. Descartes asked himself, "What is pain?" He replied, "It is clearly psychical; it is also clearly physical." We must talk about the physical, but we need not talk about the simply nonpsychical, because no evidence of any such thing exists. As Whitehead put it, simply apart from instances of experiencing or feeling, "there is nothing, nothing, bare nothing."[2] Peirce, Bergson, and Leibniz would have had little or no reason to disagree.

Buddhism arrived at the radically subjectivistic form of idealism in my opinion, the wrong form of the doctrine, well before Berkeley did so in England and Edwards in America. In another way, however, Buddhism is closer to the better type of psychical monism than other ancient traditions in the Orient or Occident. In its treatment of being and becoming, Buddhists favor becoming. Heraclitus in Greece was a solitary figure. The atomists limited becoming to locomotion. The others thought of nature, apart from animals and plants, and in much of space, as devoid of internal, qualitative changes—that is, devoid of mind as we know it in ourselves. Thinking, feeling, loving, hating, desiring, remembering, perceiving, are activities, qualitatively changing processes. Buddhism, as a method of altering our ways of thinking, feeling, and valuing, deals directly with mind as such. It anticipated the view of recent physics that nature consists of events, not things (or persons). The Greeks, even apart from the materialists, in some sense atomized reality spatially, but they tended to avoid temporal atomization or quantification, as did the materialists. Heraclitus is unclear or vague on the point. The river keeps becoming new. But is this in steps of a definite unit, or is it infinitely gradual or continuous? Buddhism seems to offer a definite pluralism of the least steps of becoming.

In our century, idealism has been either a theory of extreme cosmic oneness (Bradley, Bosanquet, Royce) or a radical pluralism of unit actualities (Whitehead's "actual entities," which are implied also by Von Wright's logical demonstration of the impossibility of purely continuous becoming). Leibniz, Peirce, and Bergson retained the old continuous or "Synechistic" view of becoming. In spatial terms, however, Leibniz was a pluralist through and through. Space was simply the order of coexistence between unit realities or monads. Yet Leibniz was in some ways the first clear-cut metaphysical idealist in East or West who was also a metaphysical realist. Nature is not there in the mere sense that we perceive it or that God perceives or thinks it. All the monads exist as truly as humans do. The frog being eaten by a snake probably feels its discomfort as truly as we perceive its misfortune, or as would normally be the case, fail to perceive it apart from extremely faint and by us undetectable differences made through the preestablished harmony to our mental states.

The overwhelming majority of monads were, for Leibniz, too insignificant or microscopic in their spatial spheres of appreciable influence to receive attention from common sense until long after physicists were convinced of their reality. Leibniz saw through an illusion that, for two thousand years of philosophizing, had caused thinkers to hesitate between a sheer mind-matter dualism and a reductive materialism that could not, in the nature of things, be comfortable for common sense. Leibniz realized that the established distinction between "animate" and "inanimate" nature rested on a failure to distinguish in principle between nature as it appears to us when perceived through our unaided senses and nature as it is in itself. Stones or bodies of water are apparently inanimate, but then (as Epicurus and his materialistic predecessors guessed) their unit constituents are as self-active, in their small scale and limited modes of action, as insects are.

Why did Leibniz succeed so little in persuading the learned world to accept his psychical monism, according to which "matter" is mind in certain very simple, individually insignificant unit forms, collectively (via God and the preestablished harmony) causing the effects on our sense organs we call seeing, hearing, smelling, tasting, tactually feeling material bodies? The answer is clear but is not found plainly stated in histories of philosophy. Leibniz had also the belief called the principle of sufficient reason and certain traditional ideas of divine omnipotence and omniscience. These destroyed the plausibility of his psychicalism, which never received attention on its merits as such, because other aspects of this philosophy were so fascinating (and also unplausible).

"Sufficient reason" is subtly ambiguous and, as intended, is an extreme intellectualist superstition lacking in rational ground. It entails strict theological determinism, which made the resulting theodicy extremely vulnerable. Voltaire had great fun with it. Becoming is creation, not the unwinding of necessities. No unqualifiedly sufficient reasons for what is done in nature are necessary. We do not live, nor does God, for the sake of making deductions from self-evident premises, but to enjoy and transmit happiness and love. Berdyaev's exhortation "Be creative and foster creativity in others" is the imperative, not "Do what the causal situations make the only possible deeds for you."

If Buddhism had been even wiser than it was, it might have done what Leibniz did, but better, to get rid of dualism and materialism. Human capacities make us dependent on the state of culture in our time. Nature is too subtle and complex for us to see through the illusion of its appearance versus its essence without much long, slow work by many cooperative thinkers, scientific and philosophical. Greeks, Egyptians, Europeans, Americans, East Indians, Chinese, and Japanese were wildly guessing for thousands of years about the nature of matter. However, when Thomas Kuhn tells us that we are still without any knowledge of what nature really is, I think he is trying to make a quarter truth into a truth. We are still far from complete knowledge of exactly what nature is, but we know that a lot of traditional statements about nature are not true, and we have a genuine cumulation of this negative knowledge.

Even Popper so emphasizes the danger of claiming too much for scientific progress that he distracts attention from his belief that it takes place. Peirce and Whitehead have similar approaches. I too believe we know that fully answering the question "What is mind in nature?" would leave no question about matter unanswered. We would know just what forms of mind matter is, including what kind of feeling the frog being swallowed and the snake swallowing it would have, and also the feelings of their cells and smaller active constituents. There are narrow limits to what we can do in this line. But we know in principle what we remain ignorant of and why. God is the one to whom all hearts are open; we are not God. That too we know, in spite of Advaita-Vedāntists (if they think they know that such things as frog or snake feelings don't exist). On this I like the saying by a Japanese Buddhist that "all things have Buddhahood."

Theism enables us to have permanence for our value achievements without having to postulate for ourselves posthumous experiences or reincarnations in other bodies. Because all concrete, actual, and intrinsic values are those of experiences, God's prehensions of our experiences, or feelings of our feelings, gives our actualities objective immortality "where rust doth not corrupt nor thieves break through or steal." Death does not cancel out our achievements. We can also value others by the same principle we use to value ourselves, that we are all cherished by divine love. This one, in a sense supernatural, belief takes the place of the many little beliefs transcending any scientific testing with which Buddhist and other religious scriptures are replete.

If belief in God is equated with belief in the supernatural, then on the Platonic principle of the divine as Cosmic Soul (here I follow Cornford), one faces the simple question: Is the cosmos or is it not besouled or minded as a whole, and not only in some of its parts? Aristotle missed the point of this question. His god is bodiless, as far as he makes clear. The universe of things and events exist besides God, for Aristotle, and God knows nothing of its contingent details. These, Aristotle says, are not worth knowing. Plato says, on the contrary, that God as soul of the cosmos orders, knows, and cares about the individuals in the world. If Aristotle missed the Platonic point, the Middle Ages (misled by him and his many admirers) adopted a weak compromise between Plato's subtle and complex theism and Aristotle's too simple unmoved mover. Plato can be quoted against the notion of a totally unmoved perfection. He clearly (in late dialogues) implies a divine becoming.

In this century, Rabbi Heschel said what had long needed to be said: "God is the most moved mover." I wish only to insert two words between "most" and "moved." These are "and best." With that addition, Heschel's remark gives exactly the right emendation to the Aristotelian formula. I add to it the phrase of Wesley, "Love divine, all [other] love excelling." Thus conceived, God becomes worthy of being loved with all of a person's mind, and soul, and strength. And so "our fleeting days acquire abiding significance," to quote another Jewish formula. I deliberately end on a Jewish note out of consideration for the terrible way in which Jews have been mistreated, especially in this century. Belief in the infallible God is one thing; belief in an infallible institutionalizing, or scriptural recording, of human beliefs about God is another. Perhaps Christians have some repenting to do and some appropriate modesty to acquire. If the claim to have certain knowledge of the absolute religious truth is not conceit, what is? And it leads to cruelty to others.

Notes

1. R. B. Levinson, ed. *A Plato Reader* (New York: Houghton Mifflin, 1967), pp. 457–462 (Timaeus), pp. 484–488 (Laws, book 10).
2. Alfred North Whitehead, *Process and Reality* (New York: Macmillan, 1929), chapter 2, section 2, paragraph 6; see also, Whitehead, *Adventures of Ideas* (New York: Macmillan, 1933), chapter 15, section 11.

7.
The Reflexive Nature of
Momentariness (*Ksana-vāda*)   *Kenneth K. Inada*

This essay was prompted by the central concept of a self-corrective society from the thinking of Nolan Pliny Jacobson.[1] In probing the concept, it became increasingly clear that the self-corrective character functions fundamentally on the basis of a mutually reflective phenomenon. For example, a function that involves the doer and the deed requires a reflexive nature inherent to both in a mutually defining sense. This led me to probe the Buddhist doctrine of impermanence that, in turn, focused on the nature of momentary existence. Rather than accept momentariness as a mere descriptive passage of events, I concentrated on the Buddhist dynamics of experiential reality. This essay attempts to understand the nature of experiential momentariness as a primary step in examining and appreciating the self-corrective process.

The concept of Buddhist reality (*Buddha-Dharma*) has challenged the best minds, including dedicated practitioners of the faith, because we do not have the means of adequately justifying its existence. The historical Buddha's initial refusal to divulge the content of his enlightenment can be understood in this vein. Eventually, however, the Buddha condescended to expound his unique experience, hoping earnestly that his followers would understand the utter fruitlessness of rational means and take up the yogic path of discipline. Thus, in the strictest sense, we should not even have the illusion that my writing this essay is not an exercise in futility. But we are not all practitioners, and I believe that if we probe further, we will clarify some doctrinal points and have a better focus on, and perhaps develop some intimacy with, Buddhist reality.

Generally speaking, three basic doctrines govern Buddhist thought: the universal nature of suffering (*duhkha*), the dynamic nonmodal nature of the self (*anātman*), and the impermanent nature of things (*anitya*). These doctrines are, in many respects, cognates that depict different phases of the same experience, interpenetrating and defining each other in the total grasp of the perspectives of reality.

Although the nature of impermanence is basic to human experience, we have, on the whole, taken it as inconsequential to our daily lives. We live with or through it without really understanding it or coming to grips with its inner working. Our understanding of ordinary experience is at best desultory. We skip and jump from place to place in our perception of things, including our mental activities. We miss and ignore the nature of the experiential continuum, thinking all along that experiences will go on, regardless of our inattention or inertia. We are, for example, unmindful of the passage of years, but at some crucial moment in our life, we become quite conscious of the years we have lived and henceforth experience a strange feeling of receding, not to the past but into an unknown future. The sensation becomes even more eerie when we focus on the microscopic passage of moments of existence. Such moments are elusive, and they go by with such rapidity that neither the mind nor the senses are able to track them down. But the passage of moments is the most tangible clue we have toward any discourse on experiential reality. This reality is, in turn, directly related to, indeed coexistent with, Buddhist reality. We must seriously turn our attention to the passage of moments or the framework of momentary existence *ksana-vāda*.

Each moment of existence is unique because qualitative differences exist among different moments—though the differences are not readily discernible in the rapidity with which these moments are evolving. Each is also unique because it can express itself in its own momentous way in any activity. Each is the focal point, the key, to the understanding of things existential. It is the locus of experiential reality as such. Unfortunately, this locus is the least focused on, because of its inherent momentary or evanescent character. Its features are invisible for the most part, and we become conscious of it only after the passage of events. We have certain bias toward what is visible and tangible. Our casual day-to-day perceptions, for example, are overwhelmingly conditioned by or based on the visibles or tangibles, so our perceptions are basically limited and distorted and revolve around the peripheral aspect of events. This limitation is the bane of mere phenomenal existence.

Due to the biased nature of our perceptions, we have built up a store of knowledge based on what is basically pseudoreality—knowledge that functions on the scientific model of a simple cause and effect affair. But this model does not apply to all cases, much less when human nature and relations are involved. It is time we seriously reflect on this simplistic framework and probe other ways of achieving knowledge. Knowing that the cause-effect paradigm we entertain, implicitly or explicitly, is not ironclad should motivate us to seek understanding in other, more subtle and profound dimensions involved in momentariness.

What is the nature of momentariness? The cardinal principle of Mahāyāna thought as expressed in *Avatamsaka* or Hua-yen philosophy is "All in one and one in all." This principle is not a simple mathematical model of an equation but an expression of dynamic reality. It means that in the dynamic nature of experiential reality, no singular moment exists alone or independently. The independent existence of a moment would be tantamount to a vacuous existence, which is utterly meaningless. Instead, each moment of existence takes on meaning and significance only as much as it is related to other moments and events and the relational context of things. Paradoxically, the moment describes the context as much as the context describes the moment.

This principle is the basic premise of the reflexive nature inherent in experiential reality. But our prejudiced ordinary minds are too feeble to penetrate this nature. The mind lacks the power, indeed glosses over this nature, because of its basic dualistic function. Every function of the mind is an instance of a dichotomy or bifurcation that covers both physical and mental spheres. Based initially and heavily on sense perceptions, the mind perceives things in the framework of subjective and objective components, as if they exist apart from each other and subsist independently. Our assumption that the mind is capable of bringing the components together is not only an oversimplification but a blatant falsehood. It is naive empiricism of the first order. On a different level, treating concepts as if they exist in the mind as separate entities fosters naive idealism.

Biased perception persists because we are attracted to, even attached to, the elements of either naive empiricism or naive idealism, without regard for the grounds in which the elements are able to be what they are. I analogize this perceptual limitation as the lighthouse effect of mentality. We only see what comes under the scrutiny of the light and tend to forget the object prior and posterior to the sighting. This narrow perception totally ignores the holistic and continuous dimensions of experiential reality. To paraphase an old saying, real perception is more than what meets the eye. Without correction, our so-called habits of perception will take a great toll and will continue to do so.

Ordinary perception has dramatically induced the selective nature of our senses. Basic Buddhism discovered this selective feature

early and concentrated on it. All perceptions have the facet of attachment (*upādāna*) built into the very function of the senses. Yet basic
Buddhism has taught us that it need not be so, that all attachments
could be removed or destroyed to enter the realm of purity, emptiness,
and nirvāna. It is time to begin to understand that ordinary perception, in virtue of its dichotomous ways, has perpetuated a process by
this phenomenon of attachment. Is it not true that no attachment exists without dichotomy and no dichotomy without attachment? The
two seem to be mutual partners in an interminable process. Is it not
also the case that the concept of a self arises in virtue of this simple
dichotomy and its attendant attachment to the elements of existence?
This rather coarse nature of perception has brought on an easy understanding by attachment to those elements whose existence is never
questioned within the total ambience of momentary existence.

Probing ordinary perception further, we can see two aspects: the
process itself, and the elements relative to perception. Of these aspects, we are mostly aware of the latter, and we do not often, if at all,
bother to consider the former. This situation is devastating because we
are attracted to and become attached to the elements and take them to
be substitutes for the reality or realities we are seeking. In David Hume's
analysis, the attachments become the basis for the ingrained habits of
perception, leaving us with what can be referred to as the predicament
of empiricism. The habits control much of our perceptual understanding, but we are left with the lingering doubt that the perception could
not completely justify the reality of things. In this regard, one of Hume's
great contributions was to explore the limits of empiricism and exhibit the nature of the predicament. He also hinted that something
other than causation is the basis of experience. But he did not pursue
the matter and probably could not pursue it because of his Western
philosophical orientation in substance thought, despite his devastating critique of the concept of substance.

We have come to rely heavily on our habits of perception for
discourse on the elements, but at the same time we have failed to account adequately for the process in which the elements thrive. The
failure is not wholly ours. Perception based on our habits is still the
sphere in which to understand the reality of things. What then needs
to be done?

Several tracks are open. In one sense, we must give a fuller vision
to what we accept as ordinary perception. The process and the elements relative to it must be perceived within the same realm or within
the singular dynamic movements. There is an identity here, or a parity

of existence. In another sense, we must begin to focus not only on the elements but on the total perceptual process. Our existential nature is deep-rooted and extensive, more than what we take it to be, and more than what ordinary perception reveals in peripheral ways. Momentary experiences show that the elements do not persist but that the process persists or continues.

To expand on the problematics of ordinary perception, we can point at the three unwholesome roots of being: greed (*rāga*), hatred (*dosa*), and delusion (*moha*). All three deviate from and distort the natural flow of the process and its elements. Each provokes an attachment to the elements either of physical or mental nature, or both, which hinders that flow. Greed provokes wanton grasping or clinging to certain elements. Hatred provokes unjustified rejection or repulsion of things and persons. And delusion provokes the inability to be decisive, which in some instances is caused by the habits of attachment to or rejection of certain things or persons. In all three, the elements of the process are blown out of proportion to their proper places within the process.

Ironically, the above analysis of the three unwholesome roots of being is not taken seriously. Life goes on as usual, without the slightest concern for the total perceptual process. Experiences are dominantly described in terms of the elements, which has brought on an atomic structural analysis of the experiences themselves. These experiences are accepted, without the slightest hesitation, as representing the nature of reality itself. This concept is wrong, but we have lived with this half-truth from time immemorial. The atomic structure of experience, however neat and clear it may be, is not reality but a skeletal view of it. Reality is fundamentally a moving phenomenon that defies any description. This great insight of Asiatic thought has been nourished throughout the centuries. On this vision of a true process philosophy, the East and West started out on an equal footing. The East preserved it in every phase of their activities, but the West somehow deviated from its original stance by being led to focus on forms and substances. In the twentieth century, however, the West is quickly recovering from its substantive treatment of nature by shifting to the novel framework of Einsteinian relativity physics. Exposure to Eastern thought is accelerating the process.

Human experience is a malleable quantity. It is paradoxical that human experience can stand a great amount of tension, pressure, and distortion while still retaining its general character. Malleability is taken for granted without questioning its very nature. In this sense, we become insensitive to one of the great features of our nature of sentiency—the fact of our vital and flexible living process. The insensitivity has given way to the structural elements and their consequent analysis. In many respects, our understanding of things is the consequence of this analytic bias.

The paradox also shows up in a way—albeit hidden by the dominance of the analytic bias—that reveals positively and effectively the nature of creativity. Without malleability, creativity would not be possible, because everything, including those elements involved in the analysis, would not take on the dynamic nature. This point has not been recognized for what it is or acknowledged for its value in understanding ordinary experience. We need to examine closely the whole fabric of experiential process in its more primitive nature. In doing so, we focus on the nature of creativity.

The Buddhist had a good look at the mechanics of experiential process and came up with the circular or wavelike theory of the famous wheel of life, or *samsāra*, the incessant turning of the wheel this side of attaining enlightenment, in virtue of the insatiable grasp for the elements of experiential process. The fundamental basis of the wheel of life is technically known as *pratītya-samutpāda*, variously translated as "conditioned origination," "relational origination," "dependent origination," "interrelational coarising," and so on. It comes closest to the Western concept of creativity in which, in the case of Alfred North Whitehead, "the many become one, and are increased by one."[2] Creativity rightly belongs to the category of the ultimate, because nothing is more ultimate on the primitive level of existence than the concepts of the many and one. Its consequences are the things, beings, and entities that we normally refer to. But Whitehead, being a process philosopher, was careful to emphasize the dynamic nature of these things, which a person can only intimate by intuitive grasp.

In both Whitehead and Buddhist thought, we have an organismic flow of existence, in which antecedent and coterminous conditions come into play at each moment of existence to exhibit the overall emergence of things or events. These events are lodged in the forms or facts with which we relate our experiences. Whitehead introduced the concept of eternal objects, clearly a Platonic influence, to round out the creative advance of these things or events. The Buddhist resorted to the so-called dharma theory of experiential reality, notably advanced by the Abhidharma school of thought.[3] In the dharma theory, each experiential event or reality is expressed by a certain dharma that dominantly manifests and becomes the distinguishing characteristics of that particular moment of existence. For example, the dharma of greed (*rāga*) will show up in the experiential nature of that particular moment in question. Or, the dharma of hatred (*dosa*) will show in that person's nature as long as hatred or anger does not cease. As long as the experiential process is in a continuum, the dharmic exhibition goes on incessantly, each replacing another in quick succession. This dharmic exhibition is another way of delineating the *samsāric* nature of things.

The *samsāric* nature was earlier described as a wavelike phenomenon. We should go further to depict it as a surging wave, like the surf that rises at the reef's edge and continues to swell as it pushes its way to the shorelines. This surging phenomenon of a wave is similar to our experiential process as it picks up its activities and displays itself accordingly. As the surf swells and surges forward, the waters within it also cycle or roll as it builds itself up. Similarly, our experiential process in the nature of relational origination is cyclic as it rolls on from the seeming past to the future, but in the strictest sense, the process always takes place as dynamic momentariness. It is specious, but this dynamic momentariness is of utmost concern to us, because it is the locus not only of experiential reality but of the understanding of and intimations with reality as such (*tathatā*). Another dimension to momentariness is the aforementioned reflexive nature. Each present moment came predominantly from the past, but although the present moment contains or reflects the past in content and form, it does so in a reflexive way that simultaneously contains the present novel conditions at play. Although the present is contiguous with the past moment, it is not wholly determined by the past but carries, to a degree, the past's form and content to surge forward.

Aside from the normal symmetric or linear flow of experiences, from past to present to future, a dynamic asymmetric movement exhibits the truly reflexive nature of the present making. In this dynamic matrix, the present sweeps the total ambience of the prevailing conditions in nonlinear ways. The symmetric flow can be labeled the horizontal flow of experiential events. The asymmetric flow in the reflexive sense depicts a vertical sweep and spread of the event. Each experiential reality is interpreted as the dynamics of both horizontal (linear) and vertical (nonlinear) flows. In this scheme, it is just as true to say that the past flows into the present as it is to say that the present gathers the past into its present total mold that involves novel conditions. This is the creative advance, not unlike what Whitehead has delineated. The past need not be related to the present, but the present is inviolably related to the past in its advancement.

In the Buddhist context, we are made cognizant that as long as we are involved in the dharmic activities, we are unable to release ourselves from *samsāra*. But there must be a break, a way out of *samsāra*. The answer from both the Theravāda and Mahāyāna traditions on this issue is united. The release will have to be found in the same realm of existence that covers the unenlightened and the enlightened nature of things. If suffering rises, the cessation of suffering also has to be within the same grounds, just as the sick recovers or regains health within the same state of existence. Because this statement is quite cryptic and puzzling, it is easily rejected or passed off as inconsequential to daily living. However, that is a mistaken view, and it calls for real dedication and seriousness to resolve all human travails. It inevitably points to yogic discipline to cleanse the whole experiential system.

The clue to the resolution of suffering may lie in the proper grasp of the dynamics of the past and present. The present vertical thrust gives credence to the past content but then goes on to carve out a novel content by being aloof to the elements in the horizontal flow. The horizontal flow is linear, as mentioned earlier, and being so, it is prone to static and elemental analysis. Such analysis, based on dichotomization and segmentation, immediately has a hold on the senses and the mind. Willy-nilly, we have been propelled by our own senses and mind to perpetuate the *samsāric* life.

The attachments are rooted in the horizontal or linear plane, and the uprooting must be achieved by breaking the bonds of the dominantly linear nature. This break is achieved by incorporating the non-linear vertical dimension in momentary existence. This incorporation is the way to a holistic accommodation of the same realm and a shift from an erstwhile *samsāric* nature to the fullness of being. The wave-like *samsāric* nature is kept intact; but on the same nature, the enlightened nature rides. This so-called ride on the *samsāric* wave is possible because it is based on the nature of emptiness (*śūnyatā*) of the dharmas. Where there is no attachment to anything but instead detachment from everything, the moment of existence becomes naturally open, fresh, and creative. All this theory is only a clue to understanding the famous dictum of Nāgārjuna: "*Samsāra* equals nirvāna."

Actually, Nāgārjuna's dictum came at the end of a long period of Mahāyāna beginnings, perhaps running for about two hundred years, in which time the basic Mahāyāna doctrines were conceived. For example, the key doctrine of the bulky *Prajñāpāramitā Sutras*, "Form is emptiness and emptiness is form," predates Nāgārjuna. So does the doctrine of "All in one and one in all" of the *Avatamsaka Sutra* and the doctrine of expedient means (*upāya-kauśalya*) of the *Saddharma-pundarīka Sutra*. In all these Mahāyāna sutras and many more, the guiding principle is the *Bodhisattvacarya*, the practice of the enlightened way of life. It is based on the mythical Bodhisattva Dharmākara's forty-eight vows, the gist of which describes a world in which sentient beings are seen as suffering and the bodhisattva wills to delay his/her entrance into nirvana until all sentients are saved. This suffering in the world is dramatized best by Vimalakīrti, who says that he is sick because sentients are suffering and that he must bestow his compassion.[4]

The practice of the bodhisattva way is a supreme example of the reflexive nature in action. That a bodhisattva suffers because sentients do means that the bodhisattva is bound to the same ground of existence as the sentients. In essence, a mutual suffering exists between two parties, one enlightened and the other unenlightened, although the latter is for the most part uncognizant of this fact. The Buddhist insight here has brought on the literal collapse of the highest form of intelligence (*prajñā*) and the universal nature of compassion (*karuna*), a feat that is little understood or appreciated because of the dichotomous ways of ordinary perception. Dichotomy generates at once attachment to elements of both sides of the split, where the objective and subjective components become frozen, as it were, in their perceptual tracks. By its own act, dichotomy has caused the elements to appear as covering, despite the natural free flow of existential process. Such is the nature of samsāra and its unsuspecting perpetuation. But the way out of samsāra consists in resolving all dichotomous natures by intimating oneself with the reflexive nature of momentary existence.

Notes

1. Nolan Pliny Jacobson, *Buddhism and the Contemporary World: Change and Self-Correction* (Carbondale and Edwardsville: Southern Illinois University Press, 1983). The subtitle already reveals the aims of the work. The sixth chapter of this work is devoted to the Buddhist self-corrective way. The other self-corrective community is modern science, which, despite controversies, has weathered quite well from Newtonian to Einsteinian physics. Although they have similar traits, the Buddhist way differs in basic ways from science and its methodology.
2. Alfred North Whitehead, *Process and Reality: An Essay in Cosmology*, corrected ed., ed. David Ray Griffin and Donald W. Sherburne (New York: Free Press, 1978), pp. 21–22.

3. The dharma theory is to be distinguished from the *Dharma*, in capital letter, which refers to the Buddhist truth of existence (e.g., *Buddha-Dharma*). The Abhidharma school thrived several centuries after the historical Buddha devised an elaborate classificatory system of seventy-five dharmas to describe every facet of human experience, from the unenlightened to the enlightened nature of things. It was the early "analytic" tradition in Buddhism. Incidentally, the term Abhidharma is variously interpreted as "higher doctrine," "study of the dharmas," "metaphysics of experience," "penetration into the dharmas," and so on.
4. Robert A. F. Thurman, trans., *The Holy Teaching of Vimalakīrti* (University Park: Pennsylvania State University Press, 1976), pp. 43–45.

8.
Buddhism, Taoism, and the Question of Ontological Difference   *David L. Hall*

Unlike Christianity, which is anchored to a system of doctrines that must be accepted on faith, and in contradistinction to Islam, which is often closely tied to concrete cultural forms and the extremes of national interest, Buddhism is a rational and empirical system, detachable in significant ways from its cultural milieu, and thus capable of functioning as a world philosophy. Among Westerners, Nolan Pliny Jacobson divined this possibility early and spent the greater portion of his life reckoning with the ecumenical potential of Buddhism. Primarily, Jacobson sought accommodation between Buddhist and Western sensibilities, but the development of something like a world civilization, if such is possible, also demands exploration of the connections between Buddhism and non-Western systems.

Comparative philosophy continues to suffer from the appearance that, with respect to the interpretations of exoteric doctrines and sensibilities, (almost) anything goes. The reasons for this have to do less with any strictly linguistic or historical confusions and more with the lack of an adequate philosophical vocabulary that translators and interpreters may access to realize the richest and most apropos constructions of the doctrines and concepts under examination.

Difficulties are increased enormously when comparisons are made between two alien or exoteric cultures, such as those of Buddhism and Taoism. Such comparisons made from the perspective of the Anglo-European philosophical tradition require a conceptual triangulation in which the interpreter's indigenous terminology is employed as the basis for translations of ideas and concepts from the Buddhist and the Taoist sensibilities, of necessity construing the exoteric doctrines by recourse to the categories of Anglo-European culture.

In this essay, I provide support for the scholars of the relation between Buddhists and Taoists, by adumbrating a schema for the interpretation of the Buddhist and Taoist responses to one of the most crucial of philosophical problematics associated with the Western tradition—the issue of ontological difference. Religious Taoism and Chinese forms of Buddhism beg the question—"What was the character of imported Buddhism and original Taoism prior to the period of their most significant interactions?" My purpose is to provide some discussion of issues crucial to the comparison of the Taoist and Buddhist sensibilities as a means of indicating the dominant conceptual background from which subsequent interactions between the two might have taken place.

The theme of ontological difference is a distinctly Western philosophical notion. It has become increasingly clear over the past several years that cross-cultural semantics presents a number of hitherto inadequately appreciated challenges to the comparative philosopher, not the least of which is the necessity to remain sensitive to the nuances associated with possible meanings of a term in the philosopher's own culture before the philosopher begins to assess either the meaning of the term, or (in the absence of a terminological equivalent) the presence of the sense of the term, in an alternative culture.

The question of ontological difference has explicitly or implicitly influenced the manner in which Anglo-European scholars have assessed Buddhist and Taoist doctrines. Important strains of philosophical Taoism, Mahāyāna Buddhism, and Anglo-European speculative philosophy present variant conceptualizations of ontological difference. Failure to recognize these variants can lead to serious misconstructions of the contrasted sensibilities. Historically, confusion between Buddhism and Taoism has involved the failure to note the precise sorts of conceptual transformations that took place in each of the two sensibilities during their several centuries of interaction in China, largely because of insensitivity to the precise differences not only between Taoism and Buddhism but between each and the dominant traditions of Western philosophy.

Cosmology, Ontology, and Difference

The most general question of difference concerns the difference between the "whatness" and the "thatness" of a thing. A rose is a rose. In addition, a rose *is*. Asking what a being is, is a cosmological question. Considering *that* it is, is an ontological appreciation. A rose as an item related with the other items in its ecosystem in complex spatiotemporal and biochemical manners is a cosmological entity. That the rose is—its "isness"—indicates its ontological character.

The contrast of cosmological and ontological cannot be imagined without the cosmogonic tradition out of which it arises. The most general problematic of Western philosophy concerns its attitude toward the chaos of beginnings. The creation and maintenance of order from out of and over against the threat of chaos is the fundamental fact that establishes our sense of beginnings. Speculative philosophy, both as general ontology and as universal science, attempts to explain the fundamental fact of order. The ontologist asks the ontological question—Why are there beings rather than no being? Or, Why is there something rather than nothing at all? The universal scientist asks the cosmological question—What kinds of things are there? The cosmogonic tradition in the Hellenic West has determined that metaphysical speculation must involve the search for beings or principles that, as transcendent sources of order, account for the order(s) experienced or observed.

Of the two questioning methods, the ontological is commonly asserted to be the more radical beginning for metaphysical speculation. Martin Heidegger has been considered a more radical thinker than, for example, Alfred North Whitehead, who seems to have remained content with the strictly cosmological concern. The ontological question need not be considered prior. Our bias toward unity over plurality, toward the being of beings rather than toward the insistent particularity of the beings themselves, may be an accident of our cultural development.

As traditionally interpreted, cosmological and ontological questions presuppose an ordered ground. This presupposition makes western philosophy *logocentric*[1]—that is, concerned with the illumination and expression of the source of order and structure in things. Since Nietzsche, however, it is perfectly plausible to argue that the cosmological question—What kinds of things are there?—is the more radical because it is open to the response: there are only interpretations, or perspectives, the sum of which is truth, the sum of which is chaos. If, as seems to be the case, the ontological question presumes an ordered or ordering ground, that question makes an assumption that the cosmological question may avoid.

The cosmological question asks about the character of things themselves, without the presumption of any single order or coherent set of orders. With Democritus, the cosmologists ask, How many and what kinds of *kosmoi* (worlds) are there? As most often understood, the ontological question, grounded as it is in the logocentric motive, may be thought to ask, Why cosmos rather than chaos? The cosmological question in its most radical form must ask the opposite question—Why chaos (*kosmoi*) rather than cosmos? It asks this question because it does not presume the existence of a cosmos, a single-ordered world.

The argument favoring the priority of the cosmological question is that it better meets the strictures of Occam's razor, because the acceptance of chaos does not require any additional principle in the form of cosmogonic activity responsible for the creation of an ordered world. Only this and this and this exist. And the *whatnesses* of these *thises*—the idiosyncratic particularities of that particular rose—are the only characters the orders own.

The issue of ontological difference is more complex than a mere exegesis of Heidegger and his epigoni suggests. We may distinguish the following interesting modes of raising the question of difference. First, a philosopher might ask after the difference between the cosmological and ontological character of things—between "beings" and "being"—presupposing the being of beings as ontological ground. Second, a philosopher might formulate a strictly cosmological vision that eschews ontology altogether and assess differences as obtaining among the beings themselves. Third, a philosopher who adopts the strictly ontological vision takes at face value the maxim grounding Parmenides' *Way of Truth*: Only being is.

In the Western philosophical and theological tradition, the first alternative has clearly dominated. God as Being is contrasted with the beings of the created order. It is important to recognize the philosophically subtle and religiously profound distinction between Parmenidean and Judaeo-Christian mysticism. Parmenides' radical ontology precludes any claim that the cosmological character of a world of manyness and change is grounded in an ontological fundament—either as creating or sustaining origin. The world of particulars is not a penultimate or second-rate being. Beings have no being at all. They are empty.

Instances of radical cosmology associated with the second mode cited above are hard to find in the Western tradition. But they are associated with the view that process and becoming are precedent over being and substance. Heraclitus and Bergson approximate this view, which has its clearest representative in philosophical Taoism.

The third response to the question of ontological difference makes of this world an illusory thing with respect to the unity of being or the absolute. This view is most closely associated with the ineffabilities of mystical experience and is approximated in the tradition of metaphysical nihilism. It is both acosmological and anontological. Neither being nor beings exist—*Nothing* exists. There is no difference, only indiffer-ence—nondifference. The mystical sense of oneness is the sense of non-difference. But this is not the only way of asserting the primacy of nondifference. A philosopher might say—or attempt to say—that non-being, the *nihil*, is fundamental. The contrast is not between being and beings but between the beings of the world and the nihil that guaran-tees their ultimately illusory or empty character. This final alternative inverts the ontological question in its classical form and asks, Why is nothingness the ultimate condition?

When, from the perspective of Anglo-European tradition, we seek to interpret Chinese Buddhism, it is necessary to ask after the interac-tions of Taoism and Indian Buddhism that came into China at the turn of the millennium. This search requires, with respect to the most gen-eral issues of the two sensibilities, some understanding of the manner in which we might employ concepts and issues entailed by the con-trast between ontological and cosmological views—or the absence of that contrast. We cannot understand the development of Chinese Bud-dhism without discussing the possible distinctiveness of the Taoist and Indian Buddhist interpretations of difference.

Taoism and Cosmological Difference

A philosophically coherent understanding of classical Taoism de-pends on a recognition that neither of the two fundamental metaphysi-cal contrasts of the Western tradition—between being and not-being and between being and becoming—is helpful in understanding the Taoist sensibility.[2] In Taoism, the sole fact is that of process or becom-ing. Being and nonbeing are abstractions from that process.

The first words of the *Tao Te Ching* may be rendered in this way: "The Tao that can be named is not the constant Tao.... The unname-able is the source of things." Throughout the *Tao Te Ching*, Tao is characterized as both nameless and nameable. Tao per se is the total process of becoming, becoming-itself. Nameless and nameable Tao function analogously to nonbeing and being, respectively. Thus being and nonbeing are abstractions from the generic process of becoming-itself. Tao is *That Which*—a name for process. That which is and that which is not[3] are the polar elements of becoming-itself.

The fundamental truth of the Taoist vision is contained in this mildly ironic send-up of Parmenides' infamous maxim: Only becom-ing is; not-becoming is not. There is only coming into being, which illustrates some mixture of being and nonbeing. Neither being nor nonbeing abstracted from its polar relationship with its opposite can be finally real.

Each particular element in the totality has its own intrinsic excellence. The Chinese term is *te*—the same word found in the title *Tao Te Ching*. *Te* may be understood as the particular focus or intrinsic excellence of a thing. The *te* of an element serves as the means in accordance with which it construes the totality of things from its perspective and thus names and creates a world.

The concepts of *tao* and *te* form a single notion, *tao-te*, which is best understood in terms of the relationships of field (*tao*) and focus (*te*). Just as in a holographic display each element contains the whole in an adumbrated form, so each item of the totality focuses the totality in its entirety. The particular focus of an item establishes its world, its environment. The totality as sum of all possible orders is adumbrated by each item.

Taoism is radically perspectival. "If a man lie down in a damp place," says Chuang-tzu, "he contracts lumbago. What of an eel?"[4] The eel will be at least as uncomfortable as the man—but for the opposite reason. The Taoist totality is horizontal; there are no hierarchies built into its ontology. No great chain of being or ladder of perfection exists in the Taoist cosmology. The anthropocentrism implicit in every form of Anglo-European ethical system is only one of a myriad of centrisms.

In the *Chuang Tzu* we find this most enlightening parable:

> The ruler of the kingdom of the north and the ruler of the kingdom of the south met on the land of Lord Hun-tun (that is, Lord Chaos), who treated them very kindly. At the end of their many visits, the two rulers discussed at length how they might repay him. Finally, they said, "All men have seven openings so they can see, hear, eat, and breathe. But Hun-tun alone doesn't have any. Let's try boring him some." So, every day they bored another hole, and on the seventh day Lord Hun-tun died.[5]

Taoism is a vision grounded not on order, but on chaos. It is a vision in which "harmony" has a special kind of meaning associated with the breechless, faceless, orifice-free Lord Hun-tun.

Assuming that Tao is becoming-itself, and therefore the sum of all orders, provides a helpful response to Benjamin Schwartz's provocative query concerning the meaning of *Tao*, in *The World of Thought in Ancient China*. "How may a word which refers to *order*," he asks, "come to have a mystical meaning?"[6] The mystical meaning of *Tao* lies in the mystery of chaos as the sum of all orders.

Tao is not organic in the sense that a single pattern or telos could be said to characterize its processes. It is not a whole but many such wholes. Its order is not rational or logical but aesthetic—that is, there can be no transcending pattern determining the existence or efficacy of the order. The order is a consequence of the particulars comprising the totality of existing things.

This interpretation of Tao makes of it a totality not in the sense of a single-ordered cosmos but in the sense of the sum of all possible cosmological orders. Any given order is an existing world that is construed from the perspective of a particular element of the totality. But as a single world, it is an abstraction from the totality of possible orders. The being of this order is not ontological but cosmological. Such an abstracted, selected order cannot serve as fundament or ground. In the Taoist sensibility, all differences are cosmological differences.

Taoism is based on the affirmation rather than the negation of chaos. In the Anglo-European tradition, chaos as emptiness, separation, or confusion is to be overcome. In Taoism it is to be left alone to thrive in its spontaneity. As Chuang-tzu says, "The myriad things manage and order themselves."[7]

In the Taoist naturalized sense of becoming, things that become are final realities, though in their processive state, these realities are not objectively, substantively, permanently real. Tao as becoming-itself names the chaotic matrix of transformations that may be spoken of only in terms of their particular, concrete differences. Any attempt to make present a ground—the being of beings—is rejected. Chuang-tzu insists, "Each thing comes into being from its own inner reflection and none can tell how it comes to be so."[8]

In Taoism, the relevant contrast is not between the cosmological whatness of things and the ontological thatness of things but between the cosmos as chaos—the sum of all orders—and the world as construed from some particular perspective—that is, one of the orders.

Pratītya-samutpāda as the Sense of Nondifference

Taoism provides a model for thinking of all difference as strictly cosmological difference. Cosmological difference can be thought to the extent that we give up the distinction between cosmological and ontological realms. The putative ontological dimension ultimately cancels the differences among cosmological entities by implicit appeal to the unity of being shared by all beings.

Is this model compatible with the principal thematics of Mahāyāna Buddhism? Buddhism's response to the question of ontological difference has received a number of different and conflicting interpretations. If we interrogate the doctrines prior to the Chinese transformations of Buddhist thought, we should be able to respond that Buddhism, as it entered China, brought with it a vision in which the contrast between cosmological and ontological perspectives was rhetorically present but was presented to be undermined.

According to Robert Neville, in his insightful essay "Buddhism and Process Philosophy," emptiness (*śūnyatā*) should not be interpreted in terms of the nihilist impulse—which dissolves everything into conditional features and thus into nothing (the nihil)—nor should we resort to mystical eternalism by identifying a thing solely with its essence and merging it with the essence of all things. But, as Neville acknowledges, both these interpretations of *śūnyatā* and of the allied doctrine of *pratītya-samutpāda* (codependent arising) have been made. I agree with Neville that, at least with respect to Chinese Buddhism, each of these interpretations is faulty. But I believe that the alternative Neville offers may be equally faulty. He interprets emptiness as a doctrine of ontological creation, which requires distinction between cosmological and ontological characters. Ontological creation involves the bringing into being of determinate things. Emptiness is then the "de facto harmony of essential and conditional features."[9]

Though Neville rings a subtle change on the traditional theological interpretation of the distinction between ontological and cosmological views, his alternative reading of Buddhist *śūnyatā* and *pratītya-samutpāda* is a controversial rendition of the Buddhist theme. The Buddhist walks a middle path between being and nonbeing. It is the way of becoming or process, as Neville appreciates. This method seems to resonate with the Taoist process vision. But there is a vast difference between the Buddhist and Taoist understandings of becoming. The closest approximation to the Mahāyāna sense of *śūnyatā* and *pratītya-samutpāda* lies in neither the radical ontological claim associated with Parmenidean mysticism, nor the acosmology of the nihilist, nor Neville's ontological interpretation.

Prajñā-pāramitā, the perfection of wisdom that permits one a sense of the truth of *śūnyatā*, is the ability to think nondifference. It is the sense of no difference between being and beings. Buddhism, thus interpreted, is the reverse of the Heideggerian project—the reverse of the need to think difference.

Neither the nihilist, the mystical, nor Neville's ontological interpretation of the Buddhist way are compatible with the sense of philosophical Taoism sketched above. *Śūnyatā* as nondifference reverses the Taoist sensibility, which stresses the independent becoming of the myriad things. Codependent arising dissolves the integrity of the cosmological sphere; Taoism holds each item of the totality to be *tzu-jan*—"so-of-itself."

Separating the one from the many, the ontological from the cosmological, cancels difference either in the cosmological sense or by contrast between being and beings, because the cosmological character of things is unreal. The Buddhist sense of emptiness need not entail an ontological problem as in the West. Nor is it a Taoist cosmological issue. The issue is epistemological, as Nāgārjuna realized. The world is not a conditioned effect of an ontological ground, nor is it determinate in respect to the indeterminate fundament. Such contrasts are irrelevant.

Mahāyāna Buddhism contains within it resources for the development of a radical negative ontology. The dissolution of the cosmological character of things leads to the ultimate experience of emptiness. Beyond the emptiness of all things is the empty—not as negation, not as nonbeing over against being—but as the emptiness of process or becoming. Is this sense of process at all compatible with the Taoist notion of becoming-itself?

Taoism and Buddhism on Cosmological Difference

Buddhism is grounded in the sense of indifference as the ground of cosmological difference—which leads, ultimately, to the dissolution of difference. Taoism stresses the cosmological difference of the insistent particularities of the totality, each with its own intrinsic character (*te*). Each of these views contrasts with the dominant Western concept of the difference of being and beings. The fundamental difference between Buddhism and Taoism lies in their distinctive conceptions of difference. Buddhism is grounded in a rhetorical use of a distinction between cosmological and ontological perspectives that ultimately denies the reality of the ontological ground and of the beings that could be so grounded. In contrast, the Judaeo-Christian tradition maintains the distinction between being and beings (the ontological difference) as fundamental. Taoism, unconcerned about that distinction, affirms the reality of the individual events or processes as sui generis.

Both Buddhism and Taoism are, in the strict sense, acosmological. Thus the notion of *the* world is problematic in both visions. Taoist acosmology asserts that *the* world is problematic because no single order exists except as an abstraction from the totality. Ultimately, Chaos is the sum of all orders. Chaos is the matrix housing all real things. Buddhism is acosmological in the more complicated sense of claiming that the things of the world are empty.

Buddhism takes ontology as problematic and dissolves the problem. Taoism effectively ignores the issue. Perhaps the Taoists should not ignore the problem, and perhaps if they did not, they would see that nameless Tao is ontological ground. But no evidence indicates that philosophical Taoists are bothered in the least by an ontological itch. If Chuang-tzu were pressed to explain the ground of things, the rationale of determinate becoming—that is, the becoming of determinate things—the textual indications are that he would go cosmological all the way.

Śūnyatā and *pratītya-samutpāda* affirm the cosmological character of Buddhism. Though its architectonic is cosmological, its problematic can plausibly be read as the contrast between cosmology and ontology that aims at the dissolution of both. Buddhism asks about being and nonbeing—and charts a middle way between the two. Acosmology and negative ontology are the consequences.

What, more precisely, is the middle way between being and nonbeing? It is the sense of process and becoming. Taoism also is based on the priority of becoming. But it asks primarily about order—conventional and spontaneous.

The Mahāyāna notion of the emptiness of selfhood entails the consequence that all things are self-less, all are functions of *pratītya-samutpāda*, which one recognizes through the attainment of *prajñā-pāramitā*. But Taoism's claim that the myriad things manage and order themselves would lead to an interpretation of codependent arising as the harmonious arising of distinctively self-caused beings. In the Taoist sensibility, we see an affirmation of the causa sui or sui generis character of individual things.

Tao as becoming-itself, as the totality of natural, correlative processes, may be thought to be the totality of things as the sum of all orders, each individual order of which is a function of the construal of a world implicit in the act of self-generation in accordance with the intrinsic character, the *te*, of each individual thing. The processes are *tzu-jan*—that is, they are spontaneous, so-of-themselves.

On such a naturalized view, codependent arising requires that the being of each thing is a consequence of its reflections in all other things, such that *śūnyatā* as emptiness, as nothing, must mean no-thing in the sense of no (particular) thing apart from the mutual reflections of all things in each and each in all. This view is not Taoism, though it may be close to the Buddhism of Ch'an and Hua Yen.

It is easy to see how Buddhists and Taoists could have understood one another to be saying essentially the same thing. When the Taoist heard the doctrine of *pratītya-samutpāda* discussed, he/she could have assented to it, believing it to refer to the ten-thousand things as acausally constituted, but as nonetheless individually sui generis. Likewise, the Buddhist could easily have (incorrectly) understood the Taoist notion of *tzu-jan*, or spontaneous arising, to be an illustration of *pratītya-samutpāda*.

At the level of strict philosophical interpretation, however, the mutual influences of Taoism and Buddhism would have involved potentially powerful consequences. Their distinctive senses of the relevance of the contrast between ontological and cosmological views would seem to guarantee this result. The interpretations of later Taoist religion that insist on the notion of transcendent Tao[10] might have resulted from accepting a (transmogrified) Buddhist doctrine of *śūnyatā*. And the naturalized versions of Ch'an and Hua Yen forms of Buddhism resonate with the radical cosmology of Taoism.

The most prominent interpretations of Mahāyāna Buddhist thinking on the issues of *śūnyatā* and *pratītya-samutpāda* as they relate to our question of ontological difference are distinctively at odds with the sense of difference derivable from the most coherent understanding of philosophical Taoism. Though I have not provided textual arguments for this conclusion and so must not claim anything more than potential heuristic value for it, I do believe that sorting out the appropriate responses to the issue of ontological difference before setting about interpreting either Buddhism or Taoism, or the relationship between the two, will be of signal value to historians, philosophers, and comparativists.

Notes

1. The term belongs to Jacques Derrida.
2. See my "Process and Anarchy: A Taoist Vision of Creativity," *Philosophy East and West* 28, no. 3 (July 1978), pp. 271–285. See also, the chapter "The Way Beyond Ways," in my *The Uncertain Phoenix: Adventures Toward a Post-cultural Sensibility* (New York: Fordham University Press, 1982).
3. In his "Being in Western Philosophy Compared with *Shan/Fei,* and *Yu/Wu* in Chinese Philosophy," in *Studies in Chinese Philosophy and Philosophical Literature* (Singapore: Institute of East Asian Philosophies, 1986), pp. 322–359, A. C. Graham has indicated that the sense of *wu* ("have not," "there is not") contrasts with locutions entailed by the sense of nothing, because nothing entails the sense of "no entity," and *wu* indicates merely the absence of concrete things. I think Graham occasionally assumes a metaphysical status for grammar and syntax that overvalues their contribution to semantics of philosophic concepts. In this instance, however, I think his conclusions are quite helpful in permitting an understanding of the contrasts between Western and Chinese views. In this essay, I have sought to provide philosophical rather than linguistic evidences for my conclusions.
4. *Complete Works of Chuang-tzu,* trans., Burton Watson (New York: Columbia University Press, 1968), p. 64.
5. Rendered freely from *ibid.,* p. 97.
6. Benjamin Schwartz, *The World of Thought in Ancient China* (Cambridge: Harvard University Press, 1985), p. 194.
7. See *Wang Pi's Commentary on the Lao Tzu,* trans. Arrienne Rump with Wing-tsit Chan, Society for Asian and Comparative Philosophy Monographs, no. 6 (Honolulu: University of Hawaii Press, 1979), p. 17.
8. See *Chuang Tzu,* chapter 8. The translation, admittedly a controversial rendering of an obscure segment of the text, is cited from Chang Chung-yuan, *Creativity and Taoism* (New York: Harper & Row, 1963), p. 66.
9. Robert Neville, *The Tao and the Daimon: Segments of a Religious Inquiry* (Albany: SUNY Press, 1982), p. 188.
10. See Michael Saso, "Buddhist and Taoist Ideas of Transcendence: A Study of Philosophical Contrast," in *Buddhist and Taoist Studies I,* ed. Michael Saso and David W. Chappell (Honolulu: University of Hawaii Press, 1977), pp. 3–22.

9.
Meanings of "The Meaning of Life" in Buddhist Perspective   *Frank J. Hoffman*

It is said that the highest compliment one philosopher can pay to another is to disagree with his views; because disagreeing indicates that the views are worthy of consideration. In this spirit, I offer a critical appreciation of one aspect of the life and work of Nolan Pliny Jacobson.[1] I pay Jacobson this highest compliment by calling attention to his work, though not always agreeing with him, and by assembling some conceptual reminders for the specific purpose of elucidating the meaning of life in Buddhism. As his life and work show, Jacobson must have regarded this as a central issue. I hope this essay will provide a much-needed counterpoint to the predominantly Western focus of the E. D. Klemke volume *The Meaning of Life.*[2]

Jacobson and the Meaning of Life

Some philosophers quote mainly to criticize, but Jacobson most often quotes other thinkers to agree—to find a point of interconnection between himself and other thinkers in a world he sees with Buddhist eyes, as interconnected by way of *paticcasamuppāda.* In so doing, he creates a symphony from diverse sources that would otherwise be cacophonous.[3] Is this sometimes taking thoughts out of context and thereby distorting them? The reader should judge only after having read several of Jacobson's works, even then remembering his holistic view of the organic universe and his conception of a symphonic truth emerging from the many voices.

"To think from the feeling side of experience" is one of Jacobson's characteristic emphases.[4] But some people are too firmly fixed by old habits and rigid socialization along parochial lines of nation, race, or culture—too firmly fixed to see the aesthetic concrescence by thinking "from the soft underside of the mind." They are, in Jacobson's often-repeated phrase, domiciled in the dictionary.[5] Nāgārjuna is seen as opposed to such "categorial" ways of thinking. The inability of Western philosophy to think from the feeling side of experience signals its decline, according to Jacobson.[6]

Abstractions cannot be the common ground unifying people, because "efforts to find common ground in abstractions, rather than in areas of experience such as shared hunger, serve more to tear into shreds our intuitive awareness of fellow-creatures."[7] Take pain, for example. Typically, Buddhists and contemporary philosophers focus on pain and pain behavior from very different perspectives. Wittgenstein was fascinated with the issue of whether and how one could have interpersonal knowledge of such prelinguistic phenomena as pain. According to Jacobson, however, instead of abstractions, humans need a "deeper-than-cultural ground" to live with deep respect for the rest of life.[8] At one point Wittgenstein emphasized that philosophy consists in showing the fly the way out of the fly bottle, but Jacobson's appropriation of the idea is to a very different effect.[9]

Jacobson asserts the uniqueness of Buddhism without clarifying in what respect it is supposed to be unique. This assertion is just as dubious as the grand claims that used to be made for the uniqueness of Christianity. Jacobson suggests that this supposed uniqueness consists in freedom from theoretical cliché, but just what this means would have to be carefully explained.[10]

Jacobson understands that Buddhism cannot be adequately rendered by any ism, such as empiricism: "All of these misconceptions depicting Buddhism as nihilism, relativism, absolutism, fatalism, mysticism, empiricism, idealism, socialism, and monasticism have been corrected over and over again, but protracted discussion usually increases the confusion."[11] Though "right view" is part of the Eightfold Āryan Path, the meaning of life in Buddhism does not consist in any sort of theoretical allegiance to an abstract philosophical position that could be encapsulated in an ism. It appears that Jacobson has grasped "the meaning of life in Buddhism." He says that his main aim in the work *Understanding Buddhism* is to show Buddhism free from Western categories, in the philosophical discussions and cultures of Asia, not as an abstract teaching but as a concrete orientation to experience.[12] In this respect, his view agrees with that of Kenneth Inada.[13]

However, in discussing the relation between Buddhism and science, Jacobson seems to think that science can confirm Buddhist views, and that it has confirmed specific ones. He writes in *Understanding Buddhism*: "It is an event of tremendous historical importance when seventy-five years of research on the front lines of particle physics confirms the Buddhist conception that the world is never the same twice, that there are no mutually independent contemporaries, and no separately and independently existing parts."[14] This comment appears to contradict his earlier view in *Buddhism: The Religion Of Analysis*, where he concludes one argument by saying: "It is not doing Buddhism a favor, therefore, to generalize as to its consistency with modern science, whatever similarities it may have with the present stage of quantum physical theory. No modern scientist would risk his reputation in defending the doctrines of karma, rebirth, the thirty-one abodes, and other metaphysical conceptions."[15] His later view (in *Understanding Buddhism*) is that research in particle physics leads us to "the aesthetic foundation of the world," and that nirvāna is "the aesthetic center of life."[16] His attack on *svabhāva* in *Buddhism: The Religion of Analysis* is not an abstract piece of philosophizing but a deeply felt truth: "I discovered in the most difficult year of my life the compulsive attachments of the self, and the suffering that is the natural expression of even the most enlightened Western life."[17]

Jacobson thinks that nothing in Buddhism is not in immediate experience. He writes in *Understanding Buddhism* that Buddhism is basically a practical rather than a speculative system, such that *"there is nothing in the teaching of Buddhism which our immediate experience does not contain."*[18]

"The Meaning of Life" in Buddhism

Jacobson's work, like my own, involves focusing Western attention on Asian thought with a view to expanding conceptual horizons for what counts as the meaning of life. When Westerners ask how Buddhists can find the meaning of life," they are likely to get in a muddle right away because of problematic presuppositions. How can there be meaning in life without God (understood as a being with specific attributes)? Is not Buddhism fatalistic and pessimistic anyway, so that there could not (logically) be any meaning to life? Such questions may rear their ugly heads in cross-cultural discussions of whether and how Buddhists can find the meaning of life. Their force and interest is diminished by understanding the various meanings of the phrase "the meaning of life" surveyed in the Buddhist context.

Meaning of Life as Goal

If we construe the question "What is the meaning of life in Buddhism?" (henceforth referred to herein simply as "the question") as a request for information about the goal of Buddhism, the answer is: *nibbāna* (Pali term for Sanskrit *nirvāna*). That would not put an end to the question (even thus specifically construed), because there are two sorts of *nibbāna*: *saupadisesa* (nirvāna while alive, literally, "with substrate") and *anupadisesa* (nirvāna in the case of the person thus gone, literally, "without substrate"). However, as some Buddhist schools (e.g., Zen) emphasize more than others, self-conscious striving after this goal is counterproductive. To achieve the goal, it is somehow necessary to abandon all goals—hence the importance of what Nolan Pliny Jacobson calls "non-calculative activity flowing with the nature of things," or *jiyū-jizai*.[19] Nevertheless, *nibbāna* is the goal (albeit a "gateless gate," *mumon-kan*). And as Ninian Smart observes, "religions and ideologies both guide men regarding the meaning of life."[20]

Meaning of Life as Intention

The question might be construed as "What do Buddhists attempt to do in life; what is their aim or intention?" Etically, or external to the system of technical terms and methods of categorization that are emic to Buddhism, the answer may be given in terms of self-actualization. Our interpretation of Buddhists' intentions may be that they are attempting self-actualization, but when one says so, the external, generic nature of the description must be apparent at once.

Meaning of Life as Role

The question might be construed as a request for a specification of what the Buddhist does to find meaning in life as a Buddhist. A major answer is meditation. In the role of the meditating Buddhist aspirant, the Buddhist finds a meaning of life in one sense. The Buddhist might also find meaning in life by filling the role of a bodhisattva, "entering the marketplace with bliss-bestowing hands" (as depicted in the tenth Zen ox-herding picture).[21]

Meaning of Life as Relation

In meaning of life as goal, the meaning of life pertains to the goal or object. In meaning of life as intention, it pertains to the intentional subject. But in meaning of life as relation, it pertains to the relation between subject and object. Cosmically considered, what is one's place in the world? The meaning of life might be found in the relation between the intentional subject, who internalizes the role of meditator, and nirvāna, which is the ultimate goal. The relation is one of being in *samsāra.*" Consequently, the meaning of life in one sense may be *samsāra*. To be alive in Buddhism is to be a being struggling to attain liberation, hoping to rise like a lotus from the mire, against all odds, as a suffering being with likes and dislikes, enmeshed in *rāga*, *dosa*, and *moha* (passion, hatred, confusion), but capable of achieving and transcending the human rebirth station in *parinibbāna* (final enlightenment). The meaning of life is thus seen as undergoing the process of *samsāra*.

Meaning of Life as Metaquestion

The question, modified with quotation marks around "life," might be construed as an entirely different question about how the term *life* (viewed as a flux, as *punabbhāva*) functions in Buddhism. Instead of "What is the meaning of life in Buddhism?" the question becomes "What is the meaning of 'life' in Buddhism?" (Compare the sentence "Socrates has eight letters" with "'Socrates' has eight letters.") Thus construed, the question is a metaquestion about the function in Buddhism of terms that may be translated as "life." What do such terms do in Buddhism? Without such terms as *bhāva*, *bhāva-tanhā*, and *punabbhāva*, the unity of things could not be understood. Life is not simply a static, fragmented entity in Buddhism but a continuous process, a somewhat tangled web, of sentient organisms.

Such contemporary philosophers as James Rachels arrived at vegetarianism on logical rather than religious grounds, in ways compatible with Buddhism's emphasis on the unity of life. In *The Elements of Moral Philosophy*, Rachels emphasizes a passage in Mill in which morality is extended "*so far as the nature of things admits, to the whole of sentient creation.*"[22] Why not mistreat animals? Following Peter Singer, the reason is the same as for humans: because they will suffer. According to Rachels: "the interests of nonhuman animals *count*. We normally assume, as the dominant tradition of our society teaches, that human beings alone are worthy of moral consideration. Utilitarianism challenges that basic assumption and insists that the moral community must be expanded to include all creatures whose interests are affected by what we do."[23] Thus a Buddhist perspective on animal rights is in accord with contemporary developments in which Peter Singer, James Rachels, and others argue as above.

Meaning of Life as Synoptic Question

The question could be understood as "What is life like overall in a Buddhist-eye view?" The answer might be that it is a mixed bag of *sukha* and *duhkha* (pleasure and displeasure, delight and pain). It is a vibrant *samsāra* wherein creative use of being in *samsāra* makes *nibbāna* a very real possibility. Life is a theater of a possible triumph of the greatest magnitude, in which there is no self to gloat in the triumph.

Some philosophers think that a question about the meaning of *all* things would be nonsensical. They think that a sweeping statement like "Nothing matters" (and consequently its denial, "Something matters") is not on the same level as a descriptive statement like "My wife chatters." "Nothing matters" is not a statement about the world and hence cannot be true or false (or so R. M. Hare's story goes). I think that the synoptic question of the meaning of life is among the most important questions that philosophers can ask.

The Meaning of Life Considered Beyond the Klemke Anthology

I would like to make some conceptual points about the logical constraints on the various meanings of the questions of life. The theistic/nontheistic metaquestions structure of the Klemke anthology *The Meaning of Life* omits reference to Buddhism or Eastern thought. Although I draw freely from Klemke's work both in exposition and as a focus for philosophical criticism, my intention is to move the discussion of the question forward in application to Buddhism. Some philosophers would hope for a general philosophical account giving the complete conceptual analysis of the idea of the meaning of life (whatever such a "complete" analysis might be like!), but I do not share their hope. I will be content with indicating a few features of the concept.

The *Meaning of Life*

The phrase "*the* meaning of life" absurdly suggests that the meaning of life can be given once and for all in a definitive way by a definite description. As John Wisdom points out: "We must however remember that what one calls answering such a question is not giving an answer. I mean we cannot answer such a question in the form: 'The meaning is this.'"[24] Wisdom does not disparage questions concerning meaning of life questions but clarifies their logical status. As Wisdom saw, no one meaning of life can be given in a word, phrase, formula, or list. This point is logical or conceptual, not empirical. In Buddhism, too, the meaning of life is not simple enough to be found in a credal formula or in a Buddhist philosopher's putative central doctrine. Pluralism is implicit in a thoughtful consideration of the questions of the meaning of life.

In a stimulating book that owes much to Zen Buddhism, Gene Blocker argues against what he calls the objectivist "non-projective theory of meaning." Blocker raises the question: "Can we, by renouncing the non-projectivist ideal of meaning, find a positive, constructive side to the sheer meaninglessness of things in themselves?"[25] Blocker argues, in his work *The Meaning of Meaninglessness*, that the nonprojectivist idea of meaning is a false, impossible ideal, which is itself a form of projection.[26] He links this objectivist view with naive realism, with religious, second-order theories of reality, and the correspondence theory of truth.[27]

Although brilliantly written, drawing together literary, philosophical, and Eastern religious material, Blocker's work may be arguing against a straw man. It is difficult to see who exactly has held the nonprojectivist theory of meaning and why Blocker is arguing against it when it follows from the claims he makes about nonprojection that it is logically incoherent[28] There are thus not two alternatives. Only the simple reminder that meaning is projected through language remains.

Is the Phrase "Nothing Matters" (and Its Denial) Descriptive?

When R. M. Hare thought he could disabuse his Swiss student of a conceptual confusion by pointing out to him that his claim "nothing matters" is not descriptive, Hare himself was the victim of a confusion. He thought that "nothing matters" was necessarily intended as a descriptive claim about someone's interests. If he had not thought so, he could not have thought that his reminder would have the force that it had on the Swiss student (the student was "cured," at least for the time being).

Hare argues that because we express concern when we say something matters, someone's concern is always implicit in claims that something matters or does not. The Swiss student's problem, according to Hare, was that he did not understand this. He thought that mattering was something that things do (an activity or process), as if "My wife matters to me" has the same logical function as "My wife chatters to me" (Hare's examples). That no one observes things mattering does not mean that they do not matter.

Although I do not think that Hare's main contention, that you cannot annihilate values because "as a matter of empirical fact, a man is a valuing creature, and is likely to remain so"[29] is mistaken, he goes too far treating "nothing matters" as a bogus empirical claim. In contrast, is "nothing matters" a metalevel statement about the unavailability of any satisfactory account of the meaning of life (which would require clarification whether this unavailability is thought to be "in principle" because of the nature of things or only "in practice" because of one's peculiar psychology at the time). If so, we have discovered another point about the logic or grammar of the phrase "meaning of life." It is a metalevel claim (not a simple erroneous descriptive claim as Hare has it), and it cannot be eliminated by the kinds of argument Hare adduces.

In rejecting Hare's point, we should not conclude rashly that claims about meaning of life are meaningless. As John Wisdom has observed, that questions about the meaning of life cannot be answered in a list, phrase, or formula does not imply that they are meaningless and cannot be answered at all. Fergus Kerr, in his stimulating work *Theology After Wittgenstein*, remarks: "There is something more to understanding language than just successfully matching words with things.... 'Words have meaning only in the stream of life,' as Wittgenstein says, with that emphasis on the primacy of 'life' which characterizes his later philosophy."[30]

It is tempting to see a parallel between Wittgenstein and Buddhism here, if one accepts Kerr's idea that Wittgenstein takes us back to "life" and away from metaphysics. Although there is sense in this possible parallel, it is ultimately misleading. Buddhism cannot completely avoid metaphysical presuppositions, despite its experientialist (but not empiricist) leanings. Buddhism can avoid what it regards as rampant, baseless metaphysical speculation, but it cannot avoid metaphysical presuppositions altogether.[31]

If it is possible in a particular case to rid someone of the obsessive grip of "nothing matters," the way is to show one (through the reality of human or divine care) that indeed "something matters." Doing so is more a matter of shaping the facts than pointing them out; it is a matter of ridding other persons of the existential grip of "nothing matters." The procedure is to convince them, by appealing to their experience, that the metalevel claim disavowing the existence of any satisfactory available account of "something matters" is false. It is a different procedure than Hare's idea of explaining to them the linguistic point that mattering is not something that life can either do or fail to do.

Questions of the Meanings of Life Are Not Nonsensical

These questions are not nonsensical. Nor are they straightforwardly factual. But facts about the world may play a role in answering such questions. John Wisdom brought out this point well by saying that because questions of the meaning of life cannot be answered
in a list, phrase, or formula does not imply that they are meaningless.
Our bewilderment does not render the question senseless. "This need
to look before or after in order to answer a question of the sort 'What
is the meaning of this?' is so common, so characteristic, a feature of
such questions that it is natural to think that when it is impossible to
answer such a question in this way then the question has no sense."[32]

In Wisdom's example of someone coming in late to a play and
leaving early, the late arriver may require information about what went
on before and after to answer his/her puzzlement as to the meaning of
the play. But Wisdom rightly goes on to point out that even if the late
arriver had seen the whole play, he/she might ask quite sensibly, "What
does it mean?" without inquiring about anything outside the play (such
as the author's intention). In the case of "What is the meaning of all
things?" no one has seen the whole drama of life, and yet our question
is not about before and after, according to Wisdom: "But with the
words 'What is the meaning of it all?' we are trying to find the order in
the drama of time."[33] We do not declare the question meaningless,
because the type of procedure it calls for is known and we may approach an answer. Specifically, we are able to find meaning in limited
wholes, whether of art or life.

Now someone might object that Wisdom's argument here involves
the fallacy of composition.[34] It might be argued that because we can
find meaning in "limited wholes" does not mean we can find the meaning of life altogether. But it would be a mistake to think that this objection undercuts Wisdom's position. He does not need to claim that
life as a whole has a meaning that will be discovered—only that if it
does have a meaning, it is reasonable to think that the meaning can be
discovered by analogous procedures.

Wisdom contends, and I believe rightly so, that the meaning of a
play, like the meaning of life itself, eludes encapsulation in a list. Historians, scientists, prophets, dramatists, poets, and religious thinkers
have said much that will help those trying to make sense of the "drama
of time." Leaving aside Paul Edwards's "super-ultimate why," questions about the meaning of life are not necessarily nonsense. But contra

Edwards, it is not a necessary presupposition of the meaningfulness of theological questions that it be demonstrable "that there is a God" lest the questions be meaningless otherwise.[35] As the work of Don Cupitt shows, theism that construes "God" as the proper name for an objectively existing object is not on the cutting edge of theology today.[36] Attempts to give a particular account of the meaning of life tell us what the world is like. As John Wisdom has observed, the essence of religion is that some belief about what the world is like should be expressed.

Metaphysical Presuppositions May Play a Role

Answers to questions of the meaning of life may have metaphysical presuppositions, but not necessarily. Someone might find meaning in just the process of life's flow, in just being. In that case, the answer is found in life itself, not outside it in a heavenly realm of metaphysical absolutes. But in the Buddhist metaphysical idea of rebirth, an answer can be found in a series of lives rather than just in the process of one lifetime's flow.[37]

It is a purely logical or conceptual point about the grammar of "meaning of life" that someone may sensibly claim that the meaning of life lies beyond this particular life, not in some heaven, but in the cycle of *samsāra*. Good Buddhists want to break out of this cycle of rebecoming (*punabbhāva*), so for them the meaning of life consists in the end of life in one sense (where "life" means the continuous cycle of a person's life-stream, but this is not *Cārvāka*, "annihilationism"). Buddhists not so high-minded may seek a better rebirth state, so for them the meaning of life consists in the end of this particular life and in a renewed life in a better situation, rather than in the end of the stream of lives altogether ("One must imagine Sisyphus happy," Camus comments in a similar but not identical vein).[38] It would be too tidy to be accurate, however, to assert that this shows a bifurcation between lay and monastic goals.

Endless Life and the Meaning of Life

Hepburn has pointed out that although questions about the meaning of life have often been rooted metaphysically in views of the afterlife, "we can and do love flowers that fade; and the knowledge that they will fade may even enhance their preciousness. To be everlasting, that is, is no necessary or sufficient condition of value and worth-whileness, nor therefore of meaningfulness. An eternity of futility is not logically impossible."[39]

The importance of the concept of boundary is an important condition for meaning. In Buddhism, *parinibbāna*, is the limit of life rather than an experience in life.[40] Without this theoretical limit to aspire to, the Buddhist would have only *samsāra*, an endless round of rebirths.

Contemporary Buddhists who have experienced a crisis of faith have sometimes wondered how we can make sense of enlightenment if rebirth and enlightenment are correlative concepts and we do not accept the existence of a realm of rebirth. Ninian Smart makes a related point:

> It might be argued that the Theravādin teaching about nirvāna would only make sense if we believe in rebirth. Perhaps so. Yet most of my previous attempt to unravel the Buddhist experience of liberation and timelessness has not depended upon the presupposition of rebirth. I mention the matter only because the Westerner's crisis about God is being echoed by the Eastern crisis concerning reincarnation. That is why arguments and evidences about reincarnation are unusually frequent in these latter days. Myself, I would adopt rebirth as a heuristic device, perchance, as it helps to contextualize Buddhist nirvāna.[41]

The concepts of Buddhist rebirth and Buddhist nirvāna are correlative. If no rebirth stations exist (in Pali Buddhism these stations are human, *deva*, *niraya*, *preta*, and animal), the idea of nirvāna without substrate (five aggregates) is nonsensical. To explicate the concept of nirvāna without substrate, reference would have to be made to rebirth stations to explain the context in which nirvāna may occur. But even in that case, the idea of nirvāna with substrate (i.e., nirvāna while alive) would still be sensical. So one solution to the Eastern crisis of which Ninian Smart speaks is to say that in one sense of enlightenment (i.e., nirvāna while alive), enlightenment may occur as a psychological experience, even if no realms other than the human one exists. Thus, as with many philosophical problems, an answer may be found by making a distinction.

Would it be wrong-headed to argue that life has no meaning because enlightenment, if it occurs at all, would occur only in the remote future? Paul Edwards's account implies that it would be wrong-headed. He argues that because we live not in the remote future but in the present and relatively near future, considerations about the remote future (or an endless cycle) are irrelevant to whether life has a meaning now. Edwards's account thus makes considerations about the remoteness of the *parinibbāna* limit irrelevant to whether *saṃsāra* can have meaning here and now.

Accordingly, Klemke argues that the meaning of life must be found in the natural universe,[42] citing with agreement Popper's claim that if life did not come to an end, it could not be lost and, hence, would have no value. I do not agree. The possible "tedium of immortality" (to use Bernard Williams's phrase)[43] has often been overlooked. Yet one could be so engrossed in the eternal here and now that the nonexistence of a foreseeable end to *saṃsāra* would not be considered at all (or would not be considered a problem).

Meaning of Life and Evil

For the Christian, the problem of evil is a great theological one. In his essay in the Klemke anthology, Hepburn says: "We can conceive of an anticipatory passage, however, which is so atrocious musically that nothing that followed it, even of high quality, could be said to fulfil or complete it. It may be argued that some 'passages' in some people's lives are so evil that nothing could conceivably justify them."[44] The Buddhist, however, is expected neither to accept Issara (Creator God) nor to deny or explain away the evident fact of evil and suffering in the world. In his philosophically interesting work *The Problem of Evil and Indian Thought*, A. L. Herman points out that because Buddhists are atheists, they are not concerned with the problem of evil as such.[45] Perhaps the Buddhists are at an advantage here over both Christian and (theistic) Hindu beliefs.

Fact Claims and Meaning of Life Statements

Nielsen, quoting Ayer with evident approval, thinks that the meaning of life is an ethical issue and that claims about it are not simple descriptive theses. I agree with the latter point, but contra Nielsen, I do not think the question reduces to an ethical or political one without remainder. He thinks that it is all right to construe the demand for the sense of things as a whole as a sociopolitical question, but not as a theological or metaphysical one.[46] But what is the basis for this distinction? Are they not both worldviews in Ninian Smart's sense? If so, is accepting the legitimacy of the ethical and political view not tantamount to implicitly accepting the legitimacy of the other? It appears that Nielsen is mired in a Marxist-style positivism that has devastating implications for his own view.

In Nielsen's favor, questions of the meaning of life cannot be radically sundered from questions of a factual sort about the world. Unless we build a conceptual system in a self-sustaining system of concepts analogous to pure mathematics, any theology and any metaphysics must take their point of departure from facts about the world. But as Thomas Kuhn has taught us, no sharp cleavage exists between observation statements and theories. Interpretation of ambiguities ("seeing as") thus becomes crucial. As Kuhn observes, "the switch of gestalt, particularly because it is today so familiar, is a useful elementary prototype for what occurs in full-scale paradigm shift."[47] And as Blocker points out, words have meaning "in the sense in which words can be used to illuminate, clarify, articulate, or call attention to certain projected aspects of the world (being-as). Language, then, is one of the ways in which we project meaning."[48] This point is not profound, but it is basic for understanding the articulation of meaning in human life.

Conclusion

In Buddhism, the meaning of life may be goal (*nibbāna*), intention (self-actualization), role (meditator), or relation (being in *saṃsāra*). It can be approached as a tangential metaquestion (the meaning of the term *bhāva* and kindred terms), or as a synoptic question (overall life as a mixture of *sukha* and *duhkha*). It is a question that has exercised the attention, directly or indirectly, of Nolan Pliny Jacobson and other Buddhistically inclined thinkers.

The meaning of life in Buddhism cannot be elucidated sufficiently without grappling with difficult conceptual issues that defy adequate solution in this brief compass. In addition, the meaning of life in Buddhism eludes simple encapsulation as long as Buddhists are being born to advance new ideas about it. Meaning here is open-textured. Nevertheless, I hope that the following conceptual reminders assembled for the specific purpose of shedding light on the meaning of life in Buddhism as sketched by Jacobson prove to be useful.

1. The meaning of life cannot be given once and for all in a definite description in a list, phrase, or formula (as John Wisdom saw).

2. Contra R. M. Hare, "nothing matters" and its denial are not necessarily descriptive claims. Consequently, a person cannot always be rid of the existential grip of "nothing matters" simply by understanding philosophical reminders (but instead, for instance, by being shown the reality of human or divine care).

3. The questions of the meaning of life are not necessarily nonsensical (or merely illustrative of the fallacy of composition); they are among the most important a philosopher can ask.

4. Meaning may be found not only in the process of living in this life but in the stream of rebirths that is saṃsāra itself, so that metaphysical presuppositions (such as rebirth) may play a role.

5. The concept of boundary may facilitate discovery of a structure in which a person's life has meaning (but that endless life does not necessarily involve the "tedium of immortality").

6. Nothing in the concepts of evil and suffering necessarily impedes life's having meaning. They provide a backdrop for the possibility of liberation in Buddhism (unlike in Hinduism or Christianity, where the existence of evil is a problem).

7. Some meaning-of-life claims are ethical, and although claims about the meaning of life cannot be radically sundered from facts about the world, it is not clear (pace Nielsen) how religion and metaphysics can be rejected as irrelevant if political thought is accepted (because both political thought and religious thought purport to provide facts about the meaning of life).

If nothing else, perhaps these concepts will stimulate further thought on questions of the meaning of life among philosophers. I believe that philosophers should not ignore these fundamental questions that twentieth-century philosophy has considered too vague to tackle.

Notes

1. I presented a shorter version of this essay at the American Philosophical Association (central division) meeting in Chicago, 27–29 April 1989, in

the Society for Asian and Comparative Philosophy panel on the meaning of life. I am grateful to the two respondents, Professors Ramakrishna Puligandla and George Sun, and to Professor Kenneth K. Inada, for their insightful comments. The shorter version will appear in *Comprehensive Harmony* and is included herein by permission of the senior editor.

2. E. D. Klemke, ed., *The Meaning of Life* (Oxford and New York: Oxford University Press, 1981). Similar material appears in Steven Sanders and David R. Cheney, *The Meaning of Life: Questions, Answers, and Analysis* (Englewood Cliffs, N.J.: Prentice-Hall, 1980).

3. Nolan Pliny Jacobson, *The Heart of Buddhist Philosophy* (Carbondale and Edwardsville: Southern Illinois University Press, 1988), p. xiii, refers to a "symphony of philosophers" to whom Jacobson is indebted.

4. Ibid., p. 47. Kant, for example, cannot do so, according to Jacobson.

5. Ibid., pp. 48–49, 57, 70.

6. Nolan Pliny Jacobson, *Understanding Buddhism* (Carbondale and Edwardsville: Southern Illinois University Press, 1986), p. 90.

7. Jacobson, *The Heart of Buddhist Philosophy*, p. 72.

8. Jacobson, *Understanding Buddhism*, pp. 34, 75. The English word *pain*, captures only a part of the semantic range of *duhkha* in Pali Buddhism; see T. W. Rhys-Davids and Wm. Stede, *Pali Text Society Pali-English Dictionary* (London: Pali Text Society, 1972), pp. 324–326. And as Jacobson points out, suffering is superficially understood in the West (*Understanding Buddhism*, p. 8). For a detailed discussion of suffering or unsatisfactoriness in Buddhism (especially in connection with false allegations of pessimism in Buddhism), see Frank J. Hoffman, *Rationality and Mind in Early Buddhism* (Delhi: Motilal Bararsidass, 1987), pp. 27–45.

9. Jacobson, *Understanding Buddhism*, p. 145: "The fly bottle is the abstractness of life with its disregard for the aesthetic foundations of the world; it is the wrong motivations acquired in the struggle to survive. The way out of the fly bottle is the way of Buddhist meditation, the gyroscope keeping an individual stable in the ups and downs of daily existence."

10. Ibid., p. 106. Jacobson refers to *jiyū-jizai* (on p. 109) in this connection, but it is not clear that it is a technical term in Buddhism. What "theoretical cliche" means requires further thought to see how the uniqueness of Buddhism could be explained with reference to freedom from theoretical cliché. (See also n. 19.)

11. Ibid., p. 4.

12. Ibid., p. 6.

13. Kenneth K. Inada, "Japanese Secularism: A Reexamination," *Free Inquiry* 8, no. 4 (Fall 1988), p. 32: "The lack of abstract thinking has long been considered a Japanese trait: this does not mean, however, that the Japanese are incapable of thinking logically or rationally. Highly meta-

physical Buddhist texts imported from China and Korea provided the Japanese with a good background in intricate analysis and a good understanding of reality, but it was not in the Japanese character to carry out a systematic treatment of reality as such. Reality simply abounded in the lives of the people and did not become an object of analysis."

14. Jacobson, *Understanding Buddhism*, p. 28.
15. Nolan Pliny Jacobson, *Buddhism: The Religion of Analysis* (New York: Humanities, 1965; reprint, Carbondale and Edwardsville: Southern Illinois University Press, 1966), p. 170.
16. Jacobson, *Understanding Buddhism*, pp. 29 and 24.
17. Ibid., p. 8.
18. Ibid., p. 133.
19. Ibid., p. 109. The source of Jacobson's idea that *jiyū-jizai* is an attribute of the bodhisattva remains mysterious. Something *jiyū-jizai* is something that can be freely applied in several contexts and is in this sense versatile.
20. Donald Wiebe, ed., *Concept and Empathy* (New York: New York University Press, 1986), p. 74.
21. Paul Reps, *Zen Flesh/Zen Bones* (New York: Doubleday Anchor, undated), pp. 154–155.
22. James Rachels, *The Elements of Moral Philosophy* (New York: Random House, 1986), p. 89.
23. Ibid., p. 89.
24. John Wisdom, "The Meanings of the Questions of Life," in Klemke, ed., op. cit., p. 208.
25. Gene Blocker, *The Meaning of Meaninglessness* (The Hague: Martinus Nijhoff, 1974), pp. 114–115.
26. Ibid., p. 115.
27. Ibid., pp. 73, 82, and 89.
28. Ibid., p. 115. Part of the difficulty in clarifying Blocker's target is perhaps caused by a confusion between questions of meaning and questions of truth. Traditional Roman Catholicism, for example, holds that it is factually or objectively true that God is a being with various attributes. But doing so does not commit them to holding the separate view that humankind does not create a world of meaning and value through language (as if they had to hold the obviously false or incoherent thesis that meaning is just a given and is not projected through linguistic and cultural filters). If traditional Roman Catholicism is not an example of what Blocker is attacking, it is not clear what would be an example of it.
29. R. M. Hare, "Nothing Matters," in Klemke, ed., op. cit., p. 247.
30. Fergus Kerr, *Theology after Wittgenstein* (Oxford and New York: Basil Blackwell, 1986), pp. 136, 134.

31. A case is made for the view expressed in this paragraph in two brief articles. See Frank J. Hoffman, "Buddhist Belief 'In,'" *Religious Studies* 21, no. 3 (1985), which takes its point of departure from H. H. Price's distinction between belief "in" and belief "that." See also my challenge to the idea that *Nikāya* Buddhism is a form of empiricism in Frank J. Hoffman, "The Buddhist Empiricism Thesis," *Religious Studies* 18, no. 2 (1982).

32. Wisdom in Klemke, ed., op. cit., p. 206.

33. Ibid., p. 207.

34. On the fallacy of composition, see Irving Copi, *Introduction to Logic*, 7th ed. (New York: Macmillan, 1986) p. 117.

35. Paul Edwards, "Why?" in Klemke, ed., op. cit., p. 234.

36. "And here God is precisely not objective, but internal to 'the heart,'" says Don Cupitt in *Taking Leave of God* (New York: Crossroads, 1981), p. 68. In this work and elsewhere in Cupitt's by now voluminous corpus, the tendency is away from construing *God* as a name for a being with various attributes.

37. In styling rebirth a metaphysical idea, I am being deliberately provocative, which Professor Puligandla rightly noticed in our symposium (see n. 1). Many contemporary scholars of South Asian thought believe that it is not metaphysical but empirical, but because they are usually unclear about in just what sense empirical, a fresh re-examination of this belief is in order. Here brevity rules, and I can make only three points: (1) to say that it is a metaphysical idea is not to imply that Buddhism holds a transcendental absolute. Metaphysics, as P. F. Strawson observes in *Individuals* (London: Metheun, 1959), may be either revisionary or descriptive; in descriptive metaphysics, the Buddhist idea of rebirth would have to be taken into account in describing "our" conceptual scheme if "we" are Buddhists; (2) rebirth is certainly not empirical in the strong sense in which in-principle falsifiability is necessary for a belief to count as verifiable (see n. 33); and (3) to deny that rebirth is an empirical doctrine is not to deny that it may be an experiential one. All religions (not just Buddhism) are based on human experience, but that neither means nor logically implies that they are empirical in the sense in which science is empirical.

38. Albert Camus, "The Absurdity of Human Existence," in Klemke, ed., op. cit., p. 80.

39. R. W. Hepburn, "Questions about the Meaning of Life," in Klemke, ed., op. cit., pp. 211–212.

40. See Hoffman, *Rationality and Mind in Early Buddhism* (Delhi: Motilal Banarsidass, 1987), p. 114.

41. Ninian Smart, "Nirvāna and Timelessness," in Wiebe, ed., op. cit., p. 124.

42. E. D. Klemke, "The Question of the Meaning of Life," in Klemke, ed., op. cit., pp. 5–6.

43. Bernard Williams, *Problems of the Self* (Cambridge and New York: Cambridge University Press, 1973; reprint 1975).

44. R. W. Hepburn, op. cit., p. 221.

45. A. L. Herman, *The Problem of Evil and Indian Thought* (Delhi: Motilal Banarsidass, 1976), p. 225. This is one of few philosophically interesting books on Buddhism written in the last two decades. But I am not certain that Herman has decisively laid to rest the hoary problem of evil. He claims "that the theological problem of evil, in all three of its formulations, can be solved by the Indian doctrine of transmigration" (p. 5). In view of the infinity of past worlds presupposed in South Asian cosmology, however, it might be argued that "the rebirth solution" favored by Herman involves an infinite regress and hence, on his admission elsewhere, is consequently an inadmissable, "absurd," explanation; see Herman, *An Introduction to Buddhist Thought* (Lanham, Md.: University Press of America, 1983), p. 194.

46. Kai Nielsen, "Linguistic Philosophy and 'The Meaning of Life,'" in Klemke, ed., op. cit., p. 203.

47. Thomas Kuhn, *The Structure of Scientific Revolutions*, 2d ed. (Chicago: University of Chicago Press, 1970), p. 85.

48. Blocker, op. cit., p. 127.

10.
Modern Science and the Rediscovery of Buddhism
Tsung-I Dow

This essay is an attempt to illustrate Nolan Pliny Jacobson's main thesis of Buddhism as a religion of analysis and of its nature of self-correction, in light of recent scientific discoveries. Without doubt, Buddhism is a religion. Yet its basic tenets do not invoke divine revelation but rely on the intellectual power of reasoning for analysis of the phenomenon of self. Its method of approach rests on analysis, knowledge, and inquiry as the keys for salvation. The advancement of quantum mechanics and related discoveries lend important support to Jacobson's views on Buddhism, and the understanding of such scientific matters in relation to Buddhism is a central part of the emerging world civilization.

On the problem of reconciling the seeming conflict between science and religion, recent advancements in science, such as in quantum mechanics, microbiology, and neurophysiology, seem to lend support to the basic assumptions of Buddhism and its historical practice. For instance, the First Noble Truth in Buddhism says that whatever we perceive and experience of the world, including our life, is phenomenal, a temporary aggregation of the elements, impermanent and subject to change. Albert Szent-Györgyi, the Nobel laureate credited with the discovery of vitamin C, confessed that in his search for the secret of life, he ended up in the phenomenal realm with atoms and electrons. Penetrating deeper into scientific phenomena, other scientists have become aware of the essential unity of all things and events of this phenomenal world.

So far as science can ascertain, we do not know how either organic life or consciousness emerged. A nuclear physicist can compute the constitution of a person averaging 165 pounds as 7.0×10^{28} U quarks $+ 6.5 \times 10^{28}$ D quarks $+ 2.5 \times 10^{25}$ electrons. But simply combining these quarks and electrons will not produce a human being. It is common sense that all chemical reactions related to the life form involve the basic carbon atom and sugar, which constitute life's main sources of energy. Yet if we mix water, ammonia, methane, carbon dioxide, and hydrogen cyanide with any type of intense energy, such as ultraviolet light or electricity, some of the molecules reassemble themselves into amino acids (e.g., the Belousov-Zhabotinski reaction), but no life appears. A neurologist can map the brain in a complete manner, but that does not explain how consciousness emerges.

Because of these few simple yet fundamental facts, it seems scientists should agree with the contention of Buddhist philosophers that life is the expression of the harmonious collaboration of fleeting elements, precious and sacred. The life we know and experience is born of the burning wish, hope, dream, and excitement of not only seeking the greatest satisfaction of immediate physical and mental needs but searching for the means to escape or transcend the limitations of the brevity and imperfection of the world into which we are born. The ultimate goal of life in the Buddhist perspective is no less than this desire to sustain, enjoy, and fulfill the meaning of life. Buddhists seek this goal by identifying the source of suffering in life and painstakingly trying to eliminate it.

The *Dhammapada* spelled out that genuine happiness will emerge once its opposite, suffering, is overcome. This approach may seem overly optimistic toward human nature. But it views the task of overcoming suffering as a matter of liberating the mind from ignorance. This Buddhist spirit of analytic inquiry as the way of salvation seems to anticipate the age of information. New discoveries in science demonstrate the awesome power of the human mind to reach, explore, comprehend, and transcend the limitations of ordinary life. These discoveries strengthen the central positive thrust of Buddhism.

Suffering Because of Ignorance in Believing the Phenomenon of Self as a Reality

Let us assume the phenomenal world consists of a twofold interactive process in being and becoming. Then, existence is relational and dependent in origination. In such a process, individuality, or the self, is a qualified reality, a temporary aggregation. Science, in our understanding of it, seems to have indicated this twofold process, although not precisely. Frank Wilczek has observed that "all the fundamental constituents of matter come in matched pairs. For every kind of particle, there is an antimatter that is identical in mass but opposite in other properties such as the negative and positive charge."[1] Everything in the diversified world—galaxies, stars, rocks, plants, and human beings—could be assembled out of two kinds of quarks, U and

D, and electrons. Nature, of which we are a part, is highly complex, yet this complexity is merely variegated manifestations of the same matter.

In their efforts to uncover the secret of life, scientists discovered that DNA is the key to understanding the biological evolution of change. DNA always comes in pairs, with a short one joined to a long one, and can only exist in pairs. The nucleotides, subunits of DNA, are strung together in pairs to form the two strands of the double helix. Base pairs link the two sides. Interestingly, cell growth follows the same pattern. In fertilization, the twenty-three chromosomes of the male sperm and the twenty-three chromosomes of the female egg pair up to form a single nucleus and then split to form two new cells. Life then begins. The human body is made up of millions of interlocking and mutually dependent components. The cells of the body are separate, but each interacts in a way that provides the greatest opportunity for mutual survival. We can break cells up and extract selected parts of them for study, much as physicists break up the atoms. But activities of cells individually do not constitute life any more than the behavior of a subatomic particle. A disrupted cell is no longer capable of continuing life.

As we gain more insight into ourselves and into the nature of our being, individually and collectively, we will realize, with sufficient evidence, that each identifiable individual in the world has a twofold nature: one as a separate being and another as related to others. Nothing in the world is entirely separable from other things. Each thing shares, to a greater or lesser extent, specific properties with other things. In the final analysis, physicists may still speak of individual electrons, protons and neutrons. If they do, they do not attribute distinctive individuality to particular entities but refer to those entities as the focal point of specific and measurable relations. These entities are not distinct and self-identical things, as in classical mechanics, but serve as a center of energy that cannot be located with exactitude in the space-time scheme. The warranty for the assertion of their existence is provided not by direct observation but by the laws of quantum mechanics. It is meaningless to talk of any space-time other than Planck's constant. Quarks and leptons are devoid of real individuality.

In the reasoning process, Buddhists have long contended that if A and B have nothing in common, A cannot transform into B. If A and B have nothing in common, change and transformation between the two is impossible. Modern science does not dispute this argument. For instance, the electron flow that underlies photosynthesis and biological oxidation is crucial for keeping living systems going. Biologists discovered that though electrons cannot move from A to B in an isolated system, they can flow without difficulty if A and B are members of a chain. Whether a theory that explains natural phenomena can explain human events may continue to disturb us, because living systems are obviously different from nonliving systems. Yet the advancement in quantum mechanics has provided us with a new conceptual framework that has uncovered a new world of possibilities in elementary particles far beyond what might have been obtained solely by experimental measurement. It also has provided a technique in logic that is well suited for analyzing the epistemological problems of human events made possible by the profound kinship between quantum theory and philosophy. Thus, the Buddhist approach to use inferences from observations of nature to explain human affairs may not be irrelevant.

Buddhists frankly admit the twofold nature of existence in happiness and suffering and the qualified reality of the self. Human beings are responsible for their suffering and their happiness. Buddha lamented that, in our ordinary way of thinking and cognition, we never go beyond the surface of the name and the appearance. The polarity of existence in the twofold process consists of two poles interacting in the principle of complementarity, but an ignorant person sees only one separate pole of happiness and clings to it for permanence, perfection, and totality. Thus, in ignorance, a person plunges into life's ocean of suffering. Suffering in one-sidedness and exclusiveness finds no end. To search for the right way to annihilate suffering, Buddhists call for in-depth analysis of cognition. Buddha argued that if we do not know where the robber is, we can never hope to catch him/her.

Ignorance in One-sidedness and Exclusiveness Because of Misunderstanding the Role of the Mind

To engage in an in-depth analysis of cognition, Buddhists embarked on two tasks: first, to examine the nature of truth; and second, to examine the essence of the mind in cognition. Two representative works dealing with these subjects may provide us a sufficient preliminary basis for evaluation. They are the proposal of the theory of double truth in two levels of knowledge in the *Prajñāpāramitā* (Great Wisdom) by Nāgārjuna and the analysis of the universal emptiness of the mind in cognition enunciated in the *Surangama Sutra* (*The Essence of Mind*) by Asvaghosha.

Knowledge is the most noble creation and the single trait that makes us human. Among our many types of knowledge, the most reliable is science. Among the theories of knowledge, that which has greatest scientific support may be materialist monism that purports true knowledge to be the genuine reflection of objective reality in our mind. Objective reality, in this sense, is defined as the phenomenal world, which by nature is twofold because of the polar relationship of its being and becoming. The nature of knowledge, then, is subject to a twofold principle in its structure and function.

Buddhism reminds us that when we assert "yes" and reject "no," it does not mean that "no" does not exist and function in our attainment of knowledge. When this occurs, we are only unconscious of this twofold nature and take it for granted. The *Prajñāpāramitā* cautioned that the root of suffering is the tendency to seize the relative as absolute. The root of skillfulness in understanding is nonexclusiveness. Aside from the subjective idealist who sees consciousness only in the manner of the *Surangama Sutra*, recent discoveries in science provide us with opportunity to conceive the double truth on a bi-level evolutionary process. It reconciles the seeming conflict between classical and quantum physics. It also invigorates the concept of emptiness of a neutral and noncommittal state of mind in a middle path, in which the mind functions as an arbiter, coordinator, harmonizer, unifier, and mediator, and ultimately as the creator of cognition. Examination of the three most essential and reliable scientific methods for acquiring knowledge illustrates these main points.

First, the primary step for scientific investigation relies on direct observation through our senses, with the assistance of instruments. Buddha warned us not to let our senses deceive us. The imperfection of the sense organs has been substantiated by the development of experimental science and sophisticated techniques. Perception is only the starting point in the study of quantities. Measurement is a complex cognition process in which abstract thinking plays an essential role. Quantum mechanics has ascertained these problems in its disclosure of the principle of uncertainty and approximation. We see colors; but color is only the reflection of light. We are blind to vast reaches of reality in the phenomenal world. The electron microscope can trick even the sharpest eyes into thinking one thing is actually another. When a small patch of hair, is magnified 500 times, it looks like a forest. In achieving coordinated unity in the Buddhist sense of understanding, the mind functions above and beyond exclusiveness and extremeness, beyond analysis and synthesis. Every act of seeing requires a visual judgment. The judgment refers to the capacity of the mind to perceive all contradictions as complementary aspects of a unified whole. A camera only records the view; it does not interpret the image. The mind has the ability to create, out of the varied experiences of the relative world, an image of the objective reality, and to perceive the workings and changes in the universe as temporary permutations of that original unitary whole.

Second, in scientific inquiry, the object of investigation, though a fundamental unity, is broken down into many parts. Generally, it is fragmented as much as necessary to isolate the object and to decipher the behaviors. Later, the inquiry is reassembled into a coherent whole and measured to formulate a statement capable of being tested and repeated for its predictability. This process of breaking the whole into parts and reassembling the parts into a reconstructed whole is the function of mind in its twofold nature of analysis and synthesis. The operation of the mind is thought, and the function of thought is judgment, which unifies two modes of thought, subject and object. This process of dissection and reassembly is a purely human construct, not an inherent nature of the cosmos. The progression from the abstract universal through further specification to the concrete singular is analytic. The process of beginning with immediacies that are incorporated through mediation into the universal is synthetic. Recent studies have shown that, beyond physiological instinct, the mind administers judgment in the middle brain of left and right hemispheres. The middle brain, from the neurological point of view, operates as the supreme unifier of the two hemispheres into a harmonious whole. Thus, only through the mediation of the mind can our microscopic and macroscopic views be integrated to gain better knowledge.

Third, assuming that true knowledge reflects objective reality, how can we be sure the object we have described retains its identity if the world is constantly changing? The knowledge we have acquired is static, a statistical average, but the world is dynamic in nature. Quantum mechanics has demonstrated that nature never turns on or off for the sake of human beings. As Martin Karplus observed "molecules, essential to life, are never at rest....In the past ten years, the static view of protein has been undergoing a fundamental revision. A protein is dynamic and is in a state of constant motion."[2] The dynamic picture makes it possible to understand phenomena that cannot be explained by the static model. Classical physics only deals with the static and macroscopic aspects of an object and is thus blind to the microscopic aspects. Theoretical approaches have uncovered details of protein motion far beyond what were accessible by experimental measurement. Theoretical physicists have relied increasingly on their analytic and intuitive abilities to uncover the secrets of nature. For instance, quantum electrodynamics (QED) is based on a theory of strong nuclear interaction known as chromodynamics. This theory works, but only as a result of "fudging the math to make it fit our observation of the world and ignore the infinities from the quantum equation."[3] This adaptation is known as renormalization.

We observe not nature itself but nature exposed to our methods of questioning. The mind is the creator, creating order out of disorder. The mind is infinitely dynamic, self-interacting in a continuum without which there would be no life and thus no knowledge. Objects vanish, but the mind does not: "When the sound of our voice ceases and all the perception arising from the sound comes to an end, the mind goes on discriminating the memory of that sound."[4] The mind does not depend on causes; nor is it subject to conditions. And it never wears out or ages.

Misunderstanding Because of Unwillingness to Use the Right Mind

Buddha did not see the improper functioning of the mind as an insurmountable problem. Throughout history, Buddhists insisted on four cardinal rules for their behavior: universal compassion that repays hatred with love, renunciation of all worldly attachments, including abstinence from sex, equality for all through brotherhood and sisterhood, and total pacificism. This ascetic mentality seems not only impractical but against human nature. But, Buddhists reasoned that our thoughts exist in opposite pairs, such as good and evil, success and failure. Our mind is endowed with the ability to reconcile this opposition by detaching attention from the evil to focus on the good. The potential power of the mind is activated, flowing to that point of attention. Then, good can be sought and attained. The opposite, evil end enables us to sharpen our mental tools, overcome the evil obstacles, and enjoy the successful experience of overcoming them. There-fore, the task necessitates the mind's functioning to concentrate on attaining the goal. This optimism is based on two assumptions, both reminiscent of Confucianism. First, ultimate reality is the basic prin-ciple of knowledge. Second, the awareness of self is a function of the mind at its highest stage and an act of free will. No scientific formula can ascertain the predictability and practicability of this optimism. But parallel developments can be suggested in science and religion by posing some questions and offering further comments.

Why does the emergence of human life observed by scientists rep-licate the seven stages of the Big Bang theory? Why does the evolution of consciousness or logic, as demonstrated by Jains in their doctrine of "may-be," appear to have a similar seven-stage structure of develop-ment? For example, the evolution of life is identified to be (1) incep-tion, (2) embryo, (3) childhood, (4) adult, (5) middle life, (6) old age, and (7) death. The evolution of consciousness is (1) infant; (2) sensory awareness; (3) hot-cold, full-hungry, happy-sad; (4) cognition; (5) ca-pacity for rationality, correct-incorrect; (6) social action, distinction of right and wrong, good and bad; and (7) free will. Moreover, does the discovery of DNA indicate a microcosm-macrocosm relationship between nature and humans like that of the deep structural similarity between the experimental field effects of consciousness and the ob-served unity of bosons and fermions in gauge supersymmetry? Lewis Thomas concluded in *The Life of a Cell* that the recognition of pat-terns and the generation of syntax are genetically established by our makeup. Thus, DNA constitutes our link with the creation of the uni-verse as a basic part of our innate nature. E. O. Wilson argued that reciprocity is contained in our genes. In view of these assertions, can we say that we know the world because we are part of it through one and the same ultimate reality?

The suggestion of a DNA link with the creation of the universe may warrant the contention that ultimate reality is the principle of knowledge. On scientific grounds, can the discovery that the auto-matic nervous system and the self-conscious nervous system exist in one and the same structure accommodate the Buddhist contention that self-awareness emerges in the thought process as the product of the function, not the essence, of the mind? In their efforts to analyze the problems of the self, which they considered to be the source of selfish-ness and thus of suffering, Buddhists noted that the function of the mind evolves in a progressive, hierarchical structure, with levels of depth. Starting from the most expressive level, the senses direct attention to the objects of sensation and desire, then to a more active level of decision making, referred to as intellect, and finally to the most subtle integrative function of individuality, the ego. Therefore, Buddhists concluded that self-awareness is the function of the mind at its highest state.

This psychological refining process, shaped by cultural values and tradition in the formation of ego consciousness, seems concomitant with Freud's ego sublimation process. Both implied a process in which a socially unacceptable behavior is changed into a socially acceptable one. In this process, only the mind's mode of expression, not its essence, is modified. On this ground, Buddhists, especially Ch'ans (Zens), based their optimism in the perfectibility of human beings. The essence of the mind, which may not be equal to the unconscious mind or the automatic nervous system, is, nevertheless, universal to us all. The conscious mind arises from the unconscious mind. The conscious mind makes us aware of the self, but the unconscious mind makes life possible. The unconscious mind seems to reflect the autonomous nervous system, and the conscious mind reflects the self-conscious nervous system. The problem is that "amid the activities of the day, we cease to realize the existence of the self-purifying process of enlightenment and, therefore, fail to activate it."[5]

Recent discoveries in science, notably computer research in artificial intelligence, further confirm the boundless power of the creativity of the mind. Computers cannot function without instructions from humans and are incapable of error, but the human mind can learn through trial and error. As a result, it can create order out of disorder, make choices, and have goals. To what extent can science be seen as supporting Ch'an's (Zen's) contention that willpower can shape ego development? Can its technique to restore the mind to its original state, one of restful alertness or nonexcited deep silence in a yet awake state, be a means for fully activating the mind's self-realization power to attain true understanding of the ego? Though science may not subscribe to precisely the same terms as the measures prescribed by Ch'an's concentration and meditation in a seated pose, suspending ordinary thought processes through dialectical negation of negation to reach a blissful nothingness, if not religious ecstasy, experimental evidence shows that such a state of mind can accelerate the rate of development of the higher consciousness, in which clarity, coherence, and attention can be increased, and anxiety, depression, and aggressiveness are decreased. Consequently, this technique of meditation, they claim, can unfreeze human development, typically fixed at the ordinary level of adult conceptual thought.

No great gap separates this conviction and the general belief in science that if the mind, being the source of thoughts and the reservoir of creative intelligence, is sufficiently organized and refined, it will lead to creative action. However, the task of organizing and refining the mind to achieve the highest level of consciousness cannot be attained through the reasoning process alone. A will of action with purposeful and deliberate effort to focus the mind's powers is also necessary. The problem of science's efforts to gain true knowledge is that it is only concerned with the rational, and ignores the role emotions play in knowledge. In the formulation of our consciousness, it has been demonstrated that if enough people believe in and think of a certain thing, a self-sustaining thought pattern is formed and perpetuates itself in the manner of a collective consciousness that is not entirely rational. History has shown that all knowledge is evolutionary. Something generally believed and accepted as true may not necessarily be true. For instance, the formulation of a religious faith is not based entirely on rational beliefs deriving from the reasoning process. In fostering religious faith, the emotional factors vested in historical tradition play a greater role than purely logical conclusion and conviction. Yet no one can deny the influence and importance of religion on an individual, a society, or even a nation. With this in mind, can the contention of Ch'an Buddhists that willpower is used to attain enlightenment be discarded as irrelevant on scientific grounds?

The discovery of nonlinear phenomena and chaos in science would seem to undermine the foundation of Buddhist religious faith in reincarnation. This retribution process is based on classical, if not mechanical, causation—A causes B. The reward or punishment for a former life by the transmigration of the soul functions on the principle of linear causality. The Twelve *Nidānas* are the best example—ignorance causes the appearance of rebirth, and so on. The discovery of uncertainty in quantum mechanics would cast doubt on the regularity and predictability of linear progression in retribution. Evil deeds or karma may not cause retribution necessarily, as predicted, especially since quantum mechanics permits events to happen without a cause. Nevertheless, questions arise. If events could evolve from nothingness, as quantum theory implies, does this concept of nothingness correspond to the Buddhist concept of nothingness? Both indicate a nondescriptiveness and nothing else. Classical physics operates as long as quantum phenomena can be ignored, and the Buddhist principle of causality can remain operating in the same manner as classical principles. Especially significant is the suggestion that the karma-rebirth cycle of the Buddhist wheel of existence infers the nature of periodicity from which modern chemistry cannot depart. The only issue that remains is the age-old controversy over whether human events can be explained by the principles of natural events. We can say that the law of causality in Buddhism may also be a statistical average (e.g., drunk driving tends to cause an accident, but it may not every time.)

It is difficult to equate the concept of soul in Buddhism to DNA, a comparatively recent discovery in biological science. So far as science can ascertain, the fate of an individual's intelligence, health, and physiological and neurological makeup is genetically determined. Environmental factors can provide the most favorable conditions for optimum development of an individual's potential, not the potential itself. The genetic makeup of an individual is merely a chance occasion, independent of the will of parents, regardless of parents' behavior. The DNA encoding is amoral, devoid of value. Thus, the concept of ethical determinism in relation to individual fate, as advocated by Buddhism, seems unsupportable in light of recent discoveries in science. Yet the force of history, in the formulation of a value system for a given group of people in a given locality, is so preponderant that no one can escape its influence. An individual's life is overwhelmingly molded in such a cultural milieu, manifested as collective consciousness. Whatever we do and think will result in our present life and in the next stage of our life, just as our present life has been influenced by whatever people did and thought in the past. Thus, the value of cultural determinants shaping individual personality are akin to the Buddhist contention of ethical determinism in a broad sense, though it might not be as automatic and mechanistic as that held by Buddhists.

According to Ch'an Buddhism, liberation from suffering is, in a sense, a realization of the twofold nature of existence, restoring the mind to its original state of nothingness through the control of the mind. A person reaches a state of knowing in which there is neither enmity nor friendship, and so on. A founder of Ch'an Buddhism, Hui Neng, spelled this out in what he called the "Law of Opposite" and "Corresponding Law," "*Dui Fa.*" He lists thirty-six pairs of opposites in three categories: five cosmological pairs, including day and night, heaven and earth; twelve epistemological pairs, including form and idea, assurance and nonassurance; and nineteen valuational pairs (application of the self-nature), including good and evil and right and wrong.

In each pair, one aspect generates or negates the other and vice versa. An analysis of the mind shows that its essence is above and beyond these opposites. Ch'ans pointed out that any wish entices suffering; hence, no wishes lead to no suffering.

From the functional perspective of analyzing the relationship of parts and wholes, the value of the efforts of an individual and the existence of its complement are equally important. For example, so far as the safety of a person and a president is concerned, the driver of a presidential car is as crucial as the president. This sort of relational approach reminds us of what Lao Tze says: You are beautiful because the other is ugly; you are intelligent because the other is stupid; you are healthy because another inherited the defective gene from the gene pool, sparing you. The relevance of this sociological analysis may remain debatable. The shift of Ch'an from linear causation to reciprocal causation seems to correspond to the shift from classical mechanics to quantum mechanics. Ch'an Buddhists attempted to awaken the individual's inner self, or higher self, through a secular approach, leading to the surrounding world awareness of the deep interconnections with others. Their stress on rational realism seems to reflect the spirit of science. Their insistence on knowledge as the key for salvation suggests an anticipation of the information age. We suffer because the world is constantly changing. Thus, we will have another chance. It is a twofold process. With this frame of reference in mind, we see this universal, nonexclusive, and pacificist doctrine the same way Nolan Pliny Jacobson did—as the religion of analysis.

Notes

1. Frank Wilczek, "The Cosmic Asymmetry Between Matter and Antimatter," *Scientific American* 243 (December 1980), pp. 82–100.
2. Martin Karplus, "The Dynamics of Proteins," *Scientific American* 243 (April 1980), p. 42.
3. John Gribbin, *In Search of Schrodinger's Cat* (New York: Bantam, 1984), pp. 255–258.
4. Asvaghosha, *Shou-Ling-yin* (Chinese translation of the *Sūrangama Sutra*), in *The Wisdom of China and India*, ed. Lin Yutang (New York: Modern Library, 1942), p. 513.
5. Ibid., p. 511.

11.
Pratītyasamutpāda and Creativity   *Ramakrishna Puligandla*

As coeditor of this memorial volume, I shall exercise editorial prerogative when I talk about my personal encounters and interactions with Nolan Pliny Jacobson. I do this not to indulge in sentimentality but to render this essay live and genuine. It is not a dry piece of scholarship but a narrative about a person, a real person, whom we have all known, loved, and admired.

I first came to know of Jacobson sometime in 1966, when I received from the publisher a copy of his book *Buddhism: The Religion of Analysis.*[1] I immediately read the book and found it a fine work, written with understanding, conviction, clarity, and enthusiasm. His treatment of Buddhism was clear and insightful, and his comparative analyses of and critical observations on Marx, Freud, Hume, and Buddhism were erudite and impressive. Nevertheless, I felt that the book suffered from a serious shortcoming because it wholly ignored Mahāyāna and exclusively dealt with Theravāda, leaving the reader who has no prior acquaintance with or knowledge of Buddhism with the impression that "Buddhism" means Theravāda Buddhism. The book is less rich for not having gained from the profound insights of Mahāyāna, particularly Nāgārjuna's Madhyamaka, Zen, and Tibetan Buddhism. Because I did not then know Jacobson personally, I did not write to inform him of my reactions to his book.

A few years later, I one day received a phone call in my office from a young man who identified himself as David Miller and told me that he was calling to invite me to serve as a commentator in a symposium where Jacobson would present a paper entitled "Creativity in Whitehead and Buddhism." I asked him how he had decided on me, and he replied, "Professor Jacobson asked me to invite you." I thanked him, accepted the invitation, and asked him whether there were any other commentators. He informed me that Professors Charles Hartshorne and Kenneth Inada would be the other commentators.

When I went to New Orleans to attend the symposium, I was informed that, owing to indisposition, Jacobson would not be able to attend. Someone would read his paper, and the symposium would go on as scheduled. I was disappointed at not having the chance to meet Jacobson. On our way to the conference hall, David Miller told me that Jacobson would like to have a copy of my comments. I told him that I am not in the habit of preparing written commentaries, but I would prepare one and send it to Jacobson (which I did a few days later). In this commentary, I said that I found Jacobson's paper predominantly Theravāda-oriented and that Mahāyāna has more in common with Whitehead's philosophy than Theravāda Buddhism does, because Mahāyāna, like Whitehead's thought, is much richer and more encompassing in scope than Theravāda. I also said that I regarded Nāgārjuna's Madhyamaka, Zen, and Tibetan Buddhism as the heart of Mahāyāna. I am not claiming that I alone brought these points to Jacobson's attention. As Jacobson told me in a conversation in Chicago, Professor Inada and I were instrumental in his subsequent larger involvement with Mahāyāna.

Jacobson came to the study of Buddhism with accomplished scholarship in American philosophy, process-theology, and Marxism. It is not surprising, then, that Jacobson should find the study of Buddhism exciting and exhilarating. He quickly discerned the kinship between process-philosophy and Buddhism, and he eventually coedited with Professor Inada *Buddhism and American Thinkers.*[2] His own essay in this volume, "A Buddhist Analysis of Human Experience," sums up his vision of Buddhist philosophy in what I consider one of his best and most insightful writings.

We are all keenly aware that the concept of creativity occupies the central place in Jacobson's understanding and interpretation of Buddhist philosophy. In light of this fact, I thought it appropriate to discuss the doctrine of dependent origination (*pratītyasamutpāda*), which, in my judgment, holds the key to creativity. Accordingly, in what follows I shall present some of my reflections on the doctrine of dependent origination and its significance to creativity. The doctrine of dependent origination is the fountainhead of the teachings of the Buddha. In his dedicatory verse for the Madhyamaka-kārikā (hereafter, *MMK*)[3] Nāgārjuna expresses profound gratitude to the Buddha for teaching the doctrine, and thereby showing the way to freedom from suffering (*duhkha*).

Let me begin with a clear statement of the doctrine of dependent origination. Put simply, it reads, "this arising, that arises; and this ceasing to be, that ceases to be." This is to say that every phenomenon arises in dependence upon other phenomena and passes away in dependence upon yet other phenomena. In other words, no phenomenon arises or passes away on its own. Thus when I plant a seed in the ground, the interaction of the seed with a variety of factors, such as the soil, water, sunshine, *etc.*, is the arising of the plant; it is not as though there were something called "plant" waiting to show up at a certain time like an actor on to the stage. The arising of the plant is none other than the interactions of the various factors (phenomena); similarly, the passing away of the plant is the interactions of a multitude of factors. The plant has no being apart from these interactions.

Before proceeding, I wish to raise a question which, to the best of my knowledge and belief, has not been raised before. We are all familiar with the fact that the doctrine of dependent origination has been widely discussed by many thinkers from different standpoints. In light of this, it is quite surprising that seldom, if ever, has anyone asked, What exactly is the status of the doctrine of dependent origination? Is it an *a priori* truth, an *a posteriori* truth, an analytic truth, a synthetic truth, a synthetic *a priori* truth, a tautology, an inductive generalization? On what grounds are we to accept or reject it? I shall not undertake here the task of answering these questions in detail; rather, I shall content myself with making certain pertinent observations.

Imagine someone saying to the Buddha, "Sir, you teach the doctrine of dependent origination. But how are we to accept this teaching? Is there some way we can determine its truth or falsity?" I conjecture that the Buddha would answer: "Your questions are indeed appropriate, and I ask no one to accept my teaching on my authority or out of veneration for me. The teaching should be accepted or rejected only on the basis of inquiry and scrutiny. The doctrine of dependent origination applies to (and therefore governs) all phenomena, without exception. To prove it false, you need to come up with a single phenomenon that is not governed by it; that is, you need to show that at least one phenomenon arises and passes away on its own. I assure you that, no matter what phenomenon you consider for examination, you will find that it is in full accord with this teaching. The reason for this is that all phenomena exist in time, and to exist in time is to be subject to arising and passing away, and to arise and pass away is to be dependent on other phenomena. Now that you have heard my answer, you should examine it, inquire into it, and determine for yourself whether or not to accept it."

Someone might object that the Buddha's answer is really no more than a definition of "phenomenon" and should be rejected because all definitions are arbitrary. Further, since, on the Buddha's own admission, the doctrine of dependent origination cannot, in principle, be falsified, someone might say that it is not a scientific truth but rather a metaphysical claim. This objection is mistaken. The Buddha's answer is not a definition of "phenomenon," but a profound insight into and observation of the fundamental trait of all phenomenal existence. If one wants to construe the Buddha's answer as a definition of "phenomenon," one should realize that this definition (observation) is not arbitrary but is fully grounded in the phenomenology of human experience. The doctrine is not potentially falsifiable, not because it is not a scientific truth, but because it is a universal truth, a truth governing all existence. It is not metaphysical, in the sense of supersensible and beyond the ken and pale of humans. Nor is it an inductive generalization. Unlike inductive generalizations, the principle of dependent origination is not potentially falsifiable.

What does it mean to falsify the doctrine of dependent origination? It means finding an existent, a phenomenon, that arises and perishes away without depending on anything other than itself. Falsifying the doctrine of dependent origination is an absurd idea because the very notion of a phenomenon that does not arise and pass away is unintelligible. The doctrine of dependent origination is not arrived at by generalizing an observation regarding a limited number of phenomena. It is a profound and luminous insight into what it is for anything to be a phenomenon at all, so it cannot be falsified. I shall now resume the discussion of the principle of dependent origination.

The heart of the doctrine of dependent origination is the teaching that no phenomenon arises or passes away on its own. Every phenomenon, without exception, arises and perishes away in dependence on other phenomena. When we examine and analyze any phenomenon, we find no ultimate residuum, or core, in it. We discover the entire being of the phenomenon to be no more and no less than the interaction among various other phenomena (the plant example). This lack of an ultimate residuum, or core, is what is meant by the declaration that "all phenomena are empty" (*svabhāva-śūnya-dharma*). Because all phenomena arise and pass away in dependence on other phenomena, no phenomenon is self-existent or has self-nature. This lack of self-existence and self-nature (own-existence and own-nature) is what is meant by saying that all phenomena are empty, empty of own-existence and own-nature. Let me ward off any misunderstanding here, by emphasizing that to say that phenomena lack self-existence and self-nature is not to say that phenomena lack existence and nature; that is, phenomena certainly exist, but they exist dependently and relatively. Thus, for example, the apple on my table exists and it is red, round, smooth, sweet, nourishing, *etc*. But its existence and nature are through and through governed by the principle of dependent origination. In short, phenomena exist and have natures dependently, relatively, not independently (and absolutely). I shall briefly digress here to make a few salient observations by comparing Hume's denial of substances with the Buddhist's denial of self-existents and self-natures, either within or without humans. ("substance" and "self-existent" are synonymous).

Hume arrived at his denial of substances, on perceptual grounds. Hume's method of analysis is the same as that of Berkeley's analysis leading to his denial of material substances, but Hume applied the method to the analysis not only of material substances but also of mental (spiritual) substances (so-called unchanging, enduring, and abiding selves). The guiding principle of Hume's analysis is, "no impression, no idea." He tells us that when he withdraws himself into his innermost recesses to discover himself, all he comes across is a sensation, an impression, an idea, a feeling, an image, a memory, and so on, not an unchanging entity, permanent self, or I to whom all these belong. According to Hume's dictum, no idea can be admitted into a body of knowledge unless it is traceable to an impression. He could not trace the idea of an unchanging self to an impression, so he declared that no mental substances exist (like Berkeley, he already had proclaimed the denial of material substances). And this is what I mean by saying that Hume arrived at his denial of substances on perceptual grounds.

How did the Buddha arrive at his denial of substances? The Buddha arrived at the denial of substances through his inquiry into existence in general—how existents (phenomena) come to be and pass away. His doctrine of dependent origination is precisely the denial of substances (self-existents), within or without humans (the teaching of *anattā*). That Hume could not find a substantial self should not surprise the Buddha. If according to the Buddha's teaching, there cannot, in principle, be any self-existents, there cannot be a substantial, enduring self, either. This is just what I mean by saying that the Buddha's declaration of the denial of substantial selves logically follows from the general principle of dependent origination; whereas Hume's denial of substantial selves is on perceptual grounds, on his failure to trace the idea of a substantial self to an impression.

To the best of my knowledge and belief, neither Berkeley nor Hume approached the question of existence (existents, phenomena) in general by way of anything that even vaguely resembles the doctrine of dependent origination. As has been shown above, their denial of substances is based on perceptual considerations. That is, Hume did not arrive at his denial of substances *via* the doctrine of dependent origination. That this is so is further attested to by the fact that, although Hume constantly appealed to the guiding principle of his inquiry, "no impression, no idea," he never bothered to ask what exactly is the status of impressions. One would think that Hume, in spite of his astute and relentless inquiry that led him to the denial of substances, regarded impressions as self-existents (substances). I am not claiming that Hume did regard impressions as substances; but by not having raised the question about the status of impressions, Hume leaves the impression that he probably regarded them as substances (self-existents). I suggest that he did not raise that question because he did not arrive at the denial of substances by way of anything like the doctrine of dependent origination.

What about the Buddha? How did he regard impressions? The Buddha, quite consistently with his teaching of dependent origination, assigns them the place of a link in the doctrine of dependent origination expressed as the twelvefold chain (*dvādaśa-nidāna*). It is appropriate to remark here that whereas Hume was greatly alarmed and profoundly disturbed by the discovery that there are no substantial selves, the Buddha rejoiced. And, I want to emphasize that this difference in their attitudes toward the discovery of the lack of self-existents and self-natures is traceable to the difference in their approaches to inquiry and the purposes of their inquiries.

I shall now pinpoint the difference between the inquiry of the Buddha and that of Hume. Hume's argument for the denial of substances may be expressed as follows: If a substantial self exists, so should an impression of it; no impression of it exists; therefore, no substantial self exists. The Buddha's reasoning is as follows: There cannot, in principle, be any self-existents (substances); therefore, a self (as a self-existent, a substance) does not exist. Hume's argument and his conclusion are in perfect accord with those of the Buddha, although their lines of inquiry are different. The reason for this is that Hume's argument follows from the Buddha's teaching of the doctrine of dependent origination (although the converse does not hold). Thus, if there cannot exist any substances, then surely there cannot exist a substantial self; for, if such a self were to exist, one would be able to trace it to an impression; that Hume could not trace the idea of a substantial self to an impression is therefore a natural, logical consequence of the Buddha's teaching that there cannot, in principle, be any self-existents, substances. Put pointedly, Hume simply concluded that there is no substantial self (on perceptual grounds), whereas the Buddha, coming at the issue *via* dependent origination, gives the primordial reason why there cannot, in principle, be substantial selves. The reason is that all existents, all phenomena, arise and pass away dependently, and hence are devoid of self-existence and self-nature.

I come now to a discussion of Emptiness (*Śūnyatā*). We have pointed out earlier that, according to the doctrine of dependent origination, all phenomena are empty—empty of self-existence and self-nature. This means that when we analyze any and all phenomena, we find no ultimate residuum (core). But the question immediately arises: If all phenomena are empty—that is, the ultimate sum of all phenomena, is Emptiness—how explain the fact that there are phenomena at all? Does this mean, then, that all phenomena arise out of Emptiness (that there are phenomena is a fact), since ultimately there is and can be nothing other than Emptiness? This is an important and complicated question. I shall present here my own answer.

That there exist phenomena is a fact; and since all phenomena are empty—devoid of any core—one wonders as to the source of phenomena; that is, since all phenomena *add up* to Emptiness, one would naturally think that Emptiness must be the source of all phenomena (since ultimately there can be nothing else than Emptiness to serve as their source). This conjecture is quite correct, but one needs to clarify certain matters in order to prevent confusion, misunderstanding, and, most seriously, unwittingly subscribing to a substantialist view of ultimate reality, of Emptiness. Let us first make the following observations concerning Emptiness. Consider, for example, any two phenomena, say, P_1 and P_2. According to the doctrine of dependent origination, both these phenomena are empty. This does not, however, mean that there are two Emptinesses, E_1 and E_2 one corresponding to P_1 and the other to P_2. To think that there are two is to commit the serious error of thinking of Emptiness as an entity, on a par with phenomena. The point here is that E_1 and E_2 are indistinguishable. It is not as though a person first looks at E_1 and then at E_2 and notices some difference between them. This is to say that the emptiness that corresponds to one phenomenon cannot be numerically distinguished from the emptiness that corresponds to another phenomenon. This in turn means that emptiness is non-dual and the same everywhere and everywhen. By saying that Emptiness is non-dual, I mean that (1) nothing ultimately exists other than Emptiness, and (2) there exist no distinctions (marks) within Emptiness itself. In a word, Emptiness is non-composite, not a thing. Thus it is clear that Emptiness is indeed the ultimate reality, and it is to be emphasized that Emptiness is not an entity, characterizable as either substance or process (or, for that matter, as anything at all).

At this point, I should register my sense of amazement at the claim of many scholars of Buddhism that the Buddha never affirmed any ultimate reality, and that the whole notion of ultimate reality was injected (smuggled) into the teaching of the Buddha by Brahmanical thinkers, such as the Vedāntins. I wish to show that such a claim is false and without foundation. The following passage clearly shows that the Buddha affirmed ultimate reality:

> There is, monks, that plane where there is neither extension nor...motion nor the plane of infinite ether...nor that of neither perception nor non-perception, neither this world nor another, neither the moon nor the sun. Here, monks, I say that there is no coming or going or remaining or decreasing or uprising, for this is itself *without support*, without continuance, without mental object—that is itself the end of suffering.

> There is, monks, an unborn, not become, not made, uncompounded, and were it not, monks, for this unborn, not become, not made, uncompounded, no escape could be shown here for what is born, has become, is made, is compounded. But because there is, monks, an unborn, not become, not made, uncompounded, therefore an escape can be shown for what is born, has become, is made, is compounded.[4]

What is the unborn, not become, not made, and uncompounded that the Buddha talks about here? It transcends all categories—neither coming nor going, neither perception nor non-perception—and is *not* governed by the doctrine of dependent origination; for categorizablity is precisely the hallmark of being subject to the doctrine of dependent origination. And I am claiming that this unborn, not become, not made, and uncompounded is indeed Emptiness, ultimate reality. To put the point straightforwardly, the doctrine of dependent origination applies only to *samsāra*, phenomenal existence, and not to Emptiness, ultimate reality, which defies all categories and characterizations. This point is clearly made by Nāgārjuna. He employs the doctrine of dependent origination to proclaim the conditionality of all phenomenal existence, and hence the denial of self-existence. However, what is often overlooked is the fact that Nāgārjuna also interprets, in full conformity with the Buddha's teaching (the passage quoted above), the doctrine of dependent origination, in such a manner as to deny conditionality *altogether*: "Neither perishing nor arising in time, neither terminable nor eternal, neither self-identical nor variant in form, neither coming nor going; Such is *pratītyasamutpāda*."[5] Further, "origination, existence, and destruction are of the nature of *māyā*, dreams, or a fairy castle."[6] That conditionality (causation, causal relations) applies only to *samsāra* is clear from the following: "That state which is the rushing in and out [of existence] when dependent or conditioned; this (state), when *not* dependent or not conditioned, is seen to be *nirvāna*"[7] (emphasis added). It is worth emphasizing that when he says that origination, existence, and destruction are *māyā*, Nāgārjuna is *not* saying that phenomenal existence (*samsāra*) is unreal and non-existent; rather, I understand him as saying that *samsāra* is fully and wholly governed by *pratītyasamutpāda* (dependent origination).

One might now object: This seems to contradict another declaration of Nāgārjuna's that there is not the slightest difference between *samsāra* and nirvāna: "There is nothing whatever which differentiates the existence-in-flux (*samsāra*) from nirvāna; and there is nothing whatever which differentiates nirvāna from existence-in-flux"; and "The extreme limit (*koti*) of nirvāna is also the extreme limit of existence-in-flux."[8] The point of this objection may be stated as follows: On the one hand, Nāgārjuna, by saying that *pratītyasamutpāda* applies only to *samsāra* but not nirvāna, seems to clearly distinguish between *samsāra* and nirvāna; but, on the other hand, he is emphatically denying any distinction between the two. How does one make sense of this glaring contradiction? I submit that there appears to be a contradiction only to those who have not fully grasped the profound point Nāgārjuna makes here.

Pratītyasamutpāda governs all existence-in-flux (*samsāra*); this is the teaching of omniconditionality. However, since conditionality—which is none other than causal relations, in the last analysis—is inexplicable,[9] omniconditionality is the same as nonconditionality. Conditionality requires self-existents and causal relations among them: According to *pratītyasamutpāda*, there cannot be any self-existents, so there cannot be any causal relations either. This is tantamount to saying that there is a way of experiencing the world with no awareness of things (self-existents) and hence of causal relations; such an experience is the experience of Emptiness.[10] This theory is in full accord with the teaching that Emptiness is non-thingness and hence nonconditionality (unborn, not become, not made, uncompounded). *Samsāra* and nirvāna are not two numerically distinguishable realities but one and the same reality, experienced in two different ways (*samvṛti* and *paramārtha*). This is just what is meant by Nāgārjuna's observation that there is not the slightest difference between *samsāra* and nirvāna, and that Emptiness is at once fullness.

Not being a thing, Emptiness transcends the "is" and the "is not." Nāgārjuna declares: "One may not say that there is 'emptiness' (*śūnya*), nor that there is 'non-emptiness.' Nor that both [exist simultaneously], nor that neither exists; the purpose for saying ['emptiness'] is for the purpose of conveying knowledge."[11] The term "emptiness" is employed only to enable one to comprehend the truth of dependent origination and nondependent nonorigination, but not to refer to some entity.

Is it correct to say, then, that Emptiness is the source of all phenomena? Yes, because "when emptiness 'works,' then everything in existence 'works.' If emptiness does not 'work,' then all existence does not 'work'";[12] and "all things prevail for him for whom emptiness prevails; nothing whatever prevails for him for whom emptiness prevails."[13] The first quotation here makes it clear that existence—things— could not be were it not for Emptiness, which is what I mean by saying that Emptiness is the source of all existence. The first half of the second quotation emphasizes this point. The second half of the second quotation emphasizes that Emptiness is not a thing, an entity, because he who understands and experiences emptiness experiences no things. Thus the first and second halves of the second quotation are the articulations of *samvṛti* and *paramārtha*, respectively.

The creativity that Jacobson speaks of is none other than *pratītyasamutpāda*; that is, dependent arising and passing away of things *is* the creativity of the world. A world consisting of self-existents, whether within or without humans, is devoid of creativity. In such a world, no change can occur, and change is a necessary condition for creativity. A word of caution is in order here; mere change is *not* creativity; rather, change which brings about novelty is creativity. Thus imagine a light which regularly changes, say, from red to blue and blue to red. There is certainly change here but no creativity; there is just monotonous repetition. *Pratītyasamutpāda* is not mere change but creativity itself, change that is unceasing creativity; and, as he himself told me in a conversation in St. Louis, Jacobson's unbounded respect and admiration for the Buddha is due to the Buddha's profound teaching of *pratītyasamutpāda*, and thereby the creativity of the world. And the thesis of the present essay is that the creativity of the world is none other than that of Emptiness (*Śūnyatā*)—Emptiness Itself. The ever-increasing emphasis on the aesthetic of our moment-to-moment experience that we find in Jacobson's later works serves to awaken us to the fact that the creativity of the world is not something hidden away and concealed from us, but rather is creativity that pervades our very existence and in which each of us has the glory of participating. Jacobson also saw and profoundly appreciated the cosmo-ecological vision and wisdom that flows from *pratītyasamutpāda*, that the world is not constituted of isolated Aristotelian substances (self-existents) with external relations, but, being through and through governed by *pratītyasamutpāda*, is interconnected existence, and that therefore the countless sentient and non-sentient beings are not alien to each other, but rather are inextricably and intricately related to each other and the weal and woe of each concerns that of all, hence the existence of unbounded care and compassion.

As some scholars remarked, Jacobson occasionally talked of reality as process, an idea inconsistent with the Buddhist insight that reality (Emptiness) transcends all categorization ("process" is a category polar to "substance"). Jacobson was fully aware of this insight, and he characterized reality as process to emphasize and call our attention to the ongoing creativity (*pratītyasamutpāda* and hence lack of self-existents), not to claim that Emptiness is process. Further, a sense exists in which the Buddhist can correctly speak of reality as process: "The 'originating dependently' we call 'emptiness'; this apprehension, *i.e.*, taking into account [all other things] is the understanding of the middle way."[14]

Few contemporary thinkers have contributed as much to the philosophy of creativity as Jacobson did. His work is unique because it brings to the study of creativity the insights of both Western and Eastern traditions. It is also unique because it shows that doing philosophy creatively is not an empty, vacuous, pointless, intellectual exercise but an activity that involves profound experimentation in the form of meditation. We are all the richer, intellectually and spiritually, for having benefitted from Jacobson's thought, and I am immeasurably grateful for his inspiration and wisdom.

Notes

1.   Nolan Pliny Jacobson, *Buddhism: The Religion of Analysis* (New York: Humanities, 1965; reprint, Carbondale and Edwardsville: Southern Illinois University Press, 1966, 1970).

2. Kenneth K. Inada and Nolan Pliny Jacobson, eds. *Buddhism and American Thinkers* (Albany: SUNY Press, 1984).

3. For an excellent translation of this work, see Kenneth K. Inada, *Nāgārjuna: A Translation of His* Mūlamadhyamakakārikā *with an Introductory Essay* (Tokyo: Hokuseido, 1970).

4. *Udāna*, 80–81 (emphasis added); in Edward Conze et al., eds., *Buddhist Texts Through the Ages* (New York: Harper & Row, 1964), pp. 94–95.

5. *MMK*, dedication.

6. Ibid., VII, 34.

7. Ibid., XXV, 9.

8. Ibid., XXV, 19, 20.

9. Ibid., I.

10. On this point, see David Loy, *Nonduality: A Study in Comparative Philosophy* (New Haven: Yale University Press, 1988).

11. *MMK*, XXII, 11.

12. Ibid., XXIV, 14.

13. Nāgārjuna, *Vigrahavyāvartanī*, II, p. 70.

14. *MMK*, XXIV, 18.

Part Three
Practical Implications

12.
The Idea of Freedom in
Chan/Zen/Son Buddhism
and Its Application to
International Conflicts   *Paul F. Schmidt*

How one author stimulates another is not easy to ascertain. When I first read Nolan Pliny Jacobson's *Buddhism and the Contemporary World*, I was attracted by his deep concern for the political and social consequences of Buddhism and by possible connections to Whitehead's chapter, "Peace," which I have long admired, in his *Adventures of Ideas*. Jacobson's hints about the influences of his year in Burma were stated more fully in the somewhat autobiographical introduction to his volume *Understanding Buddhism*, in which the epigraph from F. S. C. Northrop focuses his concern with the cultural impact of Buddhism. Jacobson felt that Buddhism was highly relevant to many problems today and could teach us much about peace and freedom. I wrote a dissertation on Whitehead (Yale, 1951) under the guidance of Northrop, who first taught me the relevance of Buddhist thought to Western philosophical problems.

All these ideas must have been percolating slowly in the recesses of my brain across the years of regularly teaching a course in Chan and Zen Buddhism at the University of New Mexico. Rereading Jacobson, I found the series of connections that suggested to me how Buddhist conceptions of freedom might be applied to contemporary world situations. So this essay came to be. I think that it directly carries on the basic spirit of Nolan Pliny Jacobson, who sought to bridge and to unify philosophical insights of East and West.

What is the idea of freedom contained in the development of Chan/Zen/Son Buddhism? Does it have applications to international conflicts? Who are some of the important teachers in the Chan/Zen/Son Buddhist tradition whose innovations provide new dimensions to the idea of freedom?

The contemporary vitality of Korean Son Buddhism enables a unique perspective on international conflicts. The original Chan tradition in China, from which Korean Son developed, seems to have lost its vitality, and since the 1949 revolution, it has been neglected, if not suppressed. The Japanese Zen tradition shares this opportunity but lacks the unique synthesis developed by Chinul in Korea in the thirteenth century and continued today. Nevertheless, each of the three traditions contributes an important aspect to the idea of freedom and may help to solve international conflicts.

At the very origin of Buddhism, with Siddhārtha's discovery of the Four Noble Truths, the first quality of freedom is made clear, a quality that permeates the entire subsequent development of Buddhism. The First Noble Truth teaches that a primary feature of human life, individual and social, is the occurrence of suffering (*duhkha*). We also experience happiness, but the historical Buddha discovered that both sides of this duality have a common cause. This cause is desire, manifested in many ways, such as clinging, attachment, possession, goal seeking, craving, pursuing ends, and striving.

In the structure of these forms of desire, we find two parts: what is and what might be. A person seeks to move from what is to the gaining or realization of what might be. I am hungry; I desire food to satisfy my hunger. If I fail to gain this goal, I suffer. If I obtain food, I am satisfied and happy. What might be may fail to come to be, which leads to suffering. Or it may come to be, creating temporary happiness during which new desires are likely to arise. Each form of desire involves a division between what is and what might be—hence, a duality. Buddha's Second Noble Truth teaches that suffering arises from unsatisfied desires. The Third Noble Truth is that if we can experience patterns of living without desires, suffering will cease. The Fourth Noble Truth, namely the Eightfold Path, usually takes the form of ethical prescriptions. The problem with this interpretation of the Eightfold Path is that these prescriptions set up goals (what might be) and hence fall into the duality of desires that causes suffering. Many Buddhist schools make this error, this misinterpretation. Part of the wisdom of Chan/Son/Zen is to see clearly how dualities produce desires and thus suffering.

Exploitation of natural resources, pollution of our earth's environment, and overpopulation are world problems that produce conflict. Each arises from a duality, issues in desires, and leads to suffering and conflict. Country X lacks oil resources in its land, but if it could conquer country Y militarily, economically, or culturally, it might gain what it lacks. In its desire to achieve this goal, its people suffer restrictions of many sorts. If it conquers, the people of country Y suffer and desire to foment change. The control of the victor creates restrictions on both X and Y. All these conflicts arise from duality and desires. The Four Noble Truths of Buddhism show us how to live without these sufferings. Pollution is a duality between toxic levels of poisons and healthy environments. The desire to manufacture a product generates toxic by-products dumped in our environment, causing suffering. If we eliminate the desire for excessive production and profit, we eliminate the suffering from toxic pollution. Overpopulation results from a desire of parents for more children than zero population growth allows and from a desire for improved medical standards that are not accompanied by cultural, religious, or sociological changes in attitudes. Sons are desired; daughters are sacrificed. Survival is desired. Disfunctional religious practices are clung to. Personal and social conflicts arise. Suffering ensues in starvation, malnutrition, infanticide, and the selling of babies.

Indian Buddhism reached another dramatic high point in the doctrine of Four-cornered Negation perfected by Nāgārjuna in his famous book *Madhyamaka Kārikās*. This doctrine appears in the Chan tradition, although modified in special ways to suit Chan, and contains another important meaning of freedom. I find Four-cornered Negation explicit in that masterful work by the third Chinese Chan teacher, Seng-ts'an, the *Hsin-hsin-ming*:

> Ignorance begets the dualism of rest and unrest,
> The enlightened have no likes and dislikes:
> All forms of dualism
> Are ignorantly contrived by the mind itself.
> ....
> When dualism does no more obtain,
> Even oneness itself remains not as such.
> ....
> In the higher realm of True Suchness
> There is neither "other" nor "self."[1]

My interpretation of Four-cornered Negation in Chan shows us that seeing into our original self-nature cannot be found in any of the four possible conceptual positions in which I can (1) affirm a standpoint; (2) deny that standpoint; (3) attempt to somehow affirm and deny the standpoint; or (4) reject both the affirmation and the denial, holding that neither the one nor the other is correct. We should abandon all four possible standpoints, realizing that any one of them excludes the others and represents a particularization of reality, one position out of four, but that the Buddha-nature is present everywhere. In place of such a particular conceptual position, Chan cultivates a direct intuition into suchness or emptiness, beyond all standpoints. Nāgārjuna's dialectical analysis in the *Kārikās* demonstrates the paradoxical results of conceptual thinking in which any one corner is espoused. *Koan (Kung-an)* shows the ineffectiveness of conceptual thinking in another way.

What meaning of freedom is contained in Four-cornered Negation? We realize that every social, political, economic, scientific, religious, educational, legal, or philosophical idea, theory, or ideological position will take one of the four corners, and that if we follow out its implications, we end in paradoxes, in the collapse of that standpoint. Conceptual positions are always partial, particular, limiting, exclusive, and self-destructing. Enlightenment suggests wholeness, totality, oneness, inclusiveness, and creativity. To show how this collapse occurs requires a lengthy analysis. Examples are in David Kalupahana's *Nāgārjuna: The Philosophy of the Middle Way.*

The modern world we live in is almost completely structured by such conceptual positions. We are taught to advocate, criticize, defend, and justify political platforms, scientific theories, religious doctrines, educational programs, legal decisions, and philosophical theses as exclusively true. Thus we imprison ourselves and lose our freedom to intuit beyond particular positions. Rigid adherence to one conceptual standpoint prevents the appreciation of other standpoints that a forbearing skepticism may allow, the readiness to see truth in opposed positions. Chan/Son/Zen recognizes that self-realization passes beyond the limitations of conceptual positions.

What is the application of this meaning of freedom to clashes between opposing economic and political systems? As long as people believe that their ideological position is the only true one, we cannot begin to resolve conflicts. Neither capitalism, nor communism, nor socialism, nor democracy, nor oligarchy has the last word in political wisdom. Beyond the Four Corners arises the compassion that extends to all sentient beings, whatever the dominant political ideology. Such compassion melts the exclusiveness that breeds conflict, and thus, in its highly unusual way, it ends conflict. Buddhist compassion contains a new kind of creativity expressed in positive tolerance, an attitude that goes beyond the acceptance of overt acts carried out by groups or nations holding intolerant standpoints.

Bodhidharma, "Darmu," the mythical historical founder of Chan, appears in China about A.D. 500, allegedly from India, to convey a transmission with "no dependence upon words and letters" through the practice of *dhyāna* meditation (*zazen*).[2] For several years, he sat silently facing a stone wall at Shaolin Temple. When I visited Shaolin Temple, I asked the abbot, an old man, "Where is the wall Bodhidharma sat facing?" Looking straight into my eyes, he replied, "Everywhere." The wall of desires confronts us wherever we turn, wherever we are, whatever we do. So Bodhidharma's transmission urges us to just sit here, free ourselves from external disturbances, from internal disturbances, from any specific particularizations. Allow them to merge into no-pointedness, which is empty of all differentiation, like a blank wall. The teachings of the historical Buddha echo in this transmission Bodhidharma passed along.

Another meaning of freedom is revealed in Bodhidharma's transmission. Beyond the freedom from holding exclusive standpoints, we here encounter the freedom of nondisturbance, exterior or interior, the freedom from all particulars, the vastness of the undifferentiated as a fertile womb from which arise particular existent entities indefinitely through all *kalpas*, or ages. Effortlessly, existence passes into nonexistence, subject into object, and conversely. This passing is symbolized by our breathing in and out in *zazen*, as dualities collapse and form, form and collapse, suddenly or gradually, ever impermanent. Hui-k'e asks Bodhidharma, "My soul is not yet pacified. Pray, master, pacify it." And Bodhidharma answers, "Bring your soul here and I will have it pacified." Hui-k'e goes on, "I have sought it these many years and am still unable to get hold of it!" Darmu comments, "There! It is pacified once for all."[3] When Hui-k'e cannot find it, when it is not, is nothing in particular, just then, it is pacified. Vast emptiness is free of disturbances.

The three meanings of freedom discussed so far pass from freedom from desires, to freedom from all standpoints, to freedom from all particularization (from any disturbance), to realization of vast emptiness. What are the applications of this last form of freedom to conflicts in our world? Ours is an age of increasing tension and stress to individuals, resulting from ever more complicated relationships in families, work, and society. The pace of living becomes frantic in a technologically developing society in which machines, especially computers, seem to drive us. All sorts of counseling, psychiatric and ordinary, are expanding. Personal conflicts break out in every direction. People are disturbed. Freedom from such disturbance, tension, stress, and conflict may be realized in *zazen* meditation. For example, among the decision-makers in schools, universities, businesses, local and national governments, specialized agencies of the United Nations, and conferences concerned with international conflicts, we might hope that quiet, serene, peaceful attitudes from *zazen* could ameliorate uncompromising opposition. Why not try it?

As the Chan School of Buddhism developed in China during the Tang Dynasty, the primary teaching method became the use of *mondo* (stories) and *kung-an* (koan puzzles). The earliest works we possess are collections of these associated with biographical sketches of teachers: Tao-hsuan, *Biographies of the High Priests* (A.D. 645); and Tao Yuan, *Records of the Transmission of the Lamp* (A.D. 1004). These *mondo* and *kung-an* produced enlightenment, that is, insight into a person's original self-nature by various shock treatments in which the student realizes the nature of existing beyond a person's usual division into subject and object. Our ordinary "consciousing" is usually intentional, a consciousness of something separate from the subject. We overcome this duality in two different directions in rare experiences. On the one hand, on rare occasions, we become so involved in what we are doing that we forget our self, forget the passage of time, and feel that we become one with the object. In such experiences, subject collapses into object. On the other hand, we sometimes experience the entire world as a dream, a projection of our mind; the object world collapses into the subject. Another experience of pure subjectivity comes, for example, with sheer happiness, devoid of any object, pure nonintentional consciousing. In the former, we become one with the object, pure objectivity; in the latter, one with the subject, pure subjectivity. These experiences constitute the undivided self. Our freedom is a positive mergence, a release from the usual separation of duality involved in consciousing.

The shock treatment of *kung-an* sometimes proceeds by stating a paradoxical claim like "What is the sound of one hand clapping?" or "Who am I when I am not?" Any effort to give a rational analysis is frustrated; an intellectual solution is impossible. What remains in our consciousing after realizing the impossibility of a rational solution is nonrational experience, which is neither rational (scientific) nor irrational (illogical, inconsistent). Nonrational experience is immediate, spontaneous, neither deductive nor inductive, neither discursive nor classificatory, unitary not polarizing, and nontemporal. The stories and puzzles offer us hints, pointers, springboards, metaphors. We approach the inexpressible but still experiential. Our freedom is the realization of a prerational experience—recognizing "your own being before your parents gave birth to you."[4]

In the arena of international conflicts, this nonrational, nonsubject/nonobject experience gives us a freedom to become one with our opponents, to get inside the other and experience the world as they do. They also can merge into our experience, from which a mutual empathy arises. Or each of us may merge with the object over which conflict exists. For example, an international conflict exists over fishing for whales. A decade of conferences has failed to resolve this issue except to limit the numbers taken. I think that both sides might become one with the whales and understand the potential extermination of this species. Another international conflict concerns nuclear missiles between the former Soviet Union and the United States. Each opponent can become one with the feelings of the other; each can become one with the potential extermination of the human species and the destruction of world environments. For such conflicts, we can realize within consciousness a prerational freedom prior to the dualities, oppositions, and particularizations of rational discourse and thinking. This kind of freedom has had little recognition in the world of international disputes, but I think it holds real promise if national leaders would explore its potential. If the parties at the successive Geneva Conferences on the reduction of nuclear missiles could genuinely practice this prerational consciousness, their experience of mutual empathy might enable them to negotiate in a way that fosters the unitary original self-nature of human persons in all societies. The exclusivity of standpoints based on rational thinking in terms of ever-finer distinctions and polarities has prevented the realization of this kind of freedom.

Another idea of freedom is contained in that development of Zen in Japan associated with Dogen (1200–1250) and the Soto school. Japan also continued to develop the Chinese school of Chan begun by Lin Chi in the Rinzai temples using the koan method. Dogen encouraged his students to "just sit" in *zazen* meditation without using koans or *mondos*, without shock treatment, without private interviews (*sanzen*) with the Roshi concerning a person's koan. Further, Dogen teaches that sitting *zazen* and *satori* (realization, liberation) are one and the same, a startling claim occasionally alluded to in the Chinese Chan tradition, especially in the so-called Northern School of Shen-hsiu (died 706) from which we possess no sutras (a major historical loss), only the remarks in the critical opposition to it from Hui Neng and the Southern School. Besides the identity of *zazen* and *satori*, of meditation and liberation, Dogen's identification implies that degrees of *satori* match degrees of concentration in *zazen*, and that the realization of *satori* comes and goes with the practice of *zazen*. Both these implications are radically different from the Rinzai tradition and hence not fully appreciated in Europe and North America, where D. T. Suzuki's books presented the Rinzai outlook of sudden complete *satori*, pervasive thereafter in a person's life.

What is the concept of freedom in Dogen's approach to Zen? He agrees with the Chinese Chan tradition concerning the prerational or nonrational consciousness of realization. But he goes further and teaches us that we realize our freedom as soon as we "just sit" quietly in *zazen* to whatever degree and whenever we "just sit." But the gradual degree and "whenever" must not be understood as stages in a temporal progression. Dogen's view of time is another crucial aspect of his position. The passages of his *Shobogenzo* concerning time are exceedingly difficult to interpret. When we "just sit," the ordinary past, present, and future divisions of time collapse into an undifferentiated present time; the passage or flow of time stops. Our original self-nature is pure presentness. Our experience of *satori*, of liberation, of freedom, is one of uninterrupted presentness, a quiet serenity, a oneness or mergence with all others who "just sit" and with the Buddha-nature in all things. A person not only "just sits" when in the lotus posture in the *zendo*, but can "just sit" in the course of any daily occupation, mundane or professional. Hence, Dogen denies any separation between *zazen* and the activities of daily living, which seems paradoxical at first. Freedom is just living in present serenity and peace, a concept so simple, yet so profound. Imagine large numbers of human beings in such realization. Conflicts of all sorts might disappear in political, social, personal, and international arenas. It would be a wonder of wonders if it could occur. Dogen teaches that it can.

The Korean tradition of Son Buddhism developed in the thought of Chinul (1158–1210). Chinul achieved a unique synthesis of apparently conflicting schools of Chan by turning these apparent conflicts into complementary approaches. In contemporary quantum physics, we see another example of the effective use of such a principle of complementarity. Chinul never went to China to study and never received certification of transmission from a Chan master. At several Korean monasteries, he studied the sutras of the various schools and had three awakening experiences: first, with study of the *Platform Sutra*; second, meditating on the *Avatamsaka Sutra*; and third, when reading the *Records of Ta-hui* (1089–1163). Meditation and sutra study reinforced each other in his life. Each heightened the power of the other. Meditation on a sutra passage was his favorite combination.

Chinul saw that each of the Chan schools isolates one aspect of training and elevates it to an exclusive position. The Northern school of Shen Hsiu (606–706) teaches gradual cultivation, in which meditation concentrates on slowly polishing the meditator's self-mirror until its brightness is free of all the dust of desires. In opposition is the sudden cultivation of the Niu Tou school of Fa Jung (594–657), in which a dramatic awareness of the utter voidness or emptiness of all dualities, desires, and theories occurs. The Southern school of Hui Neng (638–713), Ma-tsu (709–88), and Lin Chi (died 866), which use the shock treatment of shouts, blows, and *kung-an* (koans), practice the approach of sudden awakening; ordinary reasoning is utterly frustrated in trying to solve a koan, until the self suddenly bursts into an immediate realization. Its opposite is found in the Hua Yen School of Li Tung (635–730), in which a gradual awakening comes from an understanding of the total interpenetration of all things in a single totality.[5] It is possible to arrange the four training alternatives on a square of opposition as follows.

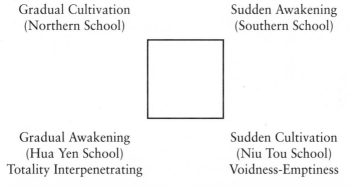

Gradual Cultivation	Sudden Awakening
(Northern School)	(Southern School)

Gradual Awakening	Sudden Cultivation
(Hua Yen School)	(Niu Tou School)
Totality Interpenetrating	Voidness-Emptiness

Chinul's genius consists in seeing how these apparent oppositions can complement each other. The flash of sudden awakening often follows a long period of gradual cultivation in meditation and monastic life, during which a slow incubation takes place while studying sutras, listening to talks on dharma, and performing daily tasks. The click of realization of the utter voidness follows a gradual awakening of the interpenetration of all things into an undifferentiated totality void of all particularity. Gradual cultivation goes hand in hand with gradual awakening, the mirror brightness illuminates the interpenetrating totality. Sudden cultivation, realizing voidness, creates an explosive vacuum that ignites the sudden awakening of "suchness." These complementary opposites provide Chinul with a synthesis that combines meditating and realization, faith and understanding (prajñā), degrees of comprehension and qualitative breakthrough, sutra study and koan study, and slow mergence and complete oneness.

The kind of freedom involved in such a synthesis is the reconciliation of opposites, the unification of disagreements, the creation of novel harmonies. Is it possible that conflicting social and political systems are complementary? That diverse goals related to different human needs can be synthesized? That individual liberties are interdependent with communal necessities? That freedom of belief and action requires sufficient levels of nutrition, health, and education? That organizational efficiency benefits from individual initiative? That personal artistic creation and enjoyment is interdependent on communal, governmental, and foundational support? The Olympic winners who break the finish tape illustrate the complementarity of gradual and sudden: they have trained for years, cultivating every facet of their bodies and minds. The freedom of Chinul's synthetic approach is the best method we have to replace exclusivity by complementarity and thus to overcome the ever-present tendency to divide and polarize. The historical Buddha's diagnosis of the relation of suffering (*duhkha*) to desires, based on dualities, receives a brilliant solution in Chinul's synthetic vision. In conclusion, Chinul's understanding of the Son tradition provides us with a unique opportunity for solving contemporary world problems.

A cluster of ideas of freedom exist in the Chan/Zen/Son tradition. The Four Noble Truths of the historical founder, Siddhārtha, teach us freedom from desires, dualities, and suffering. Nāgārjuna's Four-cornered Negation dialectically frees us from all exclusivist standpoints, yielding a compassion toward all. Bodhidharma's meditative practice paves the way to freedom from all particular disturbances in the undifferentiated vastness beyond all dualities. The technique of koans frees us to merge our separated being into oneness. Dogen's application of nondual experiencing to the practices of Chan/Zen/Son, such as *zazen* and *satori*, unveils a freedom to be at peace in the present eternal, whatever a person is doing. Finally, Chinul offers us ways of synthesizing seeming opposites as complementaries in the continuous conflict of issues and interpretations, arising and passing away on the flux of codependent origination, an ongoing, nonending impermanence of things.

Notes

1. D. T. Suzuki, *Essays in Zen Buddhism*, 1st ser. (Harper & Brothers: New York, 1949), pp. 198–199.
2. *Ibid.*, p. 174.
3. *Ibid.*, p. 188.
4. *Ibid.*, p. 240.
5. Details of my summary are from Hee-Sung Keel, *Chinul: The Founder of the Korean Son Tradition* (Berkeley: University of California, 1984), and Robert Buswell, *The Korean Approach to Zen* (Honolulu: University of Hawaii Press, 1983). I am indebted to both authors.

13.
One Out of Many: The
Way of Creation Toward
a Planetary Community   *Howard L. Parsons*

In his lifetime of global travels, conversations, and research, Nolan
Pliny Jacobson helped to open the way to creative interaction in several decisive domains in our modern world—in Christianity, Marxism, Western civilization and philosophy, science, Far Eastern civilization, and Buddhism. Flying far from the safe and fashionable havens
of analytical philosophy—which conveniently complemented the cold
war mentality of its culture—he went his way freely and courageously
across barriers of nations, cultures, and ideologies, to meet and com-
mune with peoples of varied perspectives. His mission in meeting was
not to accumulate academic mementos. It was a restless personal search
for an objective, worldwide, shared way into a fulfilled life for one
and all. He became awake, alert, and alive to the earthshaking changes
of our atomically explosive times—aware of the swift emergence of a
world of diverse peoples thrust by revolutionary transformations of
science and technology into a world of interdependencies, obligations,
and opportunities for which their isolated histories and locked-in outlooks had not prepared them. He deeply sensed the need of humankind for liberation—the need to find its way out of the stifling hovels
of impoverished personality and the suffocating tenements of past institutions, and into a way of living that would thrive on the fresh air
of a creative world community of open, free, and equal beings without want, walls, weapons (military or psychic), and wars.

The way that Jacobson took, that took him, did not lead to a
utopian place. The way sought turned out to be his own way of going.
His mission was his method of creative interaction. This modern knight
of airline and letters, in quest of the source of spiritual life, found his
Holy Grail in the traveling itself—his joyful travails, his labors of love.
In this essay, I have tried to travel in that way and to explore its relevance for understanding and dealing with some of our major planetary problems.

Out of the wombs of our mothers, out of the womb of the world, we—or more exactly, what are to become our individual bodies—begin to emerge. Each of us commences in a material matrix of many interacting things and processes, at the particular place (a Fallopian tube) where two cells, egg and sperm, have merged with one another. By the fourth day, a spherical blastocyst—a prefiguration of the great globe that awaits—forms, migrating to the wall of the womb, where some days later it burrows in, beds down, and makes itself at home. Still now more a nexus of many than an integrated one, it is by the end of one week a bundle of some 150 cells, nesting in a large One, and through its rootage drawing its nutrients from many elements. The cells divide and redivide, multiply, interact, differentiate, and integrate. They fast become one out of many. By the third and fourth weeks, the basic developmental design of an embryo has been laid down: head, rudimentary eyes, ears, brain, digestive tract, heart, bloodstream, kidneys, liver, and the buds of arms and legs. By eight weeks, the embryo has become a fetus, "recognizably human," with distinct facial features, fingers, and working internal organs. It is already a very complicated one-in-many, a wonder of creation. It is "the person in the womb."[1] Then, in time, if the bio-social-ecological context is favorable, the new creature grows into a mature adult body of sixty million million cells, all delicately and powerfully unified and unceasingly changing in the creative interactions inside the body and in interactions between the body and the many things and events of the environment.

At birth, before full bodily maturity, a new creative process takes up—the creation of the psyche. The newborn, responsive to the particular voice of its mother, begins to interact in new modes to its world, now experienced as tastes, textures, odors, sounds, sights, forms, and relations. In the first days of postnatal life, it mimics the facial and manual gestures of others. Immediately after birth, it cries in distressful response to cries of other infants. So it manifests an innate capacity for empathy, the elemental mucilage that throughout life will connect it to others in cohesive and useful ways. A few months later, the infant responds to the pain of another as if experiencing pain itself, unaware of two centers of experience. At around one year, it begins to distinguish the pain of another from its own. At two and one-half, the distinction between the two becomes clear.[2] In this whole process, the infant develops toward a unity of self by bonding with others. This empathic binding power by which it adheres to others, and selectively gives and takes with them, becomes the method of its subsequent development. Originating in this, rooted in rich emotional thickness, the sprouts of role taking arise, language leafs out, and the social self and mind grow, nourished by creative interaction with other persons and nonhuman nature.[3] This process of interchange generates both the structure and energy of individual personality; it is for the human world what the processes of photosynthesis and respiration are for the plant world.

From birth, and even before, this emergent interactive movement in medias res occurs in the mode of qualities (or feelings)—elaborated as sounds, colors, various other sense data, emotions, moods, and so on—and in the mode of forms—perceptual, geometric, syntactical, logical, and so on. Thus, as the body grows, a new unity of "consciousness" comes into being, the oneness of the psychosomatic person that is created, sustained, and transformed in the modal interactions of the body with the bodies of others, human and natural.

Still deeper and far older than individual bodily and psychic creation out of the abyss of past time, the human species has emerged, the creation of billions of years of the evolution of protoplasm on this planet, and it is still emerging into planetary unity in its interactions with other species and the earth, air, and water of the world. We continue to change this world, as it changes us. Every one, from the hydrogen atom up to the human planetary community in the making, is the gathering and integrating of many into a particular space-time region. This one is then divided, partially or wholly, to feed and sustain the ones around it. This is the rhythm of our existence, this creative interaction. We need to look at its nature, the opportunities and barriers for its advance at this point in our history, and what we must do to create the planetary community to come.

For the many ones to emerge at all, a primordial unity is presupposed as ground for existence, differentiation, and developing integration. We would need to go behind the specific laws of nature to find this. But we do know that six kinds of unity characterize our being in time and hold us in place.

1. Our bodies are integrates of material particles—hydrogen, oxygen, carbon, nitrogen, and traces of a score of other particles of many more in nature. Systematic interchanges and cyclings of materials into and out of our bodies sustain them with substance and energy. They are conglomerations and concentrations of matter and energy at particular places in our planet in our universe. As Einstein might have put it, we are local regions in that universe, warps on the manifold of

space-time, with consequent gravitational fields drawing us to other material bodies in motion in our fields; and chemical interactions—respiration, digestion, elimination—are requisite for the transformation of external materials into needed internal materials and energies.

2. Though species differ in their genetic makeup, a great portion of our genetic heritage is shared with other species, nearly 99 percent of it with the chimpanzees, and much of it with the higher plants. This linkage is lineal. It is the product of our common origin in the first forms of life on our planet and the continuity of evolutionary processes. So when we observe a chimpanzee or an oak tree, we ought not naively and self-righteously assume that we are radically "higher" than they are, with far superior "rights" of occupation and power in this particular sphere of the universe. Everyone with a domestic pet knows how it mutely or otherwise appeals for attention to its existence and how we instinctively respond to its communication.

3. Beyond our genetic similarities with other species, we share with members of our own species certain characteristics: a common human form; a common ground plan for individual development; common needs, powers, and possibilities; common promises and perils; common hopes and fears; and common mortality. Our common biosocial nature is evident in infancy. In the first few weeks of life, all infants express and communicate interest, distress, and disgust; well before the use of language, they show joy, sadness, anger, surprise, and fear.[4] This commonness, established in science, must be emphasized in a day when many seek to separate members of Homo sapiens on the basis of nation, race, class, stratum, ideology, religion, and other pseudospecies.

4. We all share a common environment, both in our evolutionary history and in our present living situation. We share a common home of land, atmosphere, and water, a common habitat and biosphere, a common space-time realm for living, and a common world economy that links us interdependently to one another. This is the one and only planet with biotic community that nurtures all of us in common and whose stewardship is jointly thrust on us.

Yet it is idealistic and misleading to speak of this terrestrial territory as "the commons" of our kind. It is the commons of the world's people as an ecological fact, but not as an economic, social, and political artifact. Nature has created and given it to us, but we have not yet recreated and appropriated it for our universal use. Much of this terrain is possessed and managed by sovereign class-ruled states, multinational and smaller corporations, and wealthy entrepreneurs and consumers. Therefore our task is to bring our economic and political order into harmony with our ecological order. A common world ecology needed equally by all calls for a common world governance, a democratic rule held equally by all.

5. We share a common future with the members of our species and with the five to thirty millions of other species that presently share the planetary environment with us. As our individual lines of ancestry lead back to common human progenitors, common prehuman species, common primeval organisms, and common star-stuff, so our ancestral lines lead forward into the future and will overlap and join in common descendants. Our only future as individuals who briefly come to pass here and pass away is the future of our one and only species in the one and only planetary community of living beings that we know. Being one and only, it carries in its present embodied process our common future.

6. Last, we are all interlocked into the nexus of a planetwide historical and ecological process, into the history of creative nature. We are born into this process, and we live, change, interchange, grow, and die under its categorical necessities, its causal powers, its disorders and destructions, its limitations and opportunities. It is our Life, in the broadest and deepest sense. It is the common creative process of the hundred billion human beings who have gone before us, of the six billion persons now living and dying on the planet at this moment, and of the countless persons who will arrive after us on this spinning and revolving ball, and who will in time—if they survive—explore and populate other celestial bodies.[5]

But today our common life and fate move under a mortal threat. For the first time in the 3.5 billion-year evolutionary history of life on our planet. the survival of living forms is imperiled and could be extinguished. Not only would an exchange of the thousands of nuclear warheads possessed by nation-states, mainly the United States and the former Soviet Union, wipe out all forms of human life on our planet but its vaporizing fireballs and sequel of dust and soot would blanket the earth in a thick shroud, blocking out sunlight and producing the cold and dark of an irreversible "nuclear winter."[6]

At the same time, many processes are driving the masses of humanity together—for better or for worse. The proliferation of lethal weapons—from conventional arms, to poisonous gases, to nuclear missiles and other weapons of mass destruction (chemical, bacterial, geological, laser, and other "modernized" weapons)—is bringing us closer to one another under the menace of state-managed terrorism and mutual assured destruction. The world economy is day by day being wrought and knotted into a wider, tighter network in industry, agriculture, and services; in production, distribution, and consumption; in trade and transport; and in monetary, financial, and fiscal policies. Thus, for example, the United States's external indebtedness of almost $350 billion in 1987—"used largely to finance government and private consumption, rather than productive investment," most of it for military purposes—has destabilized the whole world's financial system and appropriated a large surplus of the world's savings to cover one nation's expenditures.[7]

Worldwide technology, science, and a scientific community are growing and becoming integrated. The community includes the United States, the Federal Republic of Germany, Japan, and other capitalist nations, and the former Soviet Union, other centrally planned economies, and nations with undeveloped economies. Yet the network of scientific and technological cooperation is at the same time becoming a strangling noose. Half a million scientists in the world are working on weapons research, accounting for about one-half of all research and development expenditures—more than all monies spent on developing technologies for new energy sources, improving health, increasing agricultural productivity, and controlling pollution.[8] Biology has achieved the genetic knowledge and power to remove, replace, reorganize, and create genetic material. Will human selection be less costly than natural selection? Every system is limited in its perfection; it exacts a cost for its value. The cost of natural selection's profuse genetic variety and opportunism for survival is "bad genes," defect, and disease. The cost of human engineering, erasing "bad genes" and promoting "good genes," might diminish variety and hence survivability.

A revolution in information and communication—by radio, television, telephone, computer, and other equipment—is taking place, connecting nations and peoples. In 1984, 2.5 billion people, more than one-half of the world's population, viewed the Olympic games on television. Cultures with diverse lifestyles, customs, arts, languages, and worldviews are interpenetrating and changing one another.

The social and political revolutions of the poor and colored peoples of the earth—the one-third of the world's people who live in socialist countries and formerly socialist countries, another one-third in seventy ex-colonial countries—have given rise to new forms of interaction between the underdeveloped and developed nations: economic and ideological antagonism, exploitation, debilitating external indebtedness ($1 trillion), military intervention, violence, and counterviolence, including terrorism, civil strife, and war.[9] The resources of the poor are increasingly insufficient for their needs. To overcome this inadequacy, the resources of energy, food, and productive equipment must be increased, and the growth of population must be checked to match the resources. Unchecked population is one of a syndrome of problems: meager energy supplies, natural materials, and food; poor productive infrastructure; inadequate and contaminated water supplies; lack of health care, literacy, and education; refugees; and migrations. These problems are aggravated under unplanned urbanization that leads to primitive facilities, overcrowding, and disease. They cut across national boundaries and are both cause and result of a wider economic environment in a world unresponsive to the needs of the poor or exploitive of their condition. For example, the arms-producing and arms-exporting nations, mainly the United States and the former Soviet Union, spend $1 trillion each year on arms, much more than enough to feed everyone in the world.

As trucks, trains, ships, and airplanes carry cargo, and as telecommunications carry information, so these worldwide changes have carried with them the leading ideologies of the world, bringing them face-to-face in a serious way for the first time in history. The ideologies of socialist societies, capitalist economies, mixed economies, and nonindustrial nations, the ideologies of fascism, reaction, and neofascism, and the ideologies of the world's religions are stripped of their mystique and abstractions, confronting one another in armed hostility, economic competition, and ideological struggle. The socialist ideology and its variants now rule over more than one-billion people. Capitalist ideology survives in various revised forms in many advanced industrial countries. One-third of the world's six billion people subscribe to the beliefs of various religions—Christianity, Islam, Hinduism, Buddhism, Confucianism, and many others. The philosophical and political claims of these faiths—reactionary, liberal, or progressive—cannot all be true and thus are cognitively incompatible. The practical question is whether they can accommodate themselves to one another and to secular ideologies, finding common ground with them and giving creative interaction the right of way, ahead of their particular articles of faith, to deal with universal human problems.

The forces of the natural environment that bring us together around the globe are perhaps more readily grasped than the other forces. Everyone in the world every day breathes air and needs water and food, so shortage or contamination of these necessities cannot easily go unobserved. Yet our planetary estate is at grave risk. Science, technology, industry, agriculture, urbanization, and military production have profoundly disturbed the ecological context on which human life depends, by physical overloading and chemical toxification of soil, crops, water, and air, rapid extinction of plant and animal species and their ecosystems, deforestation and desertification, and alteration of the earth's climate. Environmental stress and degradation result from ignorance of the consequences of social policies, bad governmental management, and national and corporate competition for control over natural resources and peoples, with little or no concern for ecological conservation and social development. Imperialist nations resort to arms and violence to open and defend markets and investments in vulnerable regions of the world, extensively damaging both human and natural resources.

Environmental stress that results in overcultivation, erosion, and desertification marginalizes and impoverishes people, aggravates injustice, and produces violence. A case in point is apartheid in South Africa, forcing blacks onto the poor "homelands" and then into the overcrowded and segregated townships.[10] Such meshing of environmental degradation, poverty, injustice, and military conflict works massive harm on humanity, other life forms, and the commons where we all live.

This is a question of Life Itself! We are all in this ecological household together. Two hundred years ago, Robert Burns saw this intuitively as he turned up a mouse in her nest with his plow.

> I'm truly sorry man's dominion
> Has broken nature's social union,
> An' justifies that ill opinion
>   Which makes thee startle
> At me, thy poor, earth-born companion,
>   An' fellow mortal![11]

Today, of the 5 (and perhaps 30) million species on our planet (1.7 million are known to scientists), hundreds and perhaps thousands are destroyed every year. The extinguishing of living forms is caused and accompanied by the spreading plunder of the environment that supports them: overintensive agriculture, overfishing, and overgrazing; deforestation; coral reef depletion; pollution of ponds, rivers, lakes, and seas by solid wastes and toxics from industrial, municipal, and private sources; fouling of groundwater by sewage and wastes and poisoning of soil by pesticides and herbicides; contamination of the atmosphere by gases from the burning of fossil fuels in industrial and automotive use; acid rain, resulting mainly from coal-burning power plants, and the consequent killing of trees and forests; the piling up of municipal garbage, industrial wastes, and governmental nuclear reactor products; unprecedented global warming produced by an increase of heat-trapping gases like carbon dioxide and methane; and the thinning of the stratospheric ozone over Antarctica caused by nitrogen oxides (from combustion and fertilizers) and by chlorofluorocarbons used in refrigerators, air conditioners, aerosol sprays, and so on, with consequent increased radiation on the earth's surface, skin cancer, cataracts, immune deficiencies, and damage to crops and aquatic systems. All these problems spell impairment to many life forms on earth. And if they are not corrected, we could lose one-third or more of earth's species and put at risk many others.

What are the plants and animals to us? They are Life! Animals display an awareness that, though not perhaps self-awareness, intimates a domain of being far more sensitive and responsive than an inorganic thing, an awareness that commands respect—if not a respect between equals—from us. Animals have their own forms of being and experience, their own sense of value, their imperative needs, their patterns of sense, feeling, and intelligence, their sign systems, and their interactions and communities. Many also have their own interests and intentions, memories and plans, and methods of problem-solving. Some have a prevision of the future and nurture their young.[12] Even some of the most primitive animals exhibit archetypical appetites—hunger, rest, resistance to gravity, exploration, aversion, attraction, a sense of environment—which we share and with which we can identify. And only our "species solipsism" closes our appreciation to the complex life of plants. When a moving picture of a plant is greatly speeded up, it appears to behave like an animal as it perceives and responds to stimuli. We should open our own consciousness to styles of action and modes of awareness other than our own.[13]

Living forms like ours are participants in the Great Togetherness of nature. Like us, they are creatures and creators in a single system of sentient, receptive, and prehensive beings and of interactive processes—an elaborate network of rhythms, cycles, and mutualities on which we depend for our essentials, such as air, water, and nutrients, and for our essence as concrescent, experiencing beings. We are dependent on them from the bacteria and phytoplankton on—first, on the garden, shelter, and storehouse of plant life, and second, on the pyramid of animal life and food chains that nourish our life and welfare. Such a world was once our Eden. Now, after our forebears lost that paradise by reason of their own folly and

> They hand in hand, with wand'ring steps and slow,
> Through Eden took their solitary way[14]

we have more and more occupied the homes of plants and animals with tools, machines, and hungry populations, and now they greatly depend on us for survival. Our respect, knowledge, and right-relatedness toward them and toward our common system will in the long run contribute to our material and economic interest in better food, medicines, drugs, and raw materials.[15]

Plant and animal species carry in the bodies of their individual members those holy genes and helices of creativity, massed and aligned by the tens of thousands, twisted and wrapped with fantastic design, the memories of thousands of millions of years, some of them templates of reproduction, not replaceable when a unique species goes down into oblivion. From them we might learn volumes about ourselves and the evolution of life on this planet. Our own genome contains perhaps one thousand volumes of one thousand pages each, needing one thousand years to understand. Such reading of the book of nature would not be merely intellectual. It would bring in its train appreciation of this long "ascent from below" and devotion to keep it going and to improve it.

Communion and creative interaction with our world of fellow travelers on our "immense journey" can deepen and vivify our sense of who we are, of the diversity and wealth of the living process, of our identities and differences with others, of our unity and interdependence with them. Such communion merges knowledge with reverence. It magnifies our souls, makes us *magnanimous*, lifts us, in wonder and awe, from a little brief confined life to the Life that is large, liberating, and lasting. Injury to our living environment is an injury to our very selves and to the generations of our species to follow. We ought not to throw away this labor of creative power that has reared and diversified its structures on this globe against all adversities of gravity, dispersal, disorder, heat, cold, entropy, and death itself. We ought to regard with vigilant concern this gift of the ages, this blue and sunlit planet in the boundless darkness of space, this green patrimony of Eden.

What must we do to be saved? Denial, indifference, passive acceptance, safe retreat, the pursuit of immediate pleasure, and over-
powering dominance—toward nature, social organizations, or persons—are unproductive responses to our problems. The logic of safety,
pleasure, and power leads to self-contradiction, because the way to
these goods is the way to the atrophy and death of life. The way of
wisdom, for both thought and practice, is the way of creative interaction with one another and the rest of nature. It is the way things work,
the way they come to be, preserve themselves against wastage and
futility, and become transmuted into new and better beings. Things
also work in other ways, ways of obstruction and destruction. But I
do not here venture to crack the ontological nut wherein good and
evil, kernel and worm, live together.

The world is many ones that though scattered, get together, united
by various glues, into new beings. (There are four kinds of glues in the
physical world, others in the organic and human worlds). These ones
in turn unite with other ones to form still more new ones, or they
divide into many once more. Though destruction comes, the creative
process sometimes plucks the firebrand out of the burning, saves trag-
edy from disaster, and transforms loss into opportunity.

The way is there for those who have eyes to see. The Ionians,
Buddhists, and Taoists saw it. So did Marx and Darwin—for the social and biological sciences, respectively—and so do scientists in our
time, so far as they understand science as a creative process and self-
correcting method.[16] The way runs through the levels of the ladder of
emergent evolution and the lattices of natural and social structures.
From the formation of atoms, molecules, organelles, cells, organisms,
families, social systems, ecosystems, solar systems, and galaxies, the
gathering, cohering, and coworking of two or more individuals to form
a new unit is the way of creation. From a human standpoint, *to gather*
is the key concept. *Gather* comes from the Old English *gegada* (compan-
ion) and is ultimately akin to *good* (suitable). It is good to be gathered
in the company of one or more companions, breaking bread with them.
In medieval Latin, *compania* meant literally the sharing of bread with
another.[17] In sharing the bread of our pantries, we share the fare of
our spiritual cupboards and feed the souls and welfare of one another.

Creative interactions in interpersonal relations, family, workplace,
community, region, and nation are imperative if humanity is to go on
and prosper. At the same time, the big problem is global. Smaller interactions must keep in mind and aim at the health of that global
community, and it in turn must foster the life of its various parts. An

international society is struggling to be born. We must ease the birth process by our understanding and action. Four actions must be carried out.

1. We must join our knowledge of our present peril and promise to commitment to creative interaction in the international world today. Old thinking and habits must go, including individualism, narcissism, relativism, subjectivism, dogmatism, unproductive competition, national chauvinism, arrogance of power, and violence as a means of dealing with differences. In the age of modern empires, which ought to be passing, colonialism, neocolonialism, economic subjection, military adventurism and intervention, cultural imperialism, racism, and religious messianism prevailed. Today they are anarchronistic and insane. During the centuries of nationalism, *parochial* and *provincial* were terms of deprecation. Today, when creative relations between nations are paramount, nationalism (as almighty god) must likewise be discarded as unneeded and dangerous. Idols must be broken—or abandoned.

2. We must respect the existence and value of differences. Differences inhere in the life process. Their suppression, their ruinous strife, and their withdrawal and separation from one another deviate and weaken the main direction of creativity. Human living is thereby made the poorer. Totalitarian regimes, striving blindly to produce one common "order" by exterminating all dissent, end in the desolation of whole continents and the ashes of holocaust.

How can we bring together differences between governments, states, and peoples in such a way that renders them mutually vivifying, enriching, and strengthening? This task requires mutual respect and regard, courtesy and civility, and acknowledgment of the worth of the other as a distinct and autonomous being with the right to decide and determine its own affairs. It means not obtruding personal judgment and actions on the other. The doctrine of peaceful coexistence between states of different social systems summarizes what is needed: respectful recognition of the existence, sovereignty, equality, territorial integrity, independence, and self-determination of the others. Some argue that national states can never enter into such respectful give-and-take with other states because they are charged with the "defense" and "security" of their own territories and peoples. But if that is so, they need a new concept of security, an international, creative, and lifesaving concept.

3. We must acknowledge the equality of nations and states and renounce all forms of domination. As human beings, we are all born

equal and share a common human nature throughout life. Accordingly we all have an equal right to life, the means thereto, and the excellence of quality that comes with a fulfilled life (though a seriously defective newborn would not share in this equality). Correspondingly, groups of persons have an equal right to live and develop in their individual human ways, coupled with the responsibility for acknowledging the equal rights of others to enter into creative interaction with them.

The rule of equality means that we must renounce all forms of centrism. Like the astrophysical universe, the emerging global community has no centers, though many centers have been claimed: the Middle Kingdom of China, Jerusalem, Delphi, Rome, Mecca, Constantinople, Moscow, London of the British empire, Berlin of the Third Reich, and Washington of the Free World. Egocentric perception, thought, and judgment are deeply built into the human psyche. It is powered by unconscious impulse, passion, and striving and is rigidly structured by our static modes of response to the world (in gestalts, syntax, autistic logic) and by the habits, customs, and other coercions of a self-enclosed culture. Egocentricity is further aggravated when desire strikes against the prison walls of social custom, suffering ambiguity and anxiety, and when personality reacts with the protective mechanisms of selfishness.[18] The half-century obsession of the people of the United States with "the threat of communism," "security," and "defense" is explainable not so much by the red devils abroad as by the red-white-and-blue devils possessing the minds of millions at home. The psychic defense of the ego's investment in its self-centered desires and fears has been rationalized by the media and intellectuals, glorified by politicians, and objectively supported by a ruling class's defense of its investments in overseas markets threatened by established socialist states and national liberation movements.

Exorcism does not come easily. How are we to stop clutching, grasping, closing, and defending? The way of openness, of freedom from compulsive desire and domination, is best begun in childhood and nurtured in every relation and institution. It needs personal and social transformation. Not only does our personal health and joy wait on this; today's world does. It calls for new thinking in processes, interactions, interpenetrations, destructuring, and restructuring, and for holistic interchange of equals and of diverse systems of culture, society, language, economy, politics, science, religion, and art.

4. We must develop trust. Self-trust, as an assured expectation that, come what may, living is worthwhile, is the motivating power of

our existence. Because we are so profoundly social, this self-trust is the internalizing of trust received from and returned to others, the ground and roadbed over which the traffic of creative interaction travels. According to Erik Erikson, it is normally laid down early in the "basic trust" between primary care-giver and infant. It is an open outreach to the other in sign and action, a reliance on the constancy of oneself, the other, and the bonding of the two. Trust indicates undefensiveness, nonpossessiveness, and esteem and respect toward the other, and it warrants earnest and self-giving effort to communicate and cooperate with the other.

Diffidence, doubt, suspicion, withdrawal, and hostility oppose trust. They seek justification in real or imagined perceptions, reinforcing distrust. Trust can grow and deepen as it proves its pledge in the concrete evidence of successful cooperative action. The four summit meetings of President Ronald Reagan and Secretary Mikhail Gorbachev that achieved the first treaty between their nations for reducing nuclear arms illustrate the cumulative effects of mutual trust in action. Trust strides forward in the bright company of hope. Distrust shrinks from relations with the other and dwells withdrawn, listening to the dark counsels of despair. But in our world of widening interactions, seclusion is impossible, and its opposite, dominance and submission by armed hostility, is not workable. The only way is creative interaction founded on trust between equals who differ. By definition this must be a way of nonviolence.

Human development, both personal and social, is a moving balance of individualizing and integrating, of pluralizing and unifying processes. Commencing with the revolution of capitalism some five centuries ago, the modern era has been marked by accelerating individuation of personality (from the Renaissance onward), of social groups (as in cities), of cultures and nations (as in national revolutions), of industry and agriculture, of science and technology, and of military instruments and tactics. In this century, the excesses of this trend are becoming anarchic. If we are to survive through the twenty-first century, we must correct the imbalance by concentrating on the unifying processes. In doing so, we can draw instruction from the forces of creative unity already at work in prehuman nature and in the nature of humanity.

Throughout the broad globe, we must, as peoples and states, interact and constructively cooperate in the great vocation to struggle with and rectify the wrongs of our world—to displace armaments by peace, poverty by development, inequality by justice, want of learning by education, and ecological trauma by health.[19] We must take up the task of reaching across all geographical, cultural, and ideological borders to weave together the many-hued strands of persons and nations into a single human texture, strong and beautiful. We must create a human community, open and free in its home in nature, a one made out of many, wherein each one made of many returns the new wealth of its oneness to the other ones in the making. In this way, our world is woven. The way of this weaving is creative interaction.

Notes

1.   This summary is from N. J. Berrill, *The Person in the Womb* (New York: Dodd & Mead, 1968).
2.   Daniel Goleman, "Researchers Trace Empathy's Roots to Infancy," *New York Times*, 28 March 1989, pp. C1, C9.
3.   George Herbert Mead, *Mind, Self, and Society*, ed. Charles Morris (Chicago: University of Chicago Press, 1934).
4.   Robert J. Trotter, "Baby Face," *Psychology Today* 17, no. 8 (August 1983), pp. 14–20.
5.   An intriguing if not convincing case is made in Freeman Dyson, *Disturbing the Universe* (New York: Harper & Row, 1979).
6.   World Commission on Environment and Development, *Our Common Future* (New York: Oxford University Press, 1987), pp. 305–306.
7.   United Nations, Department of International Economic and Social Affairs, *World Economic Survey 1988: Current Trends and Policies in the World Economy* (New York, 1988), p. 69.
8.   *Our Common Future*, p. 298.
9.   Between 1798 and 1970, the U.S. military invaded other countries 165 times; U. S. Congress, Committee on Foreign Affairs, *Background Information on the Use of United States Armed Forces in Foreign Countries*, 91st Cong., 2d sess., 1970. This count does not include the numerous CIA initiatives to alter, undermine, and overthrow governments; see Bill Moyers, *The Secret Government* (Cabin John, Md.: Seven Locks, 1988).
10. *Our Common Future*, pp. 290–292.
11. Robert Burns, "To a Mouse," lines 7–12.
12. Donald R. Griffin, *The Question of Animal Awareness: Evolutionary Continuity of Mental Experience* (New York: Rockefeller University, 1976). Stephen R. L. Clark, *The Nature of the Beast: Are Animals Moral?* (New York: Oxford University Press, 1984).
13. A plant absorbs what it needs at its surface, but "an animal develops, through its mouth, an interior"; E. H. Corner, *The Life of Plants* (Chi-

cago: University of Chicago Press, 1964), p. 1. Animals are thus more energetically self-centered than plants. Social animals have modified this self-centeredness.

14. John Milton, *Paradise Lost*, book 12, lines 648–649.

15. *Our Common Future*, pp. 147–157.

16. Nolan Pliny Jacobson's fertile research explored some of the sources. We should not leave unnoticed his Ph.D. dissertation, "The Religious Naturalism Implicit in the Writings of Karl Marx" (University of Chicago, 1948).

17. Eric Partridge, *Origins: A Short Etymological Dictionary of Modern English* (New York: Greenwich House, 1983), pp. 247, 260, 468.

18. For a subtle exposition, see Nolan Pliny Jacobson, *Buddhism: The Religion of Analysis* (New York: Humanities, 1965; reprint, Carbondale and Edwardsville: Southern Illinois University Press, 1966, 1970). Buddhism's insight into the dynamics of egocentricity is only one of its many contributions to the emerging world civilization.

19. Skeptics in the United States doubt if cooperation is possible with the former Soviet Union. But the principle of international cooperation to solve "all-human" problems, though not forgoing class struggle, was part of the *perestroika* policy begun in 1985. Even earlier, Soviet thinkers argued that Marxism from the first had pursued the ideal of "international community" and "global approaches" in "the presence of co-existing systems of socialism and capitalism"; Ivan Frolov, *Global Problems and the Future of Mankind* (Moscow: Progress, 1982), p. 303. Circumstances in the new Commonwealth of Independent States have not altered the imperative of "constructive and creative interaction between states and peoples on the scale of the entire world"; quote from Mikhail Gorbachev, *Political Report of the CPSU Central Committee to the 27th Congress of the Communist Party of the Soviet Union* (Moscow: Novosti Press, 1986), p. 24.

Part Four
The Japan Emphasis

14.
Zen and the Art of Anything   *Hal W. French*

The phrases "Zen and" or "Zen in" are common prefixes to a variety of titles. Some of these are attached to philosophical or psychological studies (such as Masao Abe's *Zen and Western Thought*, Van Meter Ames's *Zen and American Thought*, Erich Fromm's *Zen and Psychoanalysis*, and D. T. Suzuki's *Zen Buddhism and Psychoanalysis*). Zen postulates may be correlated with those of a variety of intellectual positions in the West and in the East. Zen thought is portable, in spite of the partial disclaimer implicit in Abe's initial chapter, "Zen is Not a Philosophy, But...." Zen attitudes are also portable, and at a much more practical level, again in the tacit claims of a host of titles (Robert Pirsig's *Zen and the Art of Motorcycle Maintenance*, Eugen Herrigel's *Zen in the Art of Archery*, Joe Hyam's *Zen in the Martial Arts*, Trevor Leggett's *Zen and the Ways*, Toshimitsu Hatsumi's *Zen and Japanese Art*, and so on). This essay will focus on some common Zen assumptions and on their capacity to render a variety of other pursuits into art forms—"Zen and the Art of Anything."

Prior to a consideration of Zen's capacity to enhance artistic expression and appreciation, we need to explore Zen's contribution to *Nihon-do*, the Japan Way, or perhaps, the art of being Japanese. In that setting, where it has been indigenized most fully, how has it made its impress? In a nation whose aesthetic sensibilities have been refined peculiarly in a host of artistic disciplines, what has Zen contributed? Perhaps the access question that must be entertained first is, What is the nature of these disciplines, and how do they embody collectively *Nihon-do*, or the art of being Japanese?

Nolan Pliny Jacobson has helped us here, in his paper "Japan's Rites of Passage."[1] He is careful to explain how these are different from rites of passage in most cultures, being considered more properly as particularly intense life disciplines, identifiable as "*do*-patterns." *Do*, derived from *Tao*, or way, is abundantly evidenced, as in "the way of tea (*chado*), the way of soft combat (judo), the way of calligraphy (*shodo*), the way of the dramatic arts (Kabuki, Noh, or Bunraku), the way of the samurai (*bushido*), the way of painting (*gado*), the way of flower arranging (*kado* or *ikebana*), the way of fencing (kendo), the way of archery (*kyudo*)."[2] Many other skills, such as landscape gardening, ceramics, and weaving, might be added to this list. Once, in a home near Hiroshima, I witnessed many specimens of the art of rock carving and polishing that added beautifully to the decor. In all these practices, we see, more than the production of specific attractive objects, a deep expression of innate creativity and spontaneity. They appear to grow with integrity out of the highest refinement of the artisan's human spirit. Such persons may be designated national treasures, not only to be accorded near-veneration, but to inspire and instruct others who have more novice status on a particular path.

General forms may be taught, but a limit exists to formal instruction. Art must flow naturally from the cultivation of the artist's own humanness. An innate freedom exists here that may be expressed in a combination of two borrowed words, *jiju* and *jizai*, originally derived from Buddhism. The combined word is *jiyujizai*, which means to act freely, in absolute naturalness. One of the traits of a bodhisattva is *jiyujizai*, or perfect freedom.[3]

Though the concept is of Buddhist origin, the specifically Zen strategy of the koan may be seen as contributing to its cultivation. Typically, in traditional usage, the koan seems designed to frustrate the aspirant. After failing in successive attempts to solve the riddle by finding a logical explanation, the novice will go through a period called "The Great Doubt." In this posture, she/he may simply give up on her/his capacity to arrive at a solution by rational means, and she/he enters the presence of the master totally unarmed, with no rehearsed answer, no preplanned strategies. She/he is a blank slate, with no conclusions to defend, and in this condition, she/he may be most free to act naturally. Whatever stimulus is given her/him by the master, her/his immediate spontaneous response flows with it.

Is spontaneity what Zen offers? We somehow shuck off the carefully developed control mechanisms that have been our educational legacy and return to the guilessness of a child. We trust ourselves to be ourselves, living radically and openly in the present. Offer any group the simplest possible test: ask them if they want to take a test to check their level of spontaneity, ask them if they are ready, then say, "All right, everybody, do something spontaneous." A few moments of social paralysis almost invariably sets in, broken by one or two persons who, fairly soon, will do something, such as throwing a pencil or lightly hitting a neighbor. Then you ask even these persons to retrace the steps of their consciousness. Any act, even if it follows almost immediately from the instruction, will be preceded, by smiling collective as-

sent, with the internal question, "What am I going to do that's spontaneous?" And we realize that we have blown it. We have to get our
own permission to be ourselves. The strategy of the koan is only one
Zen device designed to short-circuit our control mechanisms and allow the natural self to emerge. In D. T. Suzuki's words, "Zen always
aims at grasping the central facts of life, which can never be brought
to the dissecting table of the intellect."[4] Or as Jacobson states in his
final volume, "The 'Japan Way' is to avoid the separation of language
from life and to keep from suffocating the vividness and rhythm of
experience in a flow of words."[5]

A specific koan, or conundrum, may serve as a skeletal frame to
explore the characteristics of the Japan Way. It was suggested to me a
few years ago in a visit to one of my classes by a friend, Richard Walker,
now returned to the University of South Carolina from his post as
U.S. ambassador to Korea. Professor Walker suggests that three qualities have characterized Japan in unusual measure. These qualities are
variations on a five-letter word, with the middle letter initially blank,
forming the koan or conundrum. The word is *ad_pt*. Fill the blank for
the first quality with the letter *o*, rendering the word *adopt*.

Someone has observed that the Japanese are perhaps the world's
greatest borrowers. They have had great facility in acquiring products, customs, and skills from other countries. Much of their culture
in their earliest historical stages was transmitted from China, including a written language, Confucian, Taoist, and Buddhist values and
forms, and so on. The quality persists, strikingly, since Perry's black
ships triggered the Meiji Revolution. Once open, Japan's doors and
windows to the world became amazingly wide. It is estimated that five
million Japanese will travel abroad this year. It is anyone's guess how
many camera clicks will be performed by those five million persons,
but I suggest that many of the recorded impressions will not be simply
those of the casual tourist. The high level of curiosity of the Japanese
is rather exceptional, and this quality is, I think, also part of the legacy
of Buddhism.

Enlightenment does not have to be thought of in ultimate, cosmic
terms. It may refer simply, as in Gautama's usage, to those who wake
up. This propensity resides not just in the Buddha, who would not
have liked the exclusive reference, but in all persons, each of whom
possesses the capacity to wake up. Buddhism, and Zen in particular,
uses some shock strategies to get us to become awake, alert, aware,
alive. The discipline of *zazen*, or "just sitting," in addition to that of
the koan, is designed to promote this facility. It is a secular, worldly,

and temporal facility. It stimulates us to be in touch with what is there, to be curious and wide-eyed. And it has not been lost on the Japanese. The Japanese Christian Toyohiko Kagawa prayed, "May I never find myself yawning at life."[6] It is a very Japanese prayer. The cardinal sin here, if the language of sin is used, is to be bored. The Japanese seem to have this quality of aliveness, the willingness to see what is there and to appropriate it without threat.

The Buddhist teaching that applies here is the doctrine of *śūnyatā*, or Emptiness. Śūnyatā is defined by Lama Anagarika Govinda as "a state of spontaneous receptivity…freedom from impediments and limitations."[7] This quality in Japan seems to have enabled them to be flexible, to be open to receive and accept a range of imported customs and teachings. This positive quality of *śūnyatā* seems to have facilitated the Japanese capacity to adopt, to be able to borrow and learn from a wide variety of sources. Emptiness means openness, a willingness to absorb from strange systems, to drink from alien wells. The Japanese word *torukumu* (to take over) perhaps expresses it, as a capacity for spiritual ingestion. Japan does not fear contamination from infidels and unbelievers as much as cultures whose religions possess a tight set of unnegotiable postulates. Emptiness implies an invitation to be filled, a welcome to what is offered by a myriad of potential hosts.

The second quality that characterizes Japan is typified in the word *adapt*. The borrowed object or trait is adapted to the Japanese setting, blended with other elements to blunt the edge of potential alienness. It is soon felt to be as fully Japanese as any other cultural expression. But this also means selectivity. Some things are too alien to be adapted and have a hard time making it in Japan. The Japanese would take over only what did not disturb, but might enhance, what was already there. Kuwabara Takeo illustrates in what may seem a surprising fashion. When asked what single factor in the Japanese temperament enabled so rapid an advance after the Meiji Revolution (the term *revolution* seems more apt to me than the more customary term, *restoration*), he answered:

> In my view, perhaps the single most important factor is the absence of "God." Over all Japan's myriad gods and deities, there is no single Allah or Jehovah, no monopolistic god that devours all the others.…For Japanese, one all knowing god would be constricting. The Japanese would begin to repress his eagerness…(for new things, new departures) as he would hear such a god asking, "Do you think that it is right to

discard tradition?" In Japan, no such voice is ever heard. None of Japan's thousands of gods has too much power. An old maxim goes, "If one god throws you out, another god will pick you up."[8]

This may sound like theological frivolity to the Westerner, but it reflects a naturalistic acceptance of the human condition, uncontaminated by any inhibiting teaching, such as that of original sin. Witness the phenomenon of the *dosojin,* or wayside gods. These gods are found extensively in rural areas, and their appearance reflects peasant values. They are humble, humorous, and often visibly interested in procreation. They are commonly found at intersections, pointing the way. And the way is *Nihon-do,* the Japan Way, as indicated by these secular deities, who reflect the worldly and temporal values of the Japanese people. The emperor himself, despite a special veneration, is of the same quality and kind of the people, and the American Occupation Forces seem to have facilitated this self-image of the late emperor, when he made his declaration of humility in 1945. The Japanese people could identify with him still more, as he was integrated into their worldview, mirroring it, not standing apart.

Conrad Hyers has a story in his book *Zen and the Comic Spirit* that illustrates this insight. It tells of a visit paid to a famous Zen master, Keichu, by the governor of Kyoto. The governor handed his card to the gatekeeper, who presented it to the Zen master, with the request for an audience. The master looked at the card and responded, impatiently, "Who is this fellow, Kitagaki, governor of Kyoto? I have no time for him." The gatekeeper returned, handing the card back with the word of rejection. The governor pondered a moment, then scratched out the title on the card, asking the gatekeeper to return it once more to the master. This time Keichu, looking at the card bearing simply the man's name, said, "Oh, is that Kitagaki! I wish to see him!"[9] The Zen teachings are those of democratization, leveling, and blending. In the words of Frederick Franck, "Among the ten thousand things, there is no ordinary thing....Zen raises the ordinariness of the ten thousand things to sacredness and it debunks much that we consider sacrosanct as being ordinary." And again, "A dandelion is in no way inferior to an orchid."[10]

In preparations for his book, *The Lotus and the Robot,* I think that Arthur Koestler must have missed, among other things, seeing the almost life-sized painting by Shohaku of three friends crossing a bridge. The old story on which it is based is that of a Zen abbot who vowed that he would never again cross the bridge that led from his monastery to the outside world. One day two friends came to visit him. They had enjoyed pleasant and happy conversation, and as it came time for them to leave, he walked with them a little, as a good host. They were talking so fast and so merrily that before they knew it, all of them had crossed the bridge. One of his friends suddenly noticed and said to the abbot, "Hey, you just broke your vow!" The painting conveys the resultant scene, with the abbot so convulsed in laughter, which immediately became contagious, that the three friends had to hold on to each other to keep from falling off the bridge.[11] If a vow, taken seriously, leads the person making the vow to take himself/herself too seriously, then the inadvertent breaking of it might lead to a kind of satori, or breakthrough moment.

Koestler saw only the robot in the Japanese psyche, and any visitor to Japan initially may be struck by much that appears stylized and uniform. But beneath the formalized structures is a great capacity for personal freedom. Nothing quite conveyed that spirit to me so much as a story related to me by Nolan Pliny Jacobson several years ago. He was scheduled to speak to a rather large group of Japanese scholars and was being introduced by Hajime Nakamura. Nakamura made a few prefatory observations about the Japanese and about religion in the Japanese setting, and one of them in particular hit the mark. "We Japanese," he said, "do not believe in religion; we *enjoy* it!" Jacobson related how the whole company validated this observation with spontaneous and extended laughter. Christianity, with its exclusive claims, has seemed to make little headway in Japan. It is hard for the Japanese to enjoy a god who appears to have so little feeling for the other less jealous gods with whom they are often on intimate terms. The Japanese spiritual hunger appears to be satisfied by what they call *chu-tohanpa* (a bit of this, a bit of that). It is what scholars call a multilayered face, and it often appears, like love in the popular Japanese setting, a "many-splendored thing."

Perhaps this is a clue to the phenomenon of *Nihon-do*, the art of being Japanese. It is life-validating, humanistic, not based on volitional assent to a doctrine. Possible, then, is the experience of truth, which is full of meaning precisely because it is empty of dogma. This experience is again an aspect of *śūnyatā*, the absence of a core of intellectual postulates that are necessarily acknowledged so that one may belong to the salvation community. Takeo Doi has suggested, "I believe in fact, that the so-called 'way of the gods'...seems consistently to have extolled the principle of no-principle and the value of no-value." Doi cites Maruyama Masao's observation that Japan lacks, in his term, "an axis of coordinates."[12] But if the Japanese people seem not to have a tightly ordered set of principles out of which one acts, it is perhaps because, according to Motoori Norinaga, the way of the gods may best be served by doing what seems best at any given moment.[13] Nolan Pliny Jacobson's phrase refers to "our holiest contact with life, the fleeting instants themselves."[14]

The lack of structural barriers and the sensitivity to imperatives generated by immediate opportunities seem to be qualities that enable the Japanese to adapt borrowed factors to what was already there. Zen's rather amorphous character reflects this adaptive quality. Thomas Merton asserts, "We find very serious and responsible practitioners of Zen first denying that it is a religion, then denying that it is a sect or school, and finally denying that it is confined to Buddhism and its 'structure.'"[15] This conclusion may make it difficult to establish Zen influence, or it may indicate that Zen's absence of institutional walls is congruent with what we find generally in the Japanese spirit, allowing it to blend borrowed elements, indigenize them, and stamp them with a characteristic Japanese spirit.

By now the reader will have anticipated the third variation on the initial conundrum: *adept*. The Japanese have the capacity to adopt quite freely, they can adapt what is borrowed, and they often prove to be more adept at the practice borrowed. We have seen it with technology "Made in Japan." Some of us can recall what that label meant a few decades ago—a cheap gadget or trinket. What changes we have witnessed in the sense of that phrase! Now it signifies highly sophisticated electronic equipment, superior automotive products, and state of the art cameras, computers, and so on. And the transition is being made quite rapidly to more concentration on what is termed the "clean" or high-tech industries. Japan's target for its computer and electronics sectors is to triple their output by the end of the decade; automotive and other industries regarded as less sophisticated are bound to decrease.

Japan's modern miracle is highlighted when we compare it with Brazil, a country of roughly the same size population, 120 million persons. On paper, Japan has all the disadvantages. It is an island with few natural resources, compared to Brazil's thousands of square miles of arable land and almost limitless mineral deposits. Yet in 1982, Japan accounted for 10 percent of the gross global product; Brazil accounted for less than 1 percent. How do we interpret this disparity?

Any visitor to Japan will be struck by the incredibly high energy level of the Japanese people. I can illustrate, anecdotally, with reference to my host in a 1978 visit to Hiroshima. He was the late Reverend Kiyoshi Tanimoto, a conspicuous A-bomb survivor featured in John Hersey's book *Hiroshima*. One day we were discussing after-effects of the bomb, such as blood diseases, which have appeared years after the blast itself. He mentioned that another is a kind of pervasive fatigue, to which his wife, who was closer to the blast center, was somewhat subject. I had observed him, in his pulpit and other activities, as something of a dynamo, however, and commented, "This doesn't seem to have affected you!" "Oh, no," he responded. "With me, atomic energy!" Despite the so obvious tragedies of Hiroshima and Nagasaki, Japan's amazing postwar resurgence exhibits many striking evidences of this atomic energy. Predictably, any nation engaged in trade or other encounters with Japan is going to be challenged by this energy. It will create both opportunities and tensions.

The United States may claim to have contributed enormously to Japan's economic recovery following World War II by picking up most of their defense tab, enabling them to devote their energies to other pursuits. But other comparative factors also may be cited. Studies have indicated the amazing statistic that the Japanese have, per capita, ten times more engineers than we do, and that we have, per capita, ten times more lawyers. The United States is a litigious society, with incredible snarls that tie up resources. Japanese society, by contrast, seems more cooperative, less internally conflictual, among different segments of the economy. The miracle is that Japan shifted from a tight, vertical hierarchy, at the beginning of the Meiji period to what the Latin philosopher Seneca once called "a concord of classes." Internally, an incredible sharing of research findings exists. Joint research patterns, across disciplinary lines, challenge the rigidities that often characterize our universities and research facilities. The cooperative ties extend to the institution of the *kairetsu*, a model of almost familial ties between large industries and banks, insuring the mutual advantage of each. Again, much of this may be part of the fallout of the total Japanese religious climate, with its low levels of dogmatism and exclusivism. These qualities, plus Japan's naturalistic spirit, may mean far fewer blocks to scientific inquiry and progress than in many other cultures.

To return to Arthur Koestler's caricature of Japan as robot, I wonder what he would do with a recent article on the Japanese robotics industry. The article, by William Boulton, notes that Japan did not enter robotics until 1968, but that, with potential uses for robots increasing rapidly through microprocessing techniques, 65 percent of the robots being used in the world are now employed in Japan. This use has expanded from initial placement in harsh and dangerous environments, such as spot and arc welding on production lines. Other simply routine jobs are now being filled by robots.[16] I submit that only the free mind can create robots; and it does so to free itself more fully. Koestler's caricature fits the Japanese product, not its psyche. The discipline, the organization, may look robotic. But, given submission to discipline, the psyche is freed, beyond the agreed-on spheres, to experience high levels of creativity. Once more, the Japanese have proven to be adept.

Boulton elaborates on the high number of engineers in the Japanese work force, noting that some 20 percent of that force is composed of engineers in a typical company that competes internationally. Almost all these people are applied engineers, not theoretical ones. Most technology is imported (the adoptive capacity again, which has not wasted time in many false starts), then perfected there. In the United States, an increasing number of our best engineers also go into Star Wars and other weapons research, with little of their work reaching consumer product areas attended to by Japan.[17]

All these skills may be elevated, as with the accompanying marketing techniques, to the level of art forms. The classical *do*-patterns discussed earlier may be expanded here. The place where kendo was practiced in ancient times was called the place of enlightenment. Perhaps that same spirit is found today in the workplace or marketplace, not in kendo, tae kwon do, or any of the traditional forms, but in a new form that we may christen *techni-do*. The Greek word *technē* means "art, skill, or craft." In its least technical use, it refers to an art. In Japan, it is characterized by the serious attempt to produce the best products available and to develop the aggressive marketing techniques to insure their distribution. It may, by its intensity, appear as a martial art, but it is an art. Following E. F. Schumacher, in an article titled "Buddhist Economics," the work that we do may be considered an art if (1) it challenges our need for creativity, (2) it helps us to overcome ego-centeredness by joining with other people in a common task, and (3) it brings forth goods and services needed for a becoming, humane existence.[18] We may measure the artistic qualities of our technological forms, East or West, by such criteria.

In Japan, the practical character of art may be illustrated with the observation by some that while the prestige of most contemporary painting and sculpture is low, designers and architects enjoy great celebrity. I am not sure of the first part of that observation, but the second part seems abundantly apparent. Art, pragmatically applied, is no less art. It does not have to be in classic form. It can lie in motorcycle maintenance, where Robert Pirsig's insight is that Zen helps us not to escape from "it all" but to get into "it all," "it all" meaning the conditions of life in technological society, East or West. We should not be intimidated by the rule of the experts, but should dive into the intricacies of the technocracy and explore its innovations as we would a treasure or scavenger hunt, with a sense of startle and wonder. Theodore Roszak speaks of our world as "purged of its sacramental capacities."[19] These can be restored. In Jacobson's memorable phrase, we may "catch the ceaseless flow of quality in the passing moment."[20]

To understand the challenge of this, consider the digital watch, a very Buddhist instrument. It has no sense of history, no past or future. All it offers you as the wearer is the moment. And it may offer you the implicit challenge to see how much quality you can invest in that fleeting moment. Life's artistry cultivates this gift of being immediately present, of pouring yourself fully and intensely into the creative possibilities that are resident now, in this instant, wherever you are. Quality is there, and you meet it in the highest artistry of your spirit.

This artistry might transfer, culturally, into a new pride of workmanship. It might help us to recover "an economy of cherished things," as opposed to mindless seasonal restyling, engineered by "pollution of taste by the mass media."[21] We need to distinguish between goods that enhance life and those that merely clutter closets. We may be challenged to value genuine creativity, especially in those goods and services we produce ourselves locally and give personally.

Van Meter Ames has explored in depth the affinity of the thought of the American philosopher George Herbert Mead to Zen. A particularly lucid passage illustrates how life's dualisms may be transcended and art may emerge: "What is needed is to heal and forget, with Mead, any split between wisdom and technology, the aesthetic and effective, the college and the garage, the man in the street and the man on the Way. Making rope, fishing for shrimps, cutting bamboo, planting pines, tilling the soil, reading, meditating, gazing at the moon, talking, laughing—life itself is the stuff of Zen, with the effort to see and say what it is."[22]

I submit, then, that Richard Walker's conundrum is reversible and may characterize something of our encounter with Japan and with Zen. Perhaps, more than Sony, Nissan, Honda, Seiko, Toyota, and so on, Zen may prove to be Japan's most exportable product. It is not segregated, bound by its Japanese setting; it may be adopted by persons of other cultures. It is adaptable; it blends. Its way of meditation can incorporate new departures. And finally, the resultant qualities that it may foster, those of creativity, spontaneity, and naturalness, may enhance a variety of life pursuits, transform them into art forms, and make us more adept at whatever we do. Marian Mountain was tempted at one point to call her book *Zen and the Art of Failure*, instead of its final title *The Zen Environment*, because she recognized what we may learn from our failures—indeed, from failure as an art form. She also proposes a response to a familiar koan, "What is Zen?" "Zen," she suggests, "is a plumber's helper."[23]

Notes

1. This lecture was given at the University of South Carolina on 9 March 1983. To my knowledge, it is unpublished, but it is contained in part in the chapter "Japan Through the Looking Glass," in Nolan Pliny Jacobson, *Understanding Buddhism* (Carbondale and Edwardsville: Southern Illinois University Press, 1986).

2. Ibid.

3. Ibid.

4. D. T. Suzuki, *Introduction to Zen Buddhism* (New York: Grove, 1963), p. 51.

5. Nolan Pliny Jacobson, *The Heart of Buddhist Philosophy* (Carbondale and Edwardsville: Southern Illinois University Press, 1988), p. 118.

6. Lecture by Toyohiko Kagawa, York, Nebraska, November 1951.

7. Lama Anagarika Govinda, *Creative Meditation and Multi-Dimensional Consciousness* (Wheaton, Ill.: Theosophical Publishing House, 1976), p. 10.

8. Kuwabara Takeo, *Japan and Western Civilization: Essays on Comparative Culture* (Tokyo: University of Tokyo Press, 1983), p. 82.

9. M. Conrad Hyers, *Zen and the Comic Spirit* (Philadelphia: Westminster Press, 1973), p. 120.

10. Frederick Franck, *The Zen of Seeing* (New York: Vintage, 1973), pp. 6, 112, 124.

11. Stewart W. Holmes and Chimyo Horioka, *Zen Art for Meditation* (Tokyo: Charles E. Tuttle, 1973), p. 99.

12. Takeo Doi, *The Anatomy of Dependence* (New York: Kodansha International/U.S.A., 1981), p. 78.

13. Ibid., p. 79.

14. Nolan Pliny Jacobson, *Buddhism and the Contemporary World: Change and Self-Correction* (Carbondale and Edwardsville: Southern Illinois University Press, 1983), p. 113.

15. Thomas Merton, *Zen and the Birds of Appetite* (New York: New Directions, 1968), p. 3.

16. William R. Boulton, "The Competitive Edge: The Japanese Robotics Industry," *The Graduate Business Alumnus* (Athens: University of Georgia, Winter 1987), p. 3.

17. Ibid., p. 2.

18. E. F. Schumacher, "Buddhist Economics," in *Sources*, ed. Theodore Roszak (New York: Harper & Row, 1972), p. 262.

19. Theodore Roszak, *Where the Wasteland Ends* (New York: Doubleday, 1972), p. 127.

20. Jacobson, *Buddhism and the Contemporary World*, p. 11.

21. Murray Bookchin, "A Technology for Life," in Roszak, op. cit., p. 253.

22. Van Meter Ames, *Zen and American Thought* (Honolulu: University of Hawaii Press, 1962), p. 279.

23. Marian Mountain, *The Zen Environment* (New York: Bantam, 1983), pp. xvii, 58.

15.
Aesthetics of Nirvāna: Nolan Pliny Jacobson on Creative Process

Morgan Gibson

According to Nolan Pliny Jacobson, Buddhism is a religion and philosophy of immanent creation, rather than of annihilation, as Schopenhauer, Rhys-Davids, and others taught. In his life and books, Jacobson practiced what he preached, freshly illuminating the teachings of Shākyamuni and his interpreters. Jacobson's original insights reshaped the massive scholarship preceding his own. Such insights, arising from Buddhist practice and from philosophical inquiry, come to us explicitly from his words and also from between the lines, in the white silence of the pages. He was at his best in comparing Buddhism to Western philosophy, especially to the other two major process-philosophies: Heraclitus's, and the modern process-thought of Peirce, James, Bergson, Dewey, Whitehead, Hartshorne, and others.

One of Jacobson's fundamental theses is that enlightenment is an aesthetic experience, but his explanation is enigmatically scattered through his books. In *Buddhism: The Religion of Analysis*, he relies on F. S. C. Northrop for the idea that Asian culture, valuing feeling more than abstract theory, has been basically aesthetic,[1] and also for the idea that nirvāna (*nibbāna* in Pali) is the "indeterminate aesthetic continuum...in man's nature and in the nature of all things," which is "undifferentiated" and which "pacifies men, giving them a compassionate fellow-feeling not merely for other men but for all nature's creatures."[2] "Man" and "fellow-feeling" do not exclude women.

Nirvāna is indeterminate because it is not caused. Nor can it be known objectively. Anything said about it (including the above) is merely suggestive of an ineffable experience. What is the aesthetic continuum? Jacobson calls it the "life continuum," "Stream of Being," and "process,"[3] the universal creative process that is immanent, incessant, and undifferentiated, until it is falsely divided by mental categories. Northrop and Jacobson were strongly influenced by Whitehead, who discovered "the foundations of the world in the aesthetic experience."[4] But Jacobson does not clarify in what senses he is using the term aesthetic. Is he referring to feeling in general (the vast spectrum of pains and pleasures)? Sensing? Contemplating? Imagining? Beauty? Form? Creative consciousness and sensibility? Artistry? The fundamental art of existing? Is the aesthetic continuum the creative process itself? Instead of exploring and clarifying these implications, Jacobson repeats Northrop's phrases without explication.

Jacobson does not focus on the aesthetics of nirvāna in "The Consummatory Experience," the chapter in which he evaluates various interpretations of nirvāna, ranging from positive assertions through skepticism to denial that it is anything but total annihilation.[5] He concludes that in the ultimate and permanent purity, peace, happiness, and deathlessness of nirvāna, "man returns to his organic unity with the totality of events and processes...with an intuitive compassion for all of life. This is what the Buddha meant by Nirvāna."[6]

How does Jacobson know? If he is deriving his conclusions from the sutras, as he seems to, he must assume that they accurately record Shākyamuni's experience. But how would this reliance on authority square with the Humean skepticism that Jacobson advocates elsewhere?[7] If Jacobson bases his conclusion on direct experience of nirvāna, how can he be sure that his experience was the same as Shākyamuni's? Moreover, if nirvāna is ineffable, any statements about it must be misleadingly reductive. Even statements attributed to Shākyamuni in the sutras must be read as intimations rather than propositions. Untroubled by the hermaneutical circle, Jacobson makes statements about nirvāna that may communicate something to readers who feel that they have had similar experiences, which they may then characterize as nirvanic. Moreover, those who do not dwell in nirvāna may acknowledge its aesthetic value as a fundamental dimension of existing, concealed and confusing though it may be. Such people may become more aware of creative process. Thus, Buddhism may enlarge the vision of people who do not deliberately practice the Way.

In *Buddhism: The Religion of Analysis*, Jacobson shows quite vividly that the interpersonal creative process generates the fiction of the self, an image or concept that refers only to streams of experience, but to which we cling for fear of being nothing.[8] Clinging to a self inhibits and represses the natural process, blinds us, and restricts compassion. Detachment from the self, a recognition that it is an illusion that comes and goes, frees us from frustrations born of egotism. Jacobson objects to the nihilistic interpretation "that Buddhism wishes to weaken and destroy human personality or to kill indiscriminately all desires, and that it would induce people to abandon the world of suffering instead of teaching them to abandon the suffering of the world."[9] Many poets, novelists, playwrights, actors, and literary critics have arrived at the notion of a fictional self or persona, independently of Buddhism. But most of these people, fearing their own non-existence and lacking the subtlety of the Buddhist view, compensate by striving to create an immortal public identity through their art. "Fame is the spur," John Milton wrote.[10]

Whatever we create, the self and its apparent products, seduces our attention from the creative process itself, and we cling to results instead of being open to perpetual renewal. In one of Jacobson's most profoundly quotable passages, we learn that "every time man dreams of new perspectives and outlets for his creative energies, the dreams become the master, especially if he manages to make them real. Thus the perfectly normal man, living out the unfolding of his powers, is taken captive by his inventions, whether thought or thing, idea or institution, product or pattern, simply because he is an uneasy, driven animal."[11] Only by living without being compelled by forces that are usually unconscious, can we become enlightened. According to Jacobson, the path is meditation, specifically *Satipatthana*.[12]

Jacobson's claim that in attaining nirvāna, "Language plays no role whatsoever,"[13] is debatable. Nirvana is ineffable and not guaranteed by means of any technique, but language plays a role in meditation as he describes it, for example, in reciting, "Calming the activity of the body, I shall breathe out." More generally, language is a skillful means for communicating compassionate insight and wisdom, as in the sutras and other Buddhist discourses, both written and oral—not by defining or explaining doctrines as absolute truths about objective reality, but by eliciting "creative interchange" with readers or listeners, to use Henry Nelson Wieman's term. Some of Shākyamuni's disciples seem to have been enlightened by his direct speech, perfectly appropriate to their suffering. Others through the centuries claimed to have been enlightened by sutras, mantras, and poetry, such as the following "Singing Image" by Kukai (Kobo Daishi), the founder of Japanese Shingon (Tantric) Buddhism.

Singing Image of a Whirling Ring of Fire

Whirling fire becomes a square and a circle as the hand moves.
Many changes are made according to our will.
One eternal word, "Ah!" turns into many others
Expressing innumerable Buddha-truths.[14]

In *Buddhism: The Religion of Analysis*, based largely on Theravāda teachings from Burma, Jacobson has no concern for the Mahāyāna tradition beyond a perfunctory rejection of Zen.[15] But Jacobson turned his attention to Mahāyāna in *Nihon-do: The Japan Way* and emphasized it in *Buddhism and the Contemporary World: Change and Self-Correction*, where he discussed the bodhisattva, the Madhyamaka philosophy of Nāgārjuna, the Pure Land or Western Paradise,[16] the Sixth Patriarch of Zen,[17] and the *Avatamsaka* image of the Jewel Net of Indra, in which each jewel reflects all the other jewels, all possible experiences and Buddha-lands.[18]

Throughout *Buddhism and the Contemporary World*, Jacobson emphasized aesthetic sensibility as essential to happiness in the profoundest sense of enlightenment. As Northrop put it, "The real world is the aesthetically breath-taking colorful world."[19] In his concluding chapter, Jacobson builds on Northrop's and Whitehead's standpoint: "The unity-giving conjunctive order within the realm of diversity—whether designated *Śūnyatā*, Nirvāna, or conditioned genesis—may best be thought of as the limitless, self-surpassing 'foster-mother of all becoming' in the flow of 'the undifferentiated aesthetic continuum' of life."[20] Jacobson seems to mean here that creative process is a cooperative interaction of temporary existents that are empty of substance. Enlightenment can therefore be understood as the realization of "conditioned genesis" (*paticcasamuppāda*, the idea that nothing exists independently of other temporary existents in creative process), of śūnyatā (Emptiness of any permanent substance), or of the perfect release and peace of nirvāna. These three doctrines are interchangeable in pure experience. Moreover, "In the *Bodhisattva* this centering of life in the aesthetic foundations of the world is associated with all-embracing service to all humankind."[21]

Curiously, the foster mother stands out as virtually the only significant feminine image in Jacobson's work, although creative process is at least as apparent in women as in men and requires interaction of feminine and masculine principles in men and women (the yin and yang of Tao). Not only do women conceive and give birth to babies; they also create homes and nurture families, as well as doing most of the things that men do. In their beauty, compassion, and concern for the arts, they are often more aesthetically aware than men. Despite overwhelming male prejudices in and out of the *sangha*, women have made important and controversial contributions to Buddhism in ancient and recent times that should not be neglected. A strong current of feminist Buddhism has been transforming Buddhism in the United

States.[22] Moreover, the symbolic value of women is crucial. *Prajñā-pāramitā* (the highest perfect wisdom) is imagined as female. The Great Bodhisattva is portrayed as female, as well as male. *Tāra, Dākini,* and other female images are prevalent in mandala. And the image of the jewel in the lotus, the union of the feminine and masculine, wisdom and skillful means, is central in Tantric Buddhism.

In the chapter called "Nirvāna: The Aesthetic Center of Life," Jacobson's opening statement is, "The whole purpose of the generalizing insights we pursue in Buddhist philosophy is to open our experience to more of the aesthetic richness flowing deep in the inarticulate rhythms of our bodies, where immense quantities of experience are stored from ages past."[23] Philosophy has a pragmatic and aesthetic value for Jacobson, as it had for James and Whitehead. If at times Jacobson's writing seems remotely abstract from the concrete experience that he celebrates and too polemical to prepare the reader for the calm of meditation, we are free to move on to an idea that opens our awareness to concrete actuality. His aim was not to construct a logically foolproof system but to open our minds to pure experience.

As Jacobson explains, most of the aesthetic richness of the universal creative process lies concealed, distorted, and perverted by personal and social "hindrances" that can be joyfully overcome by meditation, as life becomes "ever more fully a work of art." Indeed, "The power of art resembles the power of Buddhist meditation; it loosens the flow of quality from behind the frontier where precision of consciousness falls."[24] If this is so, can we conclude that artists without benefit of Buddhist meditation have been enlightened? Unfortunately, Jacobson has little more to say about art, despite its enormous relevance to his subject.

In *Understanding Buddhism,* Jacobson develops the aesthetics of nirvāna in several ways. Chapter 3 begins with a bold statement that points in a Buddhist direction but oversimplifies dharma: "The effort to create moments of awareness rich and vivid in the quality of individualized experience is what human life is all about." This aesthetic richness, inherent in human experience, is usually denied or distorted by the four "intoxicants" analyzed by the Buddha, "sensual gratifications,...obsession with life,...false views,...and ignorance; all prevent the flow of quality.[25] But these can be overcome by meditation.

The most original chapter in *Understanding Buddhism* is "Creativity and *Sūnyatā*," in which Jacobson identifies ten features of creative interrelatedness.[26] The first, fundamental feature is the "opening of experience to some new quality" before analysis or inferences can be made—the "pure experience" of James and Nishida, Pierce's "Firstness," and we might assume Jacobson's experience also. New quality emerges every instant of our lives, in every perception, though we often ignore, deny, or distort it in some way. The second feature, that "new qualities become synthesized into some novel form of togetherness; the many become one and are increased by one," is Whitehead's most famous line. Such togetherness occurs on the microlevel of perception and on the macrolevel of Jacobson's synthesis of Buddhist and Western thought.

The third feature, according to Jacobson, is that "new textures of quality lie fallow in an individual's apperceptive mass, permitting creative incubation and subliminal awakening which transform what a person can feel, appreciate and do." This creative awakening is encouraged by meditation or, I might add, by the practice of the arts, which Jacobson oddly neglects throughout his work. In the fourth aspect, communication of quality, the arts seem highly relevant, yet, again, are not mentioned. Such communication is not merely verbal but "the sharing among individuals of the novel integration."

But creative communication involves the destruction of outworn and restrictive habits of thought. And this fifth aspect melts into the seventh: "[C]onflict, criticism, friction, militant probing and clarification follow upon sharing new insights with old." Jacobson advocates a nonviolent effort at resolution in the spirit of Gandhi and Shākyamuni. My criticisms of Jacobson are offered in this grateful spirit of creative communication.

The sixth feature "is the emergence of a sense of renewal given out of the depths of things without any conscious purpose to bring it about"—a kind of trust, faith, or confidence in the processes of life, nature, and all possible universes, which requires no human manipulation or willfulness. Similarly, the ninth aspect is that "men and women get occasional glimpses of the unbroken wholeness in which their lives are embedded"—oceanic experiences, or transcendent visions of immanence.

Eighth is "the integration of new insights and alternatives for living into the linguistic and cultural system." The absorption of Buddhism in the West—in art, literature, and philosophy—is an obvious example. Finally, the tenth aspect is "the ambiguity of history": "Men and women who remain close to the concrete qualities of the *now* are prevented by this internalized richness from seeking to fulfill some glorified image or resurrect some ancient state of mind"; they are joyfully realizing the present as perfectly as possible. These ten aspects of creative interrelatedness are among Jacobson's original contributions, and it is regrettable that he does not explain them more thoroughly.

Despite Jacobson's emphasis on the aesthetic dimension of enlightenment, he had little to say about the visual arts beyond a few pages in chapter 8, "Japan Through the Buddhist Looking Glass," in which he repeats the thesis of his book, *Nihon-do: The Japan Way*, published only in Japanese translation, that the Buddhist sense of beauty and of perpetual renewal has been the distinctive foundation of Japanese life.[27] Though this thesis, depending on Daisetz Suzuki, Kitaro Nishida, Tetsuro Watsuji, Ernest Fenollosa, and others, seems true enough for Japan for most of its history, powerful technological and commercial forces are currently subverting the traditional aesthetic.

Literature, on which philosophy has directly depended, receives more attention than the other arts in Jacobson's books. But he alludes rather simplistically to themes in fiction, poetry, and plays by such authors as Rilke, Kafka, Camus, and Dostoyevsky; Auden and Shelley; Basho, Lewis Carroll, Emerson, Christopher Fry, Hemingway, Thomas Merton, Milarepa, Paz, Walker Percy, and Sartre; and Matthew Arnold, Emily Bronte, Euripides, Hesiod, Homer, Keats, Shakespeare, Sophocles, Wordsworth, and Yeats.[28] Though literary themes appropriately illustrate some of Jacobson's ideas, unfortunately lacking is any comment about the art of literature as an indispensable expression and revelation of the aesthetic dimension of existence. He might have pointed out how symbolism, imagism, surrealism, the free association of thoughts in stream of consciousness, and many other styles, techniques, and forms of modern writing have uncovered fundamental ways in which the mind works and how thoughts both express and conceal desires. This kind of literary evidence would have enriched and helped validate Jacobson's assertions about human frustrations and perhaps also Buddhist meditation and thought. Many modern writers who are unaware of Buddhist Emptiness recognize that language does not refer to fixed objective reality. The art, sensibility, and worldview of many other artists, outside of, and in Asia have been directly influenced, in various degrees, by Buddhism.[29] From America alone, artists influenced include Ezra Pound, T.S. Eliot, Amy Lowell, Gary Snyder, Richard Wright, Allen Ginsberg, Philip Whalen, Diane DiPrima, Cid Corman, Anne Waldman, Jack Kerouac, Lawrence Ferlinghetti, Joanne Kyger, Edith Shiffert, Lucien Stryk, Carol Tinker, John Solt, and philosophically most profound, Kenneth Rexroth.

One of Jacobson's comments about literature is extraordinary. Hemingway, he says, "violated the most fundamental intuitive insight;

aesthetic quality is never a means to an end, never the fruit of experience but experience itself in its vivid and harmonious flow."[30] This insight, which could be extended to the work of many, perhaps most, artists in the twentieth century, suggests that artists need to realize the aesthetic nature of the universal creative process, instead of willfully attempting to make works of art by means of craft. Beauty may best be uncovered, rather than forged.

In Jacobson's last book, *The Heart of Buddhist Philosophy*, the aesthetics of nirvāna is developed most of all in the chapter on Nāgārjuna, who affirmed "the concepts of reality as a social process and of the creativity, spontaneity, momentariness, and unrepeatability of the experiences of ordinary life." Unlike other treatments of Nāgārjuna, Jacobson's is neither technical nor threatening, but compassionately encouraging: "With rigorous logic Nāgārjuna formulates his concept of *śūnyatā*—the interrelatedness of existence—in such a way that its existence or nonexistence becomes a dead issue....From his point of view, nothing is more important than to arrive at a clear understanding of a universe that is forever surpassing itself in every momentary now, but to argue about its existence...reinforces that intellectual clinging that lies at or near the center of our major problems."[31] This passage presents some problems. First, *śūnyatā* means Emptiness, not "the interrelatedness of existence," though the interrelatedness of existence is empty. And second, Nāgārjuna had no "point of view," because he abolished all points of view. Jacobson continues to assert views and concepts throughout his writings in a way that Nāgārjuna would negate to release Jacobson from clinging to them. Would the highest enlightenment be the middle way between annihilation on the one hand and realization of universal creative process on the other? According to Nāgārjuna, "*nirvāna* is properly neither (in the realm of) existence nor non-existence."[32]

In the final chapter of *The Heart of Buddhist Philosophy*, "The Civilization of Experience," Jacobson asserts that "the supreme aesthetic achievement of the twentieth century" has been the view of the whole earth from space, because it has expanded our vision and hope for a civilization that will "foster the qualitative richness of experience, to awaken and alert us to the aesthetic foundations of the world."[33] Similarly, David Lee Miller has alluded to the astronauts' view from space in his plea for "physicians for the whole Earth" who will help humankind realize its creative potential in harmony with other beings.[34] How can a civilization fostering this enlightened aim emerge? Jacobson's answer wisely synthesizes his major ideas: "The

Buddhist solution to the problem of civilization is for each individual to live self-correctively in ultimate dependence upon the creativity operating in the original individualized experience of people everywhere in ways that bring forth the novel forms of togetherness without which human civilization would have come to an end long ago."[35]

Jacobson is perhaps overly optimistic about the future of Buddhism offering salvation for the world. I suspect Buddhism is more likely to be absorbed into other religions, the arts, philosophy, and a more comprehensive worldview, in which creativity is central. In this respect, Jacobson has made a dynamic contribution to the philosophy of creativity, as can be gathered from the works of David Lee Miller and others.

Notes

1. Nolan Pliny Jacobson, *Buddhism: The Religion of Analysis* (New York: Humanities, 1965; reprint, Southern Illinois University Press, Carbondale and Edwardsville, 1966, 1970), p. 43.
2. Ibid., pp. 116, 63–64. Jacobson has quoted from F. S. C. Northrop's *The Meeting of East and West* (New York: Macmillan, 1953), pp. 350, 472.
3. *Religion of Analysis*, pp. 83, 117.
4. Alfred North Whitehead, *Religion in the Making* (New York: Macmillan, 1953), p. 116.
5. *Religion of Analysis*, p. 146.
6. Ibid., pp. 158–59.
7. Ibid., pp. 162–77.
8. Ibid., pp. 28–31.
9. Ibid., p. 82.
10. Ibid.
11. *Religion of Analysis*, p. 136.
12. Ibid., pp. 93–123.
13. Ibid., p. 160.
14. *Tantric Poetry of Kukai (Kobo Daishi), Japan's Buddhist Saint*, translated with commentary by Morgan Gibson and Hiroshi Murakami (Fredonia, N. Y.: White Pine, 1987), p. 33. Reprinted by permission of White Pine Press. The first letter of the Sanskrit alphabet, "Ah!" is thought by Tantrists to be Mahavairocana, the universal Buddha, from whom all dharmas flow.
15. *Religion of Analysis*, p. 105–8.
16. Nolan Pliny Jacobson, *Buddhism and the Contemporary World: Change and Self-Correction* (Carbondale and Edwardsville: Southern Illinois University Press, 1983), p. 145.

17. Ibid., pp. 14, 64.
18. Ibid., p. 161.
19. Ibid., p. 10, quoted by Jacobson from F. S. C. Northrop, Foreword to *A Whiteheadian Aesthetic*, by D. W. Sherburne (New Haven: Yale University Press, 1961), p. xxv.
20. *Buddhism and the Contemporary World*, p. 157.
21. Ibid., p. 158.
22. See Rita Gross, "Buddhism and Feminism: Toward Their Mutual Transformation," *Eastern Buddhist* 19, no. 1 (Spring 1986), pp. 44–58; no. 2 (Autumn 1986), pp. 62–74. See also Gross, *Women and Buddhism*. A special issue of *Spring Wind—Buddhist Cultural Forum* 6, nos. 1–3 (1986); Deborah Hopkinson and Eileen Klera, eds., *Not Mixing Up Buddhism: Essays on Women and Buddhist Practice* (Fredonia, N. Y.: White Pine, 1986).
23. *Buddhism and the Contemporary World*, p. 65.
24. Ibid., pp. 68–69.
25. Nolan Pliny Jacobson, *Understanding Buddhism* (Carbondale and Edwardsville: Southern Illinois University Press, 1986), pp. 38, 41.
26. Ibid., pp. 82–88.
27. Ibid., pp. 101–13; Nolan Pliny Jacobson, *Nihon-do: The Japan Way*, trans. Nakazato Chieko (Tokyo: Rissosha, 1977), pp. 99–115.
28. These writers are mentioned, respectively, in *Religion of Analysis*, pp. 32, 55, 59; *Buddhism and the Contemporary World*, pp. 3, 152; *Understanding Buddhism*, pp. 3, 20, 44–45, 51–52, 70–71, 74, 78, 93, 106–7; and *The Heart of Buddhist Philosophy* (Carbondale and Edwardsville: Southern Illinois University Press, 1988), pp. 3, 41–43, 64, 86–87, 129.
29. See Earl Miner, *The Japanese Tradition in British and American Literature* (Princeton: Princeton University Press, 1958); and Sanehide Kodama, *American Poetry and Japanese Culture* (Hamden, Conn.: Shoe String, 1985); *East-West Wisdom* (Hamden, Conn.: Shoe String, 1986); and *Among Buddhas in Japan*, foreword by Nolan Pliny Jacobson (Fredonia, N. Y.: White Pine, 1988). I have listed in text some poets not mentioned in these volumes.
30. *Understanding Buddhism*, p. 71.
31. *The Heart of Buddhist Philosophy*, pp. 62, 69.
32. Kenneth K. Inada, *Nāgārjuna: A Translation of His Mūlamadhyamakakārikā with an Introductory Essay* (Tokyo: Hokuseido, 1970), p. 156.
33. *The Heart of Buddhist Philosophy*, pp. 125, 134.
34. David Lee Miller, *Philosophy of Creativity* (New York and Bern: Peter Lang, 1989), pp. 16, 181–182.
35. *The Heart of Buddhist Philosophy*, p. 135.

16.
The Lotus in the Robot:
The Emerging World
Civilization and Japan   *Stuart D. B. Picken*

Professor Nolan Pliny Jacobson's philosophical views about the past, present, and future of human civilization have been often debatable but never dull, frequently controversial but always challenging, and most important of all, without fail, illuminating and innovative. The challenge of his work to the established and accepted dogmas of the Western tradition compares to the significance of Kant's argument from incongruous counterparts.[1] But Jacobson was providing the obverse to that position in cultural terms—the need for complementarity. As I understand him, he stressed the crucial need to try to displace the powerful philosophy of substance that has dominated the Western mind since the era of Aristotle and to force it to give place, or at least to yield some ground, to the philosophy of process that in his view would not only better equip humankind to understand the deeper aspects of the universe but better prepare humankind to deal with current problems, many of which are rooted in the imprisoning perceptions of substance philosophy. His grasp of Whitehead was one key to this, and his recognition that Whitehead has been read and understood in some Japanese circles as a bridge between, for example, Christian and Buddhist thought was another key.[2] Jacobson's position is unique because he sees process philosophy not merely as a mediator between traditions but as the rectifier of the imbalances within the Western tradition.[3] This approach gave him a basis for his claims about Buddhism and its ability to have rapport with process thought as it grew in the United States.

This essay will not deal so much with Buddhism, however, as with the idea of process itself and with another source of the idea that Jacobson recognized and acknowleged but did not have time or opportunity to incorporate more fully into his thinking. I shall look at his ideas from a Japan perspective, Japan being used to denote not a country or culture but a multiplex way of thinking that contains within it more than one strand of process thought. Process thought may be recognized in Buddhism and is also found in Shinto. I believe my comments will supplement Jacobson's thesis and, perhaps while implying that a few modifications would have to be made, will confirm his basic insights as fundamentally sound.

The Japan Way

In the course of his various writings and arguments, Jacobson frequently referred to Japan as a case in point and went so far as to write a book entitled *Nihon-do: The Japan Way*.[4] The foreword was written by Hajime Nakamura, who made a number of interesting statements and observations about Jacobson's ideas. Nakamura suggested that it was an unusual book about Japan because it showed respect for certain ideas in Japanese culture that had been passed over by non-Japanese scholars and ignored by Japanese who were too close to observe it. Europeans and Americans tended often to dismiss Japan from the standpoint of their own values. Recognizing that Japanese culture has weak points, Jacobson was still interested in what contribution Japan might make to the future of humankind, according to Nakamura's estimate of his thought.

Jacobson presented these views in person at a meeting of the Asiatic Society of Japan, in June 1977, held in the German East Asiatic Club House in Akasaka, Tokyo. He focused on the heavily verbal tradition of the West, beginning with Greek civilization, and contrasted this with the relatively nonverbal culture of Japan, where ideas are transmitted in patterns learned through experience. These patterns, he argued, were identified in Japan by the suffix *do*—as in *kendo* (the way of the sword), *chado* (the way of tea), *shodo* (the way of calligraphy), and many others. He argued that these patterns were able to help people tap the energies at the center of life. He thought this characteristic would enable Japan to help make humankind wiser in certain respects by pointing to a way of living where it would be discovered that the momentum of life came from beyond what we know.

Professor Seizo Ohe noted that in Professor Jacobson's thesis was the assumption that the Japanese way of life had self-corrective elements within it. Humankind could creatively penetrate beyond itself and perhaps find the meaning of what the Japanese seemed to understand well. Process thought exists in the tradition of Japanese Buddhism, but the Japanese roots themselves are in an awareness of the natural flow of life. Therefore, the idea of process is also found in

Shinto, not just in Buddhism. Unfortunately, Shinto has not been as attractive to Western researchers as Buddhism, because it does not present a concretely worked-out philosophy in the manner of the various Buddhist groups. Shinto is intuited truth, truth perceived as the necessary ordering and explanation of experience. For the Japanese, it gives experience meaning and coherence.

The Lotus in the Robot

When reflecting on these points, I recollected Arthur Koestler's infamous book on Japan, entitled *The Lotus and the Robot*,[5] in which he depicted two incompatible facets of Japanese civilization as he saw it. One was the crude industrialization process that he designated "the Robot," with its horrific attendants, such as pollution and overcrowding. The other was "the Lotus," a symbol of Japan's aesthetic past, gone forever and displaced by the horrible new civilization Koestler encountered. Koestler was a perceptive and intelligent observer of the human scene and left many other worthwhile works, but his comments on Japan remain a classic of the worst kind of superficial and grossly oversimplified journalistic diatribe. The only saving grace in it is the observation that Zen is not the religion of Japan and that much of the then-Western interest in it was a fad. A recent sociological analysis of two Zen communities in California indicates that in that regard, he was probably not far wrong.[6] Zen is found in Japan, but the popularization of it, notably by Suzuki Daisetsu,[7] was misleading about the nature of Japanese spirituality in general and about Japanese Buddhism in particular.

Two points about Koestler's thesis struck me then, as they still do. First was what I judged to be the sound of either fear or envy in the Europocentric way of thinking that could not accept the idea that an Oriental civilization was beginning to challenge the West. Second was the absolutely peremptory dismissal implied in the idea that the axis of world civilization might ever shift from the Atlantic to the Pacific or that a people other than the descendents of the Tigris/ Euphrates civilization might ever inherit the earth or even share its inheritance. To these points, a third might be added that Koestler regrettably neither saw nor acknowledged: the "Lotus" has continued to live "within the Robot" and has helped it to create a humane society with an improved environment.[8] Through this "Lotus within the Robot" have been found ways of dealing with many of the problems that have wrought great damage in most Western urban settings: crimes of violence, lack of productivity, and the absence of social conscience. Japan's corporations have become the model their U.S. counterparts seek to study and emulate. Japan has been and is pioneering a kind of civilization that contains many hints for the West as we enter the third millennium, and one of Jacobson's contributions to human culture is that he recognized this civilization and was prepared to come to terms with it.

Jacobson perceived Buddhism as a vital part of the need to further emphasize East-West cooperation. What he saw, in my view, was Buddhism refined by Japan, a way of thinking that could be valuable in the human search for ways of thinking that will meet the world's deepest needs. Four themes belong to the Buddhist contribution to the emerging world civilization of the third millennium. These themes also have deep roots in Shinto, in the Japanese tradition, and in some of the things that Jacobson found most attractive, appealing, and challenging about Japan.[9]

In the Social Dimension—the Activation of the Ideal of Harmony of Wholeness

In the Japanese tradition, the ideal of *chowa* (harmony) may even predate the introduction of Buddhism in the sixth century, but certainly it is found in the earliest of Japan's statements of social ideals as the prime ideal of society. Shotoku Taishi (573-621), the prince regent of the seventh century, during the reign of Empress Suiko, formulated a famous Seventeen Clause Constitution in 604 (*Jushichijo no Kempo*), which was in reality a set of Buddhist guidelines for emerging Japanese civilization. Clause 1 states clearly that the implied vision of society is harmony, and clause 2 declares that only by reverencing the Buddha, the dharma, and the *sangha* can this ideal be realized.[10] With these pious thoughts and hopes, Japanese culture began to develop (after one or two unsuccessful attempts) its long rapprochement with the Buddhist tradition. The cultural flowering of this relationship is well known. And over the six centuries that it took Buddhism to settle in and become part of the total religious and cultural tradition of the nation, set of guidelines and the Confucian social ethics that accompanied it to Japan helped to mold social ideals based on harmony.

At no time did Japanese culture espouse or encourage such extreme concepts of individualism as those that grew in the West. These concepts did appear from time to time. But they were so alien to the dominant milieu that, apart from a few well-known historical instances, the Japanese have centered their existence in various forms of communal life. This aided the development of their agricultural civilization, and in modern times it has also been a vital contribution to their industrialization. Harmony in Japanese thought is not conceived of on a model principally derived from music. It also implies accord, agreement, symmetry, and conformity. It is an ideal and not the result of the incidental absence of discord. One of the basic reasons for the prohibition of Christianity in Japan in the early sixteenth century—and ultimately for the expulsion of all foreigners—was that it threatened social harmony. The Tokugawa government had seen the conflict amongst Roman Catholic orders and did not appreciate the aggressiveness and the violence of the Franciscans toward traditional Japanese religion. After long deliberation, it decided that only one solution to the problem existed, a solution Immanuel Kant praised.[11]

In total contrast to the Japanese tradition, the individual in Western thought has been protected even at the price of falsifying experience.[12] The image of the rugged individual coping with every kind of conflict and becoming strong in the process might have had truth for the nineteenth-century American frontier, but it has little application in twentieth-century urban life. In a recent work on the origins of Buddhism, Richard Gombrich points out that the earliest *sangha* members were probably urban merchants, people who knew the need for cooperation, the division of labor, and the harmonious working of different interests to produce a society.[13] "Selfhood is best achieved through Grouphood" is perhaps one way to express the ideal of Buddhist Japan.[14] Almost every analysis of Japan's social structure and behavior displays the same results—the dominance of "groupism." Contemporary Japanese social psychology is still deeply permeated by Buddhist influence. Most analysts in the field of industrial relations agree that this influence, rather than alleged low salaries or other advantages, has lifted Japan to prominence in manufacturing and export in the postwar era. The late Matsushita Konnosuke's famed *Human Resource Management* philosophy is the most humane of industrial management theories ever conceived.[15] It respects, cares for, and cultivates the individual, but it does not enshrine individualism in the manner of the West, where individualism militates against common interests when carried occasionally to ludicrous extremes.

The ideal of *chowa* is written frequently as calligraphy on office walls. It is considered with the same degree of respect as perhaps in days gone by. It is a tribute to its use in practice that Japan as a nation has fewer lawyers (around ten thousand) than the state of Illinois alone. A society that promotes harmony also promotes trust, honesty, and sincerity. These are still virtues of the Japanese people, a living part of their Buddhist heritage. Consider these moral precepts of the House of Mitsui, which date to the House of Mitsui Constitution of 1722.

> *Article 2*:…if a member of the House thinks only of his own pride and does not consider other members of the House, there will be no peace at home, and disorder and chaos may result.
> *Article 22*: It is each man's duty to believe in the *kami* and Buddha and to follow the teachings of Confucius.
> *Article 23*: The *kami* and Buddha lie within one's heart.[16]

These injunctions were first addressed to the businesspeople of eighteenth-century Japan. The corporate men and women of the West might learn something about management from this one source of Japanese commercial success.

In the Cultural Dimension—an Aesthetic Response to the Intuition of Nature

The aesthetic perception of life and nature is a frequent theme in Jacobson's literature. For Japanese culture in the sense I defined earlier—the multiplex system of value inputs from Shinto, Buddhism, and Confucianism—beauty is a value. As I pointed out in *Shinto: Japan's Spiritual Roots*, Plato originally placed truth, goodness, and beauty on the same plane, but beauty became suspect and has never again been able to enstate itself as a value in its own right in the West.[17] Beauty and the response to beauty was considered of no value, because truth (the scientific), and goodness (the moral), were all that people needed to live. Western civilization enabled itself to live with ugliness and a marked lack of interest, let alone respect, for the natural environment in its relation to the life of human beings.

Only in the years of advanced environmental crisis has nature become the focus of attention, not nature for its own sake, but nature so far as it supports human life. Western civilization confuses the replication of nature and its aesthetic charm with the true meaning of the aesthetic of experience. Courts of law will quickly punish anyone who damages a replication of nature, a painting or a mural, or something belonging to a museum or gallery. But courts of law are slow to punish those who violate nature itself by deforesting, polluting, or wasting fossil fuels. It does not make sense except in a context where only human creation has value, and where natural beauty itself is not held in any kind of awe.

The Western tradition prefers framed art, pictures that can be framed and hung on walls. Gardens, such as Versailles, are created mathematically and reflect the work of a mind that sees little or no beauty in natural form. Beauty, like everything else, must be organized. The flowers must stand like rows of colorful silent soldiers, and lawns must be cut with precision to reflect geometrical form.

Japanese art, by contrast, is an art of totality. The scroll that adorns the living room wall of a Western home was originally meant to hang inside a tokonoma, the alcove of a Japanese room that would also be decorated with a small flower arrangement. From the seat of honor in front of the scroll, the guest could look out over the tatami and out over the porch to the garden beyond as one continuous flow of beauty. The concept of a flowing aesthetic, an expression of the idea of process, stands in sharp contrast to the substance art of the West.

The adornment of daily life and the creation of objects with beauty and efficiency is basic to the Japanese tradition and belongs very much to the original tradition. The same may be said of the sense of appreciation of nature for what nature is in itself. It could be called life as an art form. This concept is not welcome to those who consider mere functionality as adequate. Part of the key is the degree to which people have become alienated from their natural environment, the degree to which they have lost the sense that they are an organic part of nature.

I recollect Jacobson shocking some U.S. undergraduates into an awareness of this alienation. They were one-year visiting students in Japan and were attending a seminar I was giving on Japanese thought. In the discussion of attitudes toward nature, I recollect him surprising some of those present by asking, obviously realizing the degree of alienation that some people were experiencing toward the environment, "Have you ever walked barefoot on the grass?" He was asking how close had they ever been to nature in a direct and unmediated sense. Excluding driving through forests or even plowing with a tractor, how close had they been to its life and its touch? His question was poignant and perceptive.

Japanese culture is profuse with songs about the micro aspects of nature, seasonal songs about dragonflies or falling cherry blossoms, about floating puffs of dandelions or insects that Westerners would stamp on rather than celebrate in song. Sounds that to the Western ear are grating or meaningless, the Japanese ear hears as music, in imitation of which a song is created.[18] There is no perception of nature through the eye of a dualism that sees what is human as moral and good and what is nature as the province of the demonic. The Japanese of old were so close to nature that when the word *nature* was introduced in English during the Meiji era, a Japanese equivalent had to be created. The distinction between subject and object was drawn. Medical science, for example, was being developed. But the attitude of human versus nature, understandable perhaps amidst desert wastes, but less so amidst the forests of Europe, never became a part of the Japanese way of thinking. The sense of nature as benign is very Japanese, and the divinities of nature, the *kami*, are benign also. Chinese Buddhist art was subtly transformed in Japan. The slim and taut faces of the Chinese Buddhas became fatter and more gentle, portraying the Buddha with the beauty the Japanese felt was appropriate to a divine being—their aesthetic response to nature.

In the Philosophical Dimension—the Reply of the Waterfall to Aristotle

The ultimate and generic ritual of Shinto is purification, ideally performed under a freestanding waterfall, with the person clad only in a loincloth (*fundoshi*) and headband (*hachimaki*). Purification is a way to enlightenment by means of direct and unmediated experience. It is unity with the cosmos that takes only seconds to achieve. It is supreme enlightenment through experience. A person may be born again and again and again. The process of rebirth is not one act of spiritual regeneration or a metaphysic of reincarnation but endless daily rebirth within life itself.

This process relates to three points I have already noted. First is the need for awareness of oneself as part of the cosmos. This need, among many other things that Jacobson attributed to Buddhism, could with equal justification be attributed to Shinto. One interesting feature of Japanese Buddhism is the degree to which Shinto thought is embedded in it. *Tendai* monks, for example, engage in mountain disciplines and practice *misogi*, as do the *shugenja*, the mountain ascetics, who combine Shinto practices and esoteric Buddhism in their own unique way. Jacobson writes, "The whole thrust of the Buddhist orientation is to return men and women to their original presence in the cosmos 'in immediate and uncontaminated grasp of the world in its full depth and without veils.'"[19] Although Jacobson quotes Erich Fromm here, the thought is essentially his. It expresses Buddhism, but it also expresses the basis of the natural spirituality of Japanese culture that is seen most clearly in the deeper meaning of Shinto rituals.

Second and related closely to the first point, the ritual of purification stimulates a closer sense of the reality and the meaning of nature for human life. When a person stands under the waterfall, it is difficult for that person to know where the fall begins and the self ends. They merge in a moment and bring the self and the cosmos into complete contact. People who think of themselves as beings in a social environment or as cogwheels of industry suddenly become aware of themselves as cosmic beings. Anyone can be more aware of humanity as part of nature when it is impossible to distinguish between the self and a flowing cascade of water. In that moment, consciousness is altered, and a new quality of experience is known. It may be called satori, enlightenment, but it is also a profound experience of nature in cosmic terms that refutes any view of humanity that offers a lesser understanding.

Third is the totally aesthetic perception of life. I often think that if Jacobson had managed to complete the work on the projected "Deep Heart of Japan," he would have found himself thinking more and more about nonverbalized aesthetic perception. This perception helps to underline the nature of reality as process, because beauty is ever effervescent and changing, yet always beauty.

The relative absence of cynicism and the almost total absence of atheism in Japan can be attributed to this way of thinking. Atheism and its various consequences are the product of Western civilization and its distinctive conception of the divine. The concept of atheism as such does not belong in cultures that are not monotheistic and in which the options of belief and unbelief are considered to be diametrically opposed positions. Nor does atheism in the "God is Dead" sense, because the waterfall never stops flowing. The energy of the universe is ever accessible. The purification and the renewal are part of the endless revitalizing process in which life exists.

Only gods of substance can die. The metaphysical imprisonment of the God and Father of Jesus of Nazareth along with himself into *tres personnae in una substantia* may have satisfied the Latinized Aristotelian thinking of the early Christian era, but it reduces the divine to terms that the human mind has created. It is more blasphemous than idolatry and more unspiritual than crude materialism. Though it pretends to portray the divine, it has encapsulated its possibility and the human relationship with it into a set of concepts that denude the *mysterium tremendum* of any experiential possibility. It also totally removes the numinous from the universe and puts in its place a legalistic formula before which the intellect may bow in deference to the cleverness of legalistic theologians of the past rather than to the reality allegedly set forth. When the divine is reduced to fit the categories of the human mind, it ceases to exist. Long before Nietzsche proclaimed the death of God, God was already dead and buried in the creeds. The universe was reduced in size, its mystery gone, and humans began to feel the hubris that damned them to centuries of medieval imprisonment of the spirit followed by agonizing wars of liberation. In all this, the ultimate victim was the name of the God who had been excluded from the world and from religion, but who may yet be found if the desire for spirituality is pursued. And spirituality seems to be one of the genuine needs of this age.

In the Spiritual Dimension—from *Homo Sapiens* to *Homo Excellens*

Spirituality is a concept that is attracting followers in the West. U.S. teenagers in cults numbered almost 14 million (52 percent of the total teenage population) in 1981.[20] Why? Conventional religious thinking is obviously not satisfying. Leaving to one side the vexing question of why so many people become attracted to fraudulent and semi-fraudulent television religious cults, that they do seems to add force to the conclusion that something is wrong with the Western religious tradition. There have been times of down and up in the history of Christianity, but with the obviously impending end of the four centuries of the Protestant era, to borrow an expression from Paul Tillich,[21] and the inability of the Roman Catholic Church and its leadership to do anything but mouth platitudes and advocate outmoded solutions to issues that fourth-century and fifth-century doctrines were never designed to comprehend, little can be expected from that source except what people would expect from any religion in decline, defensive acts of self-interest.

Western religion and spirituality have reached a crisis in an extreme form. Their traditional spirituality was cultivated in a different cosmos inhabited by the demonic and the supernatural. Now that such a milieu is repudiated by theologians of every color and credal variety, barring a few, the negative tendencies of that kind of spirituality prove totally unattractive. The heavy emphasis on self-denial and self-negation leads to a greater preoccupation with the self and its sins or its experience of grace. The personal element is at the heart of religion, but if someone is living at the center of his/her spiritual energy, the vital question to ask is where that energy is carrying the person so moved. Is it positive toward better things, or is it into greater self-torture and self-abnegation? The latter dominated the medieval world, and regrettably, Christian spirituality and discipline are still linked to that way of thinking.

In contrast, the Japanese ideal is not *via negativa* but *via positiva*. Consider simply the objectives of the discipline *Sen Nichi Kai Ho Gyo*,[22] which entails running around the peaks of Mt. Hiei in Kyoto for one thousand days from midnight (after *misogi*) until eight in the morning. It is a discipline to rehabilitate and regenerate spiritually by improving the health of the body and enriching the mind. Compare this with the sickly negative self-tortures of the medieval saints who lived with lice, the symbol of holiness, and who mutilated themselves for the sake of receiving a few days less in purgatory.

Jacobson also drew attention indirectly to one fascinating point about Japanese culture, namely, that it is, in its own way, a life science. I have long argued this point in the context of bioethics and Japan's natural life-orientation in contrast to the death-orientation of much of Western medical science.[23] Jacobson spoke of medical research that shows Japan far ahead of the West in the basic understanding of how the human organism functions in its totality.[24]

Quo Vadis?

Paul Kennedy's *Rise and Fall of Great Powers* raises crucial questions for the modern world and its future.[25] It deals in essence with the future of civilization and seems to promise the profound vision and understanding of the historian. Regrettably, however, it is little more than a modified version of Oswald Spengler's "decline and fall" thesis. It is challenging and historically interesting but fatally flawed in its conception by bad metaphysics. Cyclical conceptions of history, however appealing they may be, fail to grasp the unique nature and quality of historical events.

The emerging civilization is moving toward the meeting of cultures and the exchange of experience. One key to understanding this emergence is to recognize that though cultural heritages do not change overnight or fade, they always stand to be enriched. Japan proves that point and offers a model for seeing this mechanism in action. Seeing Japanese culture in this way raises difficulties. Japan has many critics, although I sense year by year, in the absence of abusive comments for political purposes and downright cynicism, that among enlightened circles, there is genuine respect for Japanese achievements in many fields. But the truth is not that Japan alone has the secret. The secrets are there for all. The Japanese have simply made better use of them. Jacobson's insights about Japan were soundly based and can be viewed as an interpretation of Japanese culture in the sense defined earlier. It fits meaningfully into his overall thesis about the development of human civilization in a way that points significantly and helpfully toward the future.

One final proposition about Japan that Jacobson justifiably claimed to be valid should be set alongside the Kennedy thesis. He claimed that Japanese culture is self-correcting. To avoid extinction, it has always known how to change. The same can hardly be said of many other cultures. The Heian-age Japan (794–1185), especially the eleventh to twelfth centuries, was a peak of culture, but so was the Nara age before it (711-794), in its own way, and so were Kamakura and Edo after it. Each was a response to the needs of the time. Meiji-era Japan and the post-1945 reconstruction were also responses to the age. This responsive ability is built into the way of thinking that the culture encourages. In that sense, the warning is there. Humankind must cultivate the flexibility needed to make change possible. Rigid forms of culture and ossified patterns of thinking must give way to the needs of the present and future. Otherwise, the alternative is bleak.

Most of today's pressing problems arise from desperate and belated attempts to apply inappropriate old solutions to complex new issues. Perhaps history has always been so. But the stakes have never been so high, and the danger of inflexibility, buttressed by scientific solutions and aggravated by insensitive military might, has never been greater. Therein lies the difference. The emerging world civilization will begin when the steps proposed here are applied with profound reverence for nature, a vigorous faith in humanity, and the purified energy that arises solely from deep cosmic awareness and total existential commitment. Perhaps the greatest tribute to Nolan Pliny Jacobson will not be the philosophers who expound these themes, but the courageous agents of social and cultural change who put them into practice.

Notes

1. Immanuel Kant, *Was Heisst Sich in Denken Orienteiren?* in vol. 5 of *Werke*, ed. Wilhelm Weischedel (Darmstadt: Wissenschaftliche Buchgesellschaft, 1958), p. 269.
2. John Cobb, Jr. *Beyond Dialog: Towards the Mutual Transformation of Christianity and Buddhism* (Philadelphia: Fortress, 1982).
3. Many examples could be cited. I note the following as illustrations: Nolan Pliny Jacobson, *Buddhism and the Contemporary World* (Carbondale and Edwardsville: Southern Illinois University Press, 1983), pp. 119ff; *Understanding Buddhism* (Carbondale and Edwardsville: Southern Illinois University Press, 1986), pp. 56 ff.; *The Heart of Buddhist Philosophy* (Carbondale and Edwardsville: Southern Illinois University Press, 1988), pp. 27 ff.
4. Nolan Pliny Jacobson, *Nihon-do: The Japan Way*, trans. Nakazato Chieko (Tokyo: Rissosha, 1977).
5. Arthur Koestler, *The Lotus and the Robot* (London: Hutchison, 1961). For reference to this, see *Understanding Buddhism*, pp. 107 ff.
6. David L. Preston, *The Social Organization of Zen Practice: Constructing Transcultural Reality* (London: Cambridge University Press, 1988). This book is a study of two Zen communities in California, which recognized the role of the counterculture of the 1960s in the attraction of Zen as reflected in the composition of membership. See pp. 19–21.
7. Suzuki Daisetsu is quoted by Preston (*op. cit.*, p. 24) as saying that Japanese culture is very thoroughly Zen culture. Suzuki did make claims even more exaggerated: "Zen is the keynote of Oriental culture.... Therefore I make bold to say that in Zen are found systematized, or rather crystallized, all the philosophy, religion and life itself of the Far-Eastern people, especially of the Japanese." *Introduction to Zen Buddhism* (New York: Grove, 1963), pp. 35, 37. This contention would be called into question by the majority of Japanese Buddhists, who are not practitioners of Zen.
8. Stuart D. B. Picken, *Buddhism: Japan's Cultural Identity* (New York: Kodansha International/U.S.A., 1982), p. 21.
9. These themes are developments of thought, and a large percentage is my interpretation of these phenomena as I have seen them, experienced them, and subsequently reflected on them. In terms of the scope of this volume, it is a development of new ideas taken as a starting point, a concrete insight of Jacobson, in tribute to whom we have the privilege of writing.
10. Masahiro Mori, *The Buddha in the Robot* (Tokyo: Kosei Publishing, 1980). This book contains a remarkable integration of Buddhism and modern science that is perhaps the ultimate refutation of Koestler.
11. Immanuel Kant, *Zum Ewigen Frieden: Ein Philosophischer Entwurf*, in *Werke*, op cit., vol. 9, pp. 214–215.

12. George Cabbot Lodge, "The Connection Between Ethics and Ideology," *Journal of Business Ethics* 1, no. 2 (May 1982), pp. 85-94. This essay highlights the need to recognize that the ideology of individualism is in need of being replaced by the more appropriate ideal of communitarianism.

13. Richard F. Gombrich, *Theravada Buddhism: A Social History from Ancient Benares to Modern Colombo* (London: Routledge & Kegan Paul, 1988), pp. 55 ff.

14. Stuart D. B. Picken, op. cit., pp. 49–52.

15. Konnosuke Matsushita was founder of *Matsushita Denki* (Matsushita Electronics, National Panasonic), head of the PHP Research Institute, and author of *Japan at the Brink* and other works on Japan and Japanese management.

16. House of Mitsui Rules, quoted in John G. Roberts, *Mitsui. Three Centuries of Japanese Business* (New York: Weatherhill, 1973; reprint 1989).

17. Stuart D. B. Picken, *Shinto: Japan's Spiritual Roots* (New York: Kodansha International/U.S.A., 1980) p. 57.

18. Tadanobu Tsunoda, *Right Brain and Left Brain* (Tokyo: Shogakkan, 1987).

19. Nolan Pliny Jacobson, *Understanding Buddhism*, p. 48. He is quoting Erich Fromm, "Psychoanalysis and Zen," in Erich Fromm, Daisetz Suzuki, and Richard DeMartino, *Zen Buddhism and Psychoanalysis* (New York: Harper & Row, 1960), pp. 131, 134, 136.

20. Willa Appel, *Cults in America* (New York: Hill, Rinehart & Winston, 1986), pp. 12, 181.

21. Paul Tillich, *The Protestant Era* (Chicago: University of Chicago Press, 1948).

22. Nobuya Wazaki, *Ajad no Tanjo* (New York: Kodansha International/U.S.A., 1979); John Stevens, *The Marathon Monks of Mount Hiei* (Boston: Shambhala, 1988).

23. Stuart D. B. Picken and Ono Masako, *Bioethics and Social Responsibility*, ICU GE Series, no. 10 (1981).

24. Nolan Pliny Jacobson, *Understanding Buddhism*, pp. 112 ff.

25. Paul Kennedy, *The Rise and Fall of Great Powers* (New York: Random House, 1987).

17.
Buddhism and the
Emerging World Civilization   *Seizo Ohe*

Buddhism and Science

> To study truth is to study the self.
> To study the self is to forget the self.
> To forget the self is to be enlightened by all things.
> To be enlightened by all things is to be free from attachment
>   to the body and mind of one's self and of others.

This passage is a well-known verse of the *Genjo-Koan* by Dogen-Zenji (1200–1253), which I like to recite in solitary promenade. In the above English translation, the original word *Buddhism* is intentionally replaced by *truth*. It is, I believe, essentially in accord with the spirit of religious tolerance of Buddhism, particularly of Zen Buddhism of Dogen. Thus modified, the above verse of Dogen's *Koan* induces me to meditate further on and on into the land of images of the world civilization that actually often emerged in conversation between Nolan Pliny Jacobson and me. Substantially in this connection, we shared our Buddhistic interest, and in America (Chicago) about thirty years ago, I was surprised by a Nisei preacher who declared in his Sunday sermon that among all the existing religions of the world, only Buddhism can survive the scientific civilization today and tomorrow.

To Study the Self

"Be ever master of yourself" is a fundamental teaching of Zen Buddhism. Modern scientific thought began with the Cartesian cogito (cognitive self-consciousness). For modern Western intellectuals, it was a revelation that all truth around us stands and falls with our consciousness. Some theoretical physicists even believe that all their theoretic truth might be nothing but products of human thought, though any other kinds of knowledge cannot be relied on in the human world today. Therefore, the first task for us must be to study the self. All things of the world are mirrored in it. "*Tat tvam asi*" (that art thou), said the ancient Vedic hymn. To study the self is truly the first step to Buddhist enlightenment, just as it is the foundation of all science.

To Forget the Self

A scientist absorbed in research forgets him/herself, as does an artist absorbed in creative work, and a Buddhist absorbed in selfless devotion to enlightenment. But the last case may be a little different from the other two. So far as the aim of *zazen* training is to attain the selfless personality, it also means never-ceasing self-corrective efforts toward self-perfection. To imagine a human community of such ideal personalities as an image of the emerging world civilization, however, is nothing but a quixotic dream. But it is a historical fact that the cultural treasures of the past are mostly products of great peoples' self-forgetting creative acts in science, art, and religion. On the accumulation of those creative works, though unfortunately often misused, the world history of humankind is written.

To Be Enlightened by All Things

What is the essence of self-forgetting in science? Apart from the creativity of scientific genius, the essential feature of intellectual attitude in science is to be objective, looking at things as they are. Is not this objective attitude of looking at things as they are (*tathatā*) the fundamental requirement for a Buddhist to face reality, to see the world in and around him/herself? Even the grotesque root formation of a chestnut tree that happened to shock Mr. Roquentin, the hero of a Sartrean novel, nauseated at his own existence, is only part of the ecological reality of our fellow living beings, and is nothing to be shocked at, a Buddhist would say. So we can be enlightened by all things. An American ecologist once admired the profound wisdom in the Buddha's belief that all things are our fellow beings, meaning air, water, plants, animals, men, and women, all alike. The Buddha acquired this truth without any help from modern science.

To Be Free from Attachment to the Body and Mind of One's Self and of Others

Compared with its Japanese, embarrassingly enigmatic text—"*Shin Shin Datsu Raku*" (literally, body and mind falling down)—this fourth and last stanza of the *Genjo-Koan* might sound too simple and too clear in this English version,[1] but I find it so much better and easier to understand. It hits on the core of Zen wisdom in its purest essence: detachment from all earthly existence, *śūnyatā* (Emptiness). Such an ideal Buddhist stance will never keep a civilization alive. In all likelihood, that was one of the main reasons why Buddhism as a social institution disappeared altogether in India. Therefore, I cannot imagine that genuine Buddhism will become the future world religion.

For the present time, Buddhism will be significant only as an international cultural movement rather than as a religion. Some of its essential features, such as tolerance toward other religions, compatibility with science, self-corrective creativity, and compassion for all fellow beings, living and nonliving alike, should be activated for the coming world civilization. These features are the most important qualities of the emerging world civilization.

Buddhism and Civilization

Present-day human civilization is the product of human ecological adaptation to the environment. In principle, civilization can be analyzed through three fundamental relations: relation between humans and nature (roots of natural knowledge), relation between humans and humans (roots of human and social rules), and relation of humans with themselves (roots of religion and morality). Since archaic times, human beings everywhere initially relied on religion of some kind to keep these three relationships in order for the sake of survival. From generation to generation, all the necessary things in everyday life—for example, how to do funeral services for the dead—were transmitted by means of religious tradition. Thus began human civilization.

As a rule, a tribe or nation had one language and one religion. But as international cultural communications developed and peoples of different languages and religions began to meet, violent conflicts often occurred. Religious intolerance prevailed in the West, and mostly Buddhistic tolerance prevailed in the East. In China, along with the native Taoism and Confucianism, Buddhism flourished since its introduction from India in the sixth century A.D. In Japan, Indian Buddhism and Chinese Confucianism coexist peacefully with the native Shintoism even today. Japanese Shintoism is mainly concerned with the relationship between human beings and nature; Confucianism, with the relationship between human beings and human beings; and Buddhism, with the relationship of human beings with themselves, that is, human anxiety about life and death. Each works in its respective functions quite harmoniously. Such cooperation between different religions might be an exception. But the spirit of tolerance inherent in Buddhism was evidenced already by the historic Stone Edicts of King Asoka in ancient India. This Buddhist tradition of religious toleration should be the first thing we keep in mind when we think of the future world community of humankind, which must embrace so many nations with so many different languages and cultures, including antagonistic political ideologies.

Science has universal truth, valid and useful to all human beings. But unlike religion, which has absolute truth (although only for those who believe in it), science is unable to save the human being as a whole. Science can make mistakes, but it is always ready to correct itself through free criticism. Religion usually allows no criticism against itself. Again, Buddhism is an exception. The ideal community of Buddhist priests and the international community of research scientists are self-corrective groups. Both have self-corrective creativity in common, working with each other among their fellow members toward never-ending self-perfection. This self-corrective capacity is the second important thing for us to bear in mind when we seriously think of the future world community of humankind, which will have many new difficult problems to solve.

Most people say, "Science is cool, religion is warm." But many astronauts, looking at the earth from above, seem to feel the genuine bond of all men and women who live on the green planet. And contemporary ecologists feel their sincere fellowship not only with other human beings, animals, and plants but with other nonliving things, just as the Buddha taught more than two thousand years ago. This all-embracing Buddhist compassion is originally based on the Buddha's cool intellectual attitude of looking at things as they are. Such combination of cool intelligence and warm compassion is what Buddhism surprisingly shares with science. And this approach is the third, perhaps most important, thing for us to bear in mind when we think about the future world community of humankind, bound to this planet as its irreplaceable homeland.

The characteristic compatibility between Buddhism and science can also be appreciated through another historic fact that I call Japanese immunity against "science shock." Especially since the Darwinian theory of biological evolution in the nineteenth century, a sort of "science shock" has haunted the entire Western world and has driven the intellectuals who had lost confidence in human dignity into sheer nihilism. In modern Japan, on the contrary, even after the official introduction of Western science and technology in 1868, no such devastating "science shock" is traceable. One reason may be the Buddhistic tradition congenial to the Japanese mind. The Buddha was wise and courageous, long before modern Western science, in facing squarely the nihilistic reality of human existence, and through the doctrine of dependent origination, he taught people the interconnectedness of all existence, the impermanence of all composite existents, and compassion toward all fellow beings, living and nonliving alike.[2]

The Emerging World Civilization

If we suppose that the origin of human civilization is at the center of the huge Eurasian land mass, Japan is now the eastern end of its eastern branch, America is the western end of its western branch, and the branches are separated by the largest ocean of the world, the Pacific. The classical ancient civilizations of humankind were most likely brought to maturity almost independently in the East and in the West more than two thousand years ago. In both the East and the West, the spiritual leaders of humankind at that time were teaching people the ideals of rational spirit and the morals of human love as if in unison, because at about the same time, dangerous iron weapons were beginning to circulate among civilized peoples of the world, probably at that time as dangerous for human survival as are nuclear weapons today. Later, the western branch crossed the Atlantic and, on the new American continent, pushed aside the neolithic civilization of the American Indians. The eastern branch reached off the Chinese coast to the Japanese islands and pressed steadily north to the neolithic civilization of the Ainu. By the middle of the twentieth century, modern Japan had successfully adopted Western science and technology into its Eastern tradition, and it is now flourishing as an affluent society. America and Japan, dreadful foes just a few generations ago, now seem bound together in an effort to keep the Pacific Ocean peaceful between the eastern end and the western end of human civilization—not only in industry and technology, but in culture and thought, as witnessed by such clairvoyant thinkers as Charles Morris and Nolan Pliny Jacobson.

It seems somehow to me that the two great World Wars that I experienced in my lifetime have been working in secret toward a profound structural change of the whole human world on this planet. Social classes are crushing down. Colonial empires are falling apart. Peoples are becoming independent one after another. Everybody is

growing more or less educated and freer in speech, thought, and action—a bit more civilized. Some might say, "A great Providence is at
work." Others might laugh at it, "What a ridiculous optimism!"

Consider the remarkable affinity between Buddhism and science,
the world-historical missionary encounter between the eastern end (Japan) and the western end (America) of human civilization, and the
unpredictable world events, most symbolically in and around the Soviet Union and China, at which the rest of the world is amazed. Marxism seems to have done what it had to do. The age of violent revolution and dogmatic autocracy is over, and the time of honest diplomacy
and rational calculation with a computerized information network is
coming. Sooner or later, all the seemingly fateful barriers between antagonistic nations—apartheid in South Africa, the notorious Berlin
Wall, the thirty-eighth Parallel on the Korean peninsula, and so forth—
will have fallen down.

Unfortunately, the actual present-day world situation is not that
simple. We must be courageous and wise enough to face reality as it is
and to take all possible precautions, step-by-step. We must review the
whole problem anew from the standpoint of the three fundamental
relations within civilization.

The relationship between human beings and nature is, nowadays,
more and more meticulously taken care of by ever-advancing natural
science. Environmental sciences, astrophysical and biological sciences
in particular, are warning us urgently about ever-worsening global
environmental conditions. We may hope that it is still possible to res-
cue our common home planet at the last moment of its struggle for
survival. Human intelligence with self-corrective creativity and self-
reflective consciousness is much greater than any computerized mechanism of artificial intelligence. As the famous Gödel's incompleteness
theorem suggests, mathematics of the living brain is much larger in
capacity than any rigorous axiomatic systems, such as that of *Princi-
pia Mathematica*.

In the relationship between human and human, the situation is a
little more complicated because so many peoples with so many different languages and religions contend with each other everywhere. The
present-day predicaments of humankind, such as the nuclear arms race,
environmental pollution, energy shortage and overpopulation, cannot
be solved with the most beautiful words or even with the best knowledge of science and technology as long as our thoughts, feelings, and
actions are governed by nationalism, provincialism, ethnocentrism,
and every other mechanism of divisiveness and fragmentation. We are

nationality-bound because we are a kind of gregarious animal, and at the same time, we are humanity-bound because we all belong to one and the same species, Homo sapiens. Theoretically, no reason exists why nationality and humanity must be in conflict with each other. Both must work together for human survival within the framework of the great harmony of nature. Science, philosophy, and religion were originally made for the same purpose.

As for the relationship of humans with themselves, "What I do following my heart's desire is by itself in conformity with the laws of reason," said Confucius; "Love your neighbors like yourself," said Jesus; and we have the Buddha's wonderful teaching of universal compassion toward all fellow beings, living and nonliving alike, which is in full accord with the most recent requirement of ecological science. But as long as people live, they must have their own desire to live. In a sense, it is the energy source of all activities, for better or for worse.

Try, therefore, to educate our children to like doing good things rather than bad things. Do not extinguish their inborn sentiment of universal compassion and their intellectual courage to look at things as they are. Watch science for its possible misuse. Try to protect young men and women from expanding sensual desires with recent technological progress, and keep them within the sound order of the great harmony of nature. Try to help their love of their native land continuously grow into their love of humankind, by preventing them from corruption of all sorts of sociopolitical power and monetary pollution. Watch the state authority in any excessive use of power, so that national interests are in line with interests of humankind at large. Then our grown-up children, young men and women, will be happier with themselves than they are today.

Notes

1. R. Masunaga, *The Soto Approach to Zen* (Tokyo: Layman Buddhist Society Press, 1958), p. 127.
2. In this context, I am inevitably moved to think of Nolan Pliny Jacobson's extraordinary encounter with an incurable disease (amyotrophic lateral sclerosis) that ended on 27 December 1987, after about a year of suffering, which Mrs. Jacobson described in her personal letter with placid but touching words. Professor Ramakrishna Puligandla, one of Jacobson's close friends, summarized this encounter to me perfectly, "He faced the struggle with the courage, clarity, equanimity, and wisdom characteristic only of a Bodhisattva" (personal communication).

Contributors
Bibliography
Index

Contributors

Tsung-I Dow has taught East Asian history and philosophy in China and the United States for forty years. Since the completion of his *Daily Chronicle of Li Hung-chang* and *On Humanism* (*Lun Rendao Zhuyi*) in Chinese in the late 1950s, he has focused on analyzing the philosophical creeds of Marxism and Confucianism to determine the existence and nature of compatibility between the two—to explain how a Confucian China could have been so rapidly transformed into a Marxist state—and to project possible future development of the two ideologies. Using the Marxian system as a framework, he discovered that compatibility between these two ideologies in dialectical materialism is greater than in historical materialism, and still greater than that between Confucianism and any other major philosophical system. Part of his findings were published in *Confucianism vs. Marxism* in 1977 (second edition, 1980). In the course of his studies to ascertain the claim of scientific support for Marx's philosophical system, Dow noticed that new scientific discoveries tend to support the age-old Confucian-Taoist dialectical worldview in its symbolic representation in the form of the primordial pair of the Yin-Yang interaction relationship. He contends that modification of a Yin-Yang dialectical monist system could provide the world a new conceptual framework for analyzing the twofold nature of development in things and events.

Hal W. French is professor and chairman of the Department of Religious Studies at the University of South Carolina. He authored *The Swan's Wide Waters: Ramakrishna and Western Culture*, coauthored *Religious Ferment in Modern India* with Arvind Sharma, authored *A Study of Religious Fanaticism and Responses to It*, and has authored and edited several other volumes and articles, mostly on the religious traditions of Asia. He has received the Amoco Teacher of the Year and Mortar Board Teaching awards at the University of South Carolina, and he has lectured at over thirty other universities and colleges in the United States, Canada, England, and India.

Morgan Gibson is a poet and essayist. His latest book, *Among Buddhas in Japan*, is part of his philosophical autobiography, with a foreword by Nolan Pliny Jacobson. Gibson also authored *Revolutionary Rexroth: Poet of East-West Wisdom* and coauthored *Tantric Poetry of Kukai (Kobo Daishi), Japan's Buddhist Saint* with Hiroshi Murakami. Having taught at the University of Wisconsin-Milwaukee and other American universities, he is now a professor of English at Japan Women's University.

Robert L. Greenwood is associate professor of philosophy at the University of South Alabama. His interest in Buddhism was first aroused while he was attending the Shanghai American School in 1948. His scholarly attention to the philosophy of C. I. Lewis began while he was an undergraduate at the University of Miami, Coral Gables, Florida.

Bart Gruzalski has published essays on ethical theory, animal liberation, medical ethics, environmental ethics, the work of Derek Parfit, the Chipko movement, as well as coedited *Value Conflicts in Health Care Delivery*. His current writing projects focus on ecology, ethics, and the ways in which an understanding of Buddhism and Vedanta resolves problems in contemporary Western philosophy. He has taught at Bowling Green State University and recently gave up a tenured position in the Department of Philosophy and Religion at Northeastern University in order to establish the Web of Life Center for Sustainable Living in Redway, California. This educational nonprofit focuses on our looming ecological crises, the role of economic practice in creating or mitigating these crises, the biology of watersheds and bioregions, the ethical implications of these observations for future generations and how we should live our lives, the need for "inner work" as part of the solution, and hands-on skills including organic gardening, low-impact housing, solar energy, compost toilets, stream restoration, fishery restoration, and forestry restoration.

David L. Hall, a graduate of Texas Western College, Chicago Theological Seminary, and Yale University (Ph.D., 1967), is professor of philosophy at the University of Texas at El Paso and managing review editor of *Philosophy East and West*. He is the author of several books on the philosophy of culture, including *Eros and Irony: A Prelude to Philosophical Anarchism* and *The Uncertain Phoenix: Adventures Toward a Post-cultural Sensibility*. He is coauthor, with Roger Ames, of *Thinking Through Confucius*. He and Ames are completing *Anticipating China: The Circle and the Square*, a sequel to their Confucius book.

Charles Hartshorne is Distinguished Service Professor Emeritus of Philosophy at the University of Texas at Austin. He has taught at four universities in this country, at The New School for Social Research, at Colorado College, and overseas at universities in Germany,

Belgium, Australia, Japan, and India. He has been the president of five philosophical societies and is an elected member of the American Ornithological Union. He has lectured in forty-five states in this country and in England, Scotland, and France. Born on 5 June 1897, he was educated at Haverford College and Harvard University, from which he holds three degrees. He did postdoctoral study in England and Europe, served in the United States Army Medical Corps, and was Instructor and Research Fellow at Harvard University. Senior editor of *The Collected Papers of Charles S. Peirce*, he is the author of many books and hundreds of articles in philosophy and of one book and twelve articles in ornithology. He specializes in philosophy of religion, metaphysics, the psychology of sensation, and the study of songbirds and other singing animals.

Cedric Lambeth Heppler has pursued his scholarly interests and encouraged that of others in his position as reference librarian at North Carolina State University at Raleigh since 1975. He is editor of two books by Henry Nelson Wieman, *Seeking a Faith for a New Age* (Scarecrow, 1975) and *The Organization of Interests* (University Press of America, 1985). This area of specialty has continued, and he is editing Wieman's manuscript on the philosophy of history and writing another about Wieman's religious philosophy. Through earlier educational endeavors, he earned the B.A. from Stetson University, DeLand, Florida; the Th.M. from Southeastern Baptist Seminary (with his thesis on Charles Hartshorne's concept of God); and the M.S.L.S. from University of North Carolina at Chapel Hill. Among Heppler's published works is the essay "Creative Naturalism and Creative Interchange," in *Creative Interchange*, edited by John A. Broyer and William S. Minor.

Frank J. Hoffman was educated in St. Louis, Honolulu, and London. He received his Ph.D. degree from the University of London in 1981 and is assistant professor of philosophy at West Chester University. He is the author of *Rationality and Mind in Early Buddhism* and has published over twelve papers and numerous book reviews. He serves on the editorial advisory board of the journal *Asian Philosophy*, is on the advisory board of the Mid-Atlantic Regional Association for Asian Studies, and is a member of the Oriental Club of Philadelphia. He is currently doing research on early Indian (Pali) Buddhism and the philosophy of religion.

Kenneth K. Inada is the author, editor, and translator of five books. He has contributed chapters and articles on Asian and comparative philosophy, with focus on Buddhist thought, to a variety of publications, nationally and internationally. He is currently a Distinguished Service Professor of Philosophy at the State University of New York at Buffalo.

David Lee Miller is professor and chair of the philosophy department at the University of Wisconsin—La Crosse. From 1974 to 1982, he served as chair of the Society for Philosophy of Creativity in the central division of the American Philosophical Association, and he is presently a member of the society's board of directors. He is the author of *Philosophy of Creativity* and numerous essays investigating the nature of creativity.

Hajime Nakamura is the founder and director of the Eastern Institute in Tokyo. He is the author of *Ways of Thinking of Eastern People* and *A History of Early Vedanta Philosophy*. He has also completed a nineteen-volume anthology, *Selected Works of Hajime Nakamura*.

Seizo Ohe, Litt.D., graduated from the Imperial University of Tokyo (philosophy) in 1928. He studied in Europe (mostly at Heidelberg) for the subsequent four years, where he lived as a private scholar until about 1948, because of ill health. He was professor of philosophy at Nihon University, Tokyo, from 1949 to 1975, where he was a lecturer at the graduate school of philosophy until 1985. His professional honors include: national delegate (observer) at the XI International Congress of Philosophy, Brussels, 1953; Fulbright exchange scholar and Rockefeller Fellow at Chicago and Harvard, 1955–56; fellow at the Center for Advanced Study in the Behavioral Sciences, Stanford, 1958–59; member of l'Institut International de Philosophie, Paris, since 1971; and president of Japan Philosophy of Science Society, 1975–81. He is now advisor to the Institute of Seizon and Life Sciences, Tokyo.

Howard L. Parsons is professor emeritus of philosophy at the University of Bridgeport, Connecticut. He is the author of *Man Today: Problems, Values, and Fulfillment*; *Man East and West*; *Marxism, Christianity, and Human Values*; *Buddhism as Humanism*; *Christianity Today in the USSR*; and other works.

Stuart D. B. Picken is director of the Center for Japanese Studies at the International Christian University in Tokyo. His published works include *Shinto: Japan's Spiritual Roots* and *Christianity and Japan: Meeting, Conflict, Hope*.

Ramakrishna Puligandla, educated in his native India and in the United States, holds graduate degrees in physics and engineering and the Ph.D. in philosophy from Rice University. His areas of specialty are logic, philosophy of science, and comparative philosophy and religion, with emphasis on Madhyamaka and Advaita-Vedānta. Among his published works are *Fact and Fiction in B. F. Skinner's Science and Utopia; An Examination of the Copenhagen Interpretation of Quantum Theory; Fundamentals of Indian Philosophy; An Encounter with Awareness; Jñāna Yoga;* and over sixty articles in scholarly journals and periodicals. He is professor of philosophy at the University of Toledo and senior editor of *Comprehensive Harmony: International Journal for Comparative Philosophy and Culture.* He was Fulbright visiting professor at the Radhakrishnan Institute for Advanced Study in Philosophy, University of Madras, India, in 1992.

Paul F. Schmidt taught at Oberlin College (1951–65) and the University of New Mexico (1965–89) until his retirement. He served as chair of the Department of Philosophy at the University of New Mexico from 1965 to 1976. Among his published works are *Religious Knowledge; Perception and Cosmology in Whitehead's Philosophy; Rebelling, Loving, and Liberation; Temple Reflections;* and *Buddhist Meditation on China.* Born in Rochester, New York, on 14 September 1925, Schmidt received the A.B. with high honors, from the University of Rochester in 1947 and the Ph.D. at Yale University in 1951.

Bibliography

Alt, Wayne. "There Is No Paradox of Desire in Buddhism." *Philosophy East and West* 30 (October 1988).

Ames, Van Meter. *Zen and American Thought*. Honolulu: University of Hawaii Press, 1962.

Appel, Willa. *Cults in America*. New York: Hill, Rinehart & Winston, 1986.

Asvaghosha. *Shou-Ling-Yin* (Chinese translation of the *Sūrangama Sutra*). In *The Wisdom of China and India*, edited by Lin Yutang. New York: Modern Library, 1942.

Babbitt, Irving. "Buddha and the Occident." In *The Dhammapada*. New York and London: Oxford University Press, 1936.

Berill, N. J. *The Person in the Womb*. New York: Dodd & Mead, 1968.

Blocker, Gene. *The Meaning of Meaninglessness*. The Hague: Martinus Nijhoff, 1974.

Bookchin, Murray. "A Technology for Life." In *Sources*, edited by Theodore Roszak. New York: Harper & Row, 1972.

The Book of Kindred Sayings. London: Pali Text Society, 1980.

Boulton, William R. "The Competitive Edge: The Japanese Robotics Industry." *The Graduate Business Alumnus* (Athens: University of Georgia, Winter 1987).

Buchler, Justin, ed. *Philosophical Writings of Peirce*. New York: Dover, 1955.

Buswell, Robert. *The Korean Approach to Zen*. Honolulu: University of Hawaii Press, 1983.

Camus, Albert. "The Absurdity of Human Existence." In *The Meaning of Life*, edited by E. D. Klemke. Oxford and New York: Oxford University Press, 1981.

Chang Chung-yuan. *Creativity and Taoism*. New York: Harper & Row, 1963.

Clark, Stephen R. L. *The Nature of the Beast: Are Animals Moral?* New York: Oxford University Press, 1984.

Cobb, John, Jr. *Beyond Dialog: Towards the Mutual Transformation of Christianity and Buddhism*. Philadelphia: Fortress, 1982.

Complete Works of Chuang Tzu. Translated by Burton Watson. New York: Columbia University Press, 1968.

Conze, Edward, et al., eds. *Buddhist Texts Through the Ages*. New York: Harper & Row, 1964.

Copi, Irving. *Introduction to Logic*. 7th ed. New York: Macmillan, 1986.

Corner, E. H. *The Life of Plants*. Chicago: University of Chicago Press, 1964.

Cupitt, Don. *Taking Leave of God*. New York: Crossroads, 1981.

Danto, Arthur. *Mysticism and Morality.* New York: Harper & Row, 1972.

Dogen, trans. *Shobogenzo Zuimonki.* Honolulu: East-West Center Press, 1971.

Doi, Takeo. *The Anatomy of Dependence.* New York: Kodansha International/U. S. A., 1981.

Dyson, Freeman. *Disturbing the Universe.* New York: Harper & Row, 1979.

Edwards, Paul. "Why?" In *The Meaning of Life,* edited by E. D. Klemke. Oxford and New York: Oxford University Press, 1981.

Franck, Frederick. *The Zen of Seeing.* New York: Vintage, 1973.

Frolov, Ivan. *Global Problems and the Future of Mankind.* Moscow: Progress, 1982.

Fromm, Erich, Daisetz Suzuki, and Richard DeMartino. *Zen Buddhism and Psychoanalysis.* New York: Harper & Row, 1960.

Goldman, Alvin. *A Theory of Human Action.* Englewood Cliffs, N. J.: Prentice-Hall, 1970.

Gombrich, Richard F. *Theravada Buddhism: A Social History from Ancient Benares to Modern Colombo.* London: Routledge & Kegan Paul, 1988.

Gorbachev, Mikhail. *Political Report of the CPSU Central Committee to the 27th Congress of the Communist Party of the Soviet Union.* Moscow: Novosti, 1986.

Govinda, Lama Anagarika. *Creative Meditation and Multi-Dimensional Consciousness.* Wheaton, Ill.: Theosophical Publishing House, 1976.

Graham, A. C. "Being in Western Philosophy Compared with *Shan/Fei,* and *Yu Wu* in Chinese Philosophy." In *Studies in Chinese Philosophy and Philosophical Literature.* Singapore: Institute of East Asian Philosophies, 1986.

Gribbin, John. *In Search of Schrodinger's Cat.* New York: Bantam, 1984.

Griffin, Donald R. *The Question of Animal Awareness: Evolutionary Continuity of Mental Experience.* New York: Rockefeller University, 1976.

Gross, Rita. "Buddhism and Feminism: Toward Their Mutual Transformation." *Eastern Buddhist* 19, no. 1 (Spring 1986); no. 2 (Autumn 1986).

———. *Women and Buddhism.* A special issue of *Spring Wind—Buddhist Cultural Forum* 6, nos., 1–3 (1986).

Hall, David. L. "Process and Anarchy: A Taoist Vision of Creativity." *Philosophy East and West* 28, no. 3 (July 1978).

———. *The Uncertain Phoenix: Adventures Toward a Post-Cultural Sensibility.* New York: Fordham University Press, 1982.

Hare, R. M. "Nothing Matters." In *The Meaning of Life,* edited by E. D. Klemke. Oxford and New York: Oxford University Press, 1981.

Hepburn, R. W. "Questions About the Meaning of Life." In *The Meaning of Life,* edited by E. D. Klemke. Oxford and New York: Oxford University Press, 1981.

Herman, A. L. *An Introduction to Buddhist Thought.* Lanham, Md.: University Press of America, 1983.

———. *The Problem of Evil and Indian Thought.* Delhi: Motilal Banarsidass, 1976.

Hershey, John. *Hiroshima*. New York: A. A. Knopf, 1946.

Heschel, Rabbi Abraham Joshua. *Man Is Not Alone: A Philosophy of Religion*. New York: Farrar, Straus & Giroux, 1951.

Hoffman, Frank J. "Buddhist Belief 'In.'" *Religious Studies* 21, no. 3 (1985).

———. "The Buddhist Empiricism Thesis." *Religious Studies* 18, no. 2 (1982).

———. *Rationality and Mind in Early Buddhism*. Delhi: Motilal Banarsidass, 1987.

Holmes, Stewart W., and Chimyo Horioka. *Zen Art for Meditation*. Tokyo: Charles E. Tuttle, 1973.

Hopkinson, Deborah, and Eileen Klera, eds. *Not Mixing Up Buddhism: Essays on Women and Buddhist Practice*. Fredonia, N. Y.: White Pine, 1986.

Hyers, M. Conrad. *Zen and the Comic Spirit*. Philadelphia: Westminster Press, 1973.

Inada, Kenneth K. "Japanese Secularism: A Reexamination." *Free Inquiry* 8, no. 4 (Fall 1988).

———. *Nāgārjuna: A Translation of His* Mūlamadhyamakakārikā *with an Introductory Essay*. Tokyo: Hokuseido, 1970.

Inada, Kenneth K., and Nolan Pliny Jacobson, eds. *Buddhism and American Thinkers*. Albany: SUNY Press, 1984.

Jacobson, Nolan Pliny. *Buddhism and the Contemporary World: Change and Self-Correction*. Carbondale and Edwardsville: Southern Illinois University Press, 1983.

———. *Buddhism: The Religion of Analysis*. New York: Humanities, 1965. Reprint. Carbondale and Edwardsville: Southern Illinois University Press, 1966, 1970.

———. "A Buddhist Analysis of Human Experience." In *Buddhism and American Thinkers*, edited by Kenneth K. Inada and Nolan Pliny Jacobson. Albany: SUNY Press, 1984.

———. *The Heart of Buddhist Philosophy*. Carbondale and Edwardsville: Southern Illinois University Press, 1988.

———. "Hume on the Uses of Reason in Religion." *The Iliff Review* 15, no. 2 (Spring 1958).

———. "Marxism and Religious Naturalism." *Journal of Religion* 29, no. 2 (April 1949).

———. "Niebuhr's Philosophy of History." *Harvard Theological Review* 37, no. 4 (October 1944).

———. *Nihon-do: The Japan Way*. Translated by Nakazato Chieko. Tokyo: Rissosha, 1977.

———. "The Possibility of Oriental Influence in Hume's Philosophy." *Philosophy East and West* 19, no. 1 (January 1969).

———. "The Problem of Civilization." *Ethics, an International Journal of Social, Political and Legal Philosophy* 63, no. 1 (October 1952).

———. "Religion and Fragmentation of Man." *Journal of Religion* 32, no. 1 (January 1952).

———. "The Religious Naturalism Implicit in the Writings of Karl Marx." Ph.D. diss., University of Chicago, 1948.

———. *Understanding Buddhism*. Carbondale and Edwardsville: Southern Illinois University Press, 1986.

———. "The Uses of Reason in Religion: A Note on David Hume." *Journal of Religion* 39, no. 1 (January 1959).

Kalupahana, David. *Nāgārjuna: The Philosophy of the Middle Way*. Albany: SUNY Press; Honolulu: University of Hawaii Press, 1983.

Kant, Immanuel. *Was Heisst Sich in Denken Orienteiren?* In *Werke*, edited by Wilhelm Weischedel, vol. 5. Darmstadt: Wissenschaftliche Buchgesellschaft, 1958.

———. *Zum Ewigen Frieden: En Philosophischer Entwurf*. In *Werke*, edited by Wilhelm Weischedel, vol. 9. Darmstadt: Wissenschaftliche Buchgesellschaft, 1958.

Karplus, Martin. "The Dynamics of Proteins." *Scientific American* 243 (April 1980).

Keel, Hee-Sung. *Chinul: The Founder of the Korean Son Tradition*. Berkeley: University of California Press, 1984.

Kennedy, Paul. *The Rise and Fall of Great Powers*. New York: Random House, 1987.

Kerr, Fergus. *Theology after Wittgenstein*. Oxford and New York: Basil Blackwell, 1986.

Klemke, E. D. "The Question of the Meaning of Life." In *The Meaning of Life*. Oxford and New York: Oxford University Press, 1981.

Klemke, E. D., ed. *The Meaning of Life*. Oxford and New York: Oxford University Press, 1981.

Kodama, Sanehide. *American Poetry and Japanese Culture*. Hamden, Conn.: Shoe String, 1986.

———. *Among Buddhas in Japan*. Foreword by Nolan Pliny Jacobson. Fredonia, N. Y.: White Pine, 1986.

———. *East-West Wisdom*. Hamden, Conn.: Shoe String, 1986.

Koestler, Arthur. *The Lotus and the Robot*. London: Hutchison, 1961.

Kuhn, Thomas. *The Structure of Scientific Revolutions*. 2d ed. Chicago: University of Chicago Press, 1970.

Lewis, Clarence Irving. *Collected Papers of Clarence Irving Lewis*. Edited by John D. Goheen and John L. Mothershead, Jr. Stanford: Stanford University Press, 1970.

———. *Mind and the World Order: Outline of a Theory of Knowledge*. New York, Chicago, and Boston: Charles Scribner's Sons, 1929.

Lodge, George Cabbot. "The Connection Between Ethics and Ideology." *Journal of Business Ethics* 1, no. 2, (May 1982).

Loy, David. *Nonduality: A Study in Comparative Philosophy.* New Haven: Yale University Press, 1988.

Majjhima-nikāya. In *Pali Canon,* vol. 1, no. 63. London: Pali Text Society, 1972.

Marx, Karl. *Critique of Hegel's "Philosophy of Right."* Translated by Annette Jolin and Joseph O'Malley. Cambridge: Cambridge University Press, 1970.

Masunaga, R. *The Soto Approach to Zen.* Tokyo: Layman Buddhist Society Press, 1958.

Mead, George Herbert. *Mind, Self, and Society.* Edited by Charles Morris. Chicago: University of Chicago Press, 1934.

Merton, Thomas. *Zen and the Birds of Appetite.* New York: New Directions, 1968.

Miller, David Lee. *Philosophy of Creativity.* New York and Bern: Peter Lang, 1989.

Miner, Earl. *The Japanese Tradition in British and American Literature.* Princeton: Princeton University Press, 1958.

Mori, Masahiro. *The Buddha in the Robot.* Tokyo: Kosei Publishing, 1981.

Mountain, Marian. *The Zen Environment.* New York: Bantam, 1983.

Moyers, Bill. *The Secret Government.* Cabin John, Md.: Seven Locks, 1988.

Nāgārjuna. *Madhyamaka Kārikās.* Translated by K. Inada, in *Nāgārjuna: A Translation of His* Mūlamadhyamakakārikā *with an Introductory Essay.* Tokyo: Hokuseido, 1970.

———. *Vigrahavyāvartanī.* London: Pali Text Society, ?.

Nagel, Thomas. "The Absurd." In *Mortal Questions.* Cambridge: Cambridge University Press, 1979.

Neville, Robert. "Buddhist and Taoist Ideas of Transcendence: A Study of Philosophical Contrast." In *Buddhist and Taoist Studies I,* edited by Michael Saso and David W. Chappell. Honolulu: University of Hawaii Press, 1977.

———. *The Tao and the Daimon: Segments of a Religious Inquiry.* Albany: SUNY Press, 1982.

Nielsen, Kai. "Linguistic Philosophy and 'The Meaning of Life.'" In *The Meaning of Life,* edited by E. D. Klemke. Oxford and New York: Oxford University Press, 1981.

Northrop, F. S. C. Foreword to *A Whiteheadian Aesthetic,* by D. W. Sherburne. New Haven: Yale University Press, 1961.

———. *The Meeting of East and West.* New York: Macmillan, 1953.

Parfit, Derek. *Reasons and Persons.* Oxford: Clarendon, 1984.

Partridge, Eric. *Origins: A Short Etymological Dictionary of Modern English.* New York: Greenwich House, 1983.

Picken, Stuart D. B. *Buddhism: Japan's Cultural Identity.* New York: Kodansha International/U. S. A., 1982.

————. *Shinto: Japan's Spiritual Roots.* New York: Kodansha International/ U. S. A., 1980.

Picken, Stuart D. B., and Ono Masako. *Bioethics and Social Responsibility.* ICU GE Series, no. 10. 1981.

Plato, The Works of. Translated by B. Jowett. New York: Tudor Publishing, undated.

Preston, David L. *The Social Organization of Zen Practice: Constructing Transcultural Reality.* London: Cambridge University Press, 1988.

Rachels, James. *The Elements of Moral Philosophy.* New York: Random House, 1986.

Rahula, Walpola. *What the Buddha Taught.* New York: Grove, 1974.

Reps, Paul. *Zen Flesh/Zen Bones.* New York: Doubleday Anchor, undated.

Rhys-Davids, T. W., trans. *Buddhist Suttras.* Vol. 11 of *Sacred Books of the East.* Oxford: Clarendon, 1881.

————, trans. *Dialogues of the Buddha.* Vols. 2 and 3 of *Sacred Books of the Buddhists.* Edited by H. Frowde. London: Oxford University Press, 1899, 1957.

Rhys-Davids, T. W., and Wm. Stede. *Pali Text Society Pali-English Dictionary.* London: Pali Text Society, 1972.

Roberts, John G. *Mitsui: Three Centuries of Japanese Business.* New York: Weatherhill, 1973. Reprint 1989.

Roszak, Theodore. *Where the Wasteland Ends.* New York: Doubleday, 1972.

Ryle, Gilbert. *The Concept of Mind.* London: Barnes & Noble, 1949.

Samyutta-nikāya. In *Pali Canon,* vol. 3. London: Pali Text Society, 1972.

Sanders, Steven, and David R. Cheney. *The Meaning of Life: Questions, Answers, and Analysis.* Englewood Cliffs, N.J.: Prentice-Hall, 1980.

Saso, Michael. "Buddhist and Taoist Ideas of Transcendence: A Study of Philosophical Contrast." In *Buddhist and Taoist Studies I,* edited by Michael Saso and David W. Chappell. Honolulu: University of Hawaii Press, 1977.

Schumacher, E. F. "Buddhist Economics." In *Sources,* edited by Theodore Roszak. New York: Harper & Row, 1972.

Schwartz, Benjamin. *The World of Thought in Ancient China.* Cambridge: Harvard University Press, 1985.

Seng-ts'an. *Inscription on the Believing Mind (Hsin-hsin Ming).* In *Taisho shinshu daizokyo,* vol. 48, no. 2010.

Smart, Ninian. "Nirvāna and Timelessness." In *Concept and Empathy,* edited by Donald Wiebe. New York: New York University Press, 1986.

Smith, Houston. *The Religions of Man.* New York: Harper & Row, 1965.

Stevens, John. *The Marathon Monks of Mount Hiei.* Boston: Shambhala, 1988.

Strawson. P. F. *Individuals.* London: Methuen, 1959.

Suttanipāta. In *Pali Canon,* vol. 1. London: Pali Text Society, 1980.

Suzuki, D. T. *Introduction to Zen Buddhism.* New York: Grove, 1963.

Ta-hui Tsung-kao. *Recorded Dialogues of Ch'an Master Ta-hui P'u-chio* (Ta-hui P'u-chio Ch'an-shih Yu-lu), compiled by Yun-wen in 1171. In *Taisho shinshu daizokyo*, vol. 47, no. 1998A.

Taisho Tripitaka. In *Pali Canon*, vol. 4. London: Pali Text Society, 1972.

Takeo, Kuwabara. *Japan and Western Civilization: Essays on Comparative Culture*. Tokyo: University of Tokyo Press, 1983.

Tantric Poetry of Kukai (Kobo Daishi), Japan's Buddhist Saint. Translated with commentary by Morgan Gibson and Hiroshi Murakami. Fredonia, N. Y.: White Pine, 1987.

Tao-hsuan. *Biographies of the High Priests*.

Tao-yuan, Shih. *Records of the Transmission of the Lamp*. New York: Pantheon, 1969.

Thurman, Robert A. F., trans. *The Holy Teaching of Vimalakīrti*, University Park: Pennsylvania State University Press, 1976.

Tillich, Paul. *The Protestant Era*. Chicago: University of Chicago Press, 1948.

Trotter, Robert J. "Baby Face." *Psychology Today* 17, no. 8 (August 1983).

Tsunoda, Tadanobu. *Right Brain and Left Brain*. Tokyo: Shogakkan, 1987.

United Nations. Department of International Economic and Social Affairs. *World Economic Survey 1988: Current Trands and Policies in the World Economy*. New York, 1988.

U. S. Congress. Committee on Foreign Affairs. *Background Information on the Use of United States Armed Forces in Foreign Countries*. 91st Cong., 2d sess., 1970.

Wang Pi's Commentary on the Lao Tzu. Translated by Arrienne Rump with Wing-tsit Chan. Society for Asian and Comparative Philosophy Monographs no. 6. Honolulu: University of Hawaii Press, 1979.

Warren, Henry Clarke. *Buddhism in Translation*. Harvard Oriental Series, vol.3, no. 9. Cambridge, Mass.: Harvard University Press, 1947.

Wazaki, Nobuya. *Ajad no Tanjo*. New York: Kodansha International/U. S. A., 1979.

Whitehead, Alfred North. *Adventures of Ideas*. New York: Macmillan, 1933.

———. *Process and Reality*. New York: Macmillan, 1929.

———. *Process and Reality: An Essay in Cosmology*. Corrected ed., edited by David Ray Griffith and Donald W. Sherburne. New York: Free Press, 1978.

———. *Religion in the Making*. New York: Macmillan, 1953.

Wiebe, Donald, ed. *Concept and Empathy*. New York: New York University Press, 1986.

Wilczek, Frank. "The Cosmic Asymmetry Between Matter and Antimatter." *Scientific American* 243 (December 1980).

Williams, Bernard. *Problems of the Self*. Cambridge and New York: Cambridge University Press, 1973. Reprint 1975.

Winternitz, Maurice. *A History of Indian Literature*. Translated by S. Ketkar and H. Kohn and revised by the author. 2 vols. Berkeley: University of California Press, 1927, 1933.

Wisdom, John. "The Meanings of the Questions of Life," In *The Meaning of Life*, edited by E. D. Klemke. Oxford and New York: Oxford University Press, 1981.

Wittgenstein, Ludwig. *Tractatus Logico-philosophicus*. London: Routledge & Kegan Paul, 1961.

Woodward, F. L., trans. *Udana: Versus of Uplift and Itivuttaka: As it Was Said*. The Minor Anthologies of the Pali Canon, pt. 2. Vol. 8 of *Sacred Books of the Buddhists*. London: Pali Text Society.

World Commission on Environment and Development. *Our Common Future*. New York: Oxford University Press, 1987.

Index